Praise for *Beyond Denial*

"Sonorous essays that weave progressive spirituality into a seamless garment . . . [and] open up thoughtful reinterpretations of Christian doctrine."

—*Kirkus Reviews*

"An inspired synthesis of wisdom, these essays are both practical and luminous. From a mind fully engaged, and with a heart that is always intelligently compassionate, these ruminations are clear evidence that the humane is entirely possible within humanity so long as we are rigorously alert, and (to borrow from Mr. Acheson), 'we begin with a commitment to realness.'"

—LYNN STEGNER,
author of *For All the Obvious Reasons*

"These religion-page musings from a Vermont minister reveal both the obstinacy of our collective denial and the necessity of a well-grounded spirituality to move us beyond it. Only then can we bridge the many impasses threatening our sanity, our democracy, and our planet."

—CHRISTINE MARIE EBERLE,
author of *Finding God in Ordinary Time*

"*Beyond Denial* is a series of essays written with a big heart by an ordained minister. The author invites us to practice forms of spirituality that promote self-empowerment, while also leading us to care beyond ourselves through protecting the earth as well as meeting human need in the wider communities of our society."

—JOYCE SLAYTON MITCHELL, author of
Landmark Memories: A Vermont Village, 1930s-1960s

"These beautifully crafted essays invite humane and tolerant reflection on our shared responsibility to build a better world."

—T.H. BREEN, author of *Will of the People: The Revolutionary Birth of America*

"In *Beyond Denial* Rev. Acheson weaves together such diverse topics as personal self-awareness and climate change; the Gnostic Gospels and the pressures of Christmas; enjoying Vermont summers, and engaging in social action. These essays offer ways to find resources of "lasting hope and value" in a time of dizzying change and social disruption."

—THE REV. MAREN C. TIRABASSI, author of *Christmas Eve at the Epsom Circle McDonald's and Other Poems*

"Anthony Acheson's deep wisdom in easy-to-read language reminds me of the teachings of Buddhist sages like Pema Chodron. His reflections will feed you with an understanding of love as the highest form of Intelligence to heal our world and ourselves."

—NANCY KILGORE, author of *Bitter Magic*

BEYOND DENIAL

Essays on Consciousness,
Spiritual Practice,
and Social Repair

BEYOND DENIAL

*Essays on Consciousness,
Spiritual Practice,
and Social Repair*

ANTHONY E. ACHESON

GREEN PLACE BOOKS   *Brattleboro, Vermont*

Printed in the United States

10 9 8 7 6 5 4 3 2 1

Green Writers Press is a Vermont-based publisher whose mission is to spread
a message of hope and renewal through the words and images we publish.
Throughout we will adhere to our commitment to preserving and protecting
the natural resources of the earth. To that end, a percentage of our proceeds
will be donated to environmental activist groups. Green Writers Press
gratefully acknowledges support from individual donors, friends, and readers
to help support the environment and our publishing initiative.

Giving Voice to Writers & Artists Who Will Make the World a Better Place
Green Writers Press | West Brattleboro, Vermont
www.greenwriterspress.com

Library of Congress Cataloging-in-Publication Data available upon request.
ISBN: 978-1-950584-66-6

Cover design by Asha Hossain Design LLC

*This book is dedicated to my daughter, Emma,
to her mother, Nancy, and to our
grandchildren, Vivian, Celia, and Nelle,
who bring so much joy and hope to this world.
For better or worse our younger generations will reap
the full harvest of their elders' choices—whether they be for denial
or committed, wise action—about the environmental, social,
and ethical challenges facing our larger human family.*

Everything is related, and we human beings are united as brothers and sisters on a pilgrimage, woven together by the love of the Divine for each (person). . . a love which unites us in fond affection with brother sun, sister moon, brother river, and mother earth.

—POPE FRANCIS

The time has come for the creation of a new idea of God; a God reflected in the creation itself, and in the brave creations of self-reliant social pioneers; a religion based not upon surrender or submission, but on a new birth of confidence in life and in the God of life.

—RABBI JOSHUA LOTH LIEBMAN, 1946

Your own worst enemy cannot harm you as much as your own unguarded thoughts.

—THE BUDDHA

CONTENTS

Words of Thanks   xiii

Introduction   xv

THE CENTRALITY OF CONSCIOUSNESS   3

BEYOND DENIAL   9

SOCIAL LOVE   12

HAS GOD FALLEN SILENT?   16

DEALING WITH THE SHADOW   20

A CALL TO SPIRITUALITY   24

LOOK TO THE LIGHT   28

CHANGES   31

IN SEARCH OF REAL LEADERSHIP   33

THE CONTINUUM OF CONSCIOUSNESS (PART 1)   36

THE CONTINUUM OF CONSCIOUSNESS (PART 2)   42

THE LESSONS OF OKLAHOMA CITY   49

A WEEKEND FOR MEMORIALS   52

SUMMERTIME   54

ASKING THE RIGHT QUESTIONS   56

RELIGIONS MUST ALSO GROW   59

THE WORTH OF WORSHIP   63

HANDLING THE HOLIDAY BLUES   67

BETWEEN CLINTON AND STARR, NO WHITE HATS   71

A STUNNING INSTANCE OF DENIAL   75

SPIRITUAL DEMOCRACY   79

BLESSINGS, MY SON   81

SCAPEGOATING, AMERICAN STYLE   83

TRUTH IN FOCUSING   87

FROM GRACE SLICK TO SLICK BILL   90

IN PRAISE OF FALLING LEAVES   94

BELOVED AND UNBELOVED GHOSTS   97

"THANK U" FOR EVERYTHING   100

RELIGION AS RESOURCE NOT AUTHORITY   102

BEYOND GOD THE JUDGE   105

OF LOVE AND COMPASSION   110

A TALE OF TWO LEADERS   113

THE WORK OF WINTER   116

RISEN INDEED   118

THE LESSONS OF LITTLETON   121

ME AS THE MANTRA OF ALL THINGS   124

ON PARADES AND THE FOURTH   127

FINDING GOD IN NATURE   129

THE UNIVERSAL MIND   132

IN PRAISE OF FASTING   136

MEETING JESUS AGAIN FOR THE FIRST TIME   139

THE DEEP MANTRA OF THE AMERICAN MIND   144

ALWAYS AND FOR EVERYTHING   147

GAYNESS, PORK, AND PERIODS   150

RECLAIMING CHRIST FROM CHRISTIANITY   155

NOT BY BREAD ALONE   158

THE PRODIGAL BROTHERS   160

LIVING IN PRESENT TIME   162

THE CROSS REVISITED   165

NECESSARY SUFFERING   168

RELIGION AND POLITICS   172

RELIGION AND POLITICS REVISITED   174

A MORE HUMBLE CHURCH   177

IT'S BEYOND BELIEF   179

SHIFT HAPPENS   182

SIFTING THE TRADITION   184

MY SAME NEW FACE   187

RELIGION AS SURRENDER TO LOVE   189

AN EPIPHANY OF RADICAL SIGNIFICANCE   193

NO TO NORTON   196

THE REAL PRESENT DANGER   199

SACRAMENTAL CHOCOLATE   203

COMPASSIONLESS CONSERVATISM   205

A GOD WITH SOME SKIN   208

BLAME AS ANESTHESIA   211

THE WOUNDS OF THE FATHERS   214

BEYOND ECO-DENIAL   218

SPORTS, SPIRIT, AND PRACTICE   222

WITH WHAT YOU HAVE LEFT   225

WITHOUT YOUR CONSENT   227

BEYOND THE FREEZE-FRAME   230

THE POST-9/11 WORLD   234

A POST-PATRIARCHAL VIEW OF LOVE   237

THE POWER OF INTELLIGENT LOVE   242

A TALE OF TWO VICTORS   248

LOOKING IN THE MIRROR   254

VIETNAM REDUX?   257

THE EMPIRE GAME   260

"HOW COULD GOD ALLOW . . . ?" (PART 1)   264

"HOW COULD GOD ALLOW . . . ?" (PART 2)   266

"HOW COULD GOD ALLOW . . . ?" (PART 3)   270

TWO PAPER BAGS   274

About the Author   278

WORDS OF THANKS

⮾

S EVERAL YEARS AGO, my life-partner, Nancy, started asking me a question every evening when we sat down to eat: What are you grateful for? Over time, asking that question to each other (and sometimes to family or guests) has become a regular ritual in our household at dinner time.

Just as that has become a rich practice both for beginning a meal and for nearing the end of our daily schedule at home, I have a parallel sense of gratitude in the face of a simultaneous beginning (of this book being physically published) and ending (of writing and preparing the manuscript). And in relation to that, I am enormously grateful for several people who have played a key role of support in that process.

I'll start with my aforementioned partner, who has been an important gratefulness teacher in my life. Over and above her support for writing this book, she has consistently supported and encouraged me to find and express my own voice, and to do so in a range of ways: literarily and musically, interpersonally, psychologically, and spiritually. She has been, and is, a great gift indeed for whom I am deeply grateful.

Additional major thanks go to my editor, Michael Fleming, whose care, thoroughness, and thoughtful observations are woven into virtually every page that follows. In addition to being very good at the technical side of his work, Mike has a remarkably balanced ability to make pointed suggestions about possible textual changes, while also affirming—strongly and sincerely—that the final decisions must remain, legitimately, with the author. As the editing process unfolded, I followed Mike's suggestions a substantial majority of the time, even as I also sometimes stuck with my own original (or differently modified) phrasing. Mike was fully supportive of that process, and of those choices. And the synergy of his and my collaboration has resulted in a much, much better manuscript than the one I first presented him with all those months ago. (And in the process, we had a lot of fun to boot.)

I also want to express my enormous appreciation to all the people who have helped bring this project into tangible form. My thanks go to Dede Cummings at Green Writers Press (in Brattleboro, VT) for agreeing to publish the book, and for her many shows of affirmation, support, and help, including her beautiful interior book design; to Suzanne Kingsbury for her wise counsel about how to approach the publishing world; to Asha Hossain, whose artwork for the cover is brilliant, and whose skillful listening and dialogue with me were instrumental in crafting an image that is both visually arresting and consonant with the themes of the book; to Emma Irving, whose consistent, thorough, and patient efforts to walk me through the publicity process have been invaluable; to Ellen Keelan for her remarkable proofreading skills; and to the folks at Guilford Sound (in Guilford, VT)—Matt Hall, the sound engineer, and Cindy Larsen, the office manager—whose skill and flexibility have made the recording process for the audiobook version a genuine pleasure.

And finally, to those of you who may be holding this book, or viewing or hearing it digitally, thanks to you also for giving it a look. I hope you will find your time here well spent.

INTRODUCTION

IN 1990, not long after becoming the minister of All Souls Church in Brattleboro, Vermont, one of my parishioners began suggesting that I submit some columns to appear on the religion page of our local newspaper, the *Brattleboro Reformer*. (That parishioner was its editor, Stephen Fay.)

Although I accepted Steve's invitations only rarely at first, I became more and more intrigued by the challenge of writing such pieces, and eventually produced a few hundred of them. (I wrote them most frequently between 1998 and 2002, when they appeared almost weekly in the *Reformer*, and eventually in several other newspapers in New England.) This book is a collection of eighty-two of those essays.

One reason I *did* come to write those articles more frequently was because they helped me fulfill what I see as a central task for today's clergy: finding a wider range of ways to "translate" the core insights of humankind's wisdom-traditions into articulations that speak effectively to today's people. Over time, a rich dialogue developed between me and many of my readers through mail, e-mail, and face-to-face talks.

Those conversations fed my awareness of how many people there were who, though mostly disconnected from organized religion, were nonetheless vitally interested in spiritual themes and questions. Even as I heard many examples of why they saw religion as the province of outdated thinking, narrow-mindedness, or bigotry, I also heard that their hunger for spiritual experience—and intellectually viable spiritual paradigms—was every bit as strong as what I heard about from church-attenders (whether in Brattleboro or in my subsequent churches). Those unchurched readers, though, were finding scant spiritual food in either formal religion or secular society.

But many of those readers, although they had no interest in Sunday-morning church, were more than open to reading an ordained minister's thoughts as they sipped their Saturday-morning coffee. Their interest in spiritual themes, coupled with their *lack* of interest in church involvement, signaled the emerging divide in our culture between religion and spirituality. And addressing that tension became an increasingly frequent theme both in my writing and in my ministry generally.

This divide between religion and spirituality highlights an ongoing tension between what we might describe as the "needed old" and the equally "needed new." And this, in turn, calls us to a devilishly difficult balance. On the one hand, we need to preserve the tried and true insights (and human connections) offered by our faith traditions. But we also need, simultaneously, to *critique and correct* those same faith traditions, even as we are working to sustain them. And after nearly forty years of ministry in churches, I can tell you that maintaining both sides of that balancing act at one and the same time is a difficult dance indeed.

For those of us involved in a specific faith tradition, another significant part of that balance (between both preserving *and* evolving our religious-spiritual perspectives) lies in acknowledging the legitimate insights in traditions other than our own. This summons us to the great work of culling the core commonalities that *transcend* the particular religions in which they appear (including, for me, my own native Christianity).

Of those commonalities, what I see as being the most central is this: all of the great faiths call their people—in one form or another—to grow into an expanded spiritual consciousness of a kind that allows and empowers us to be transformed into people who live lives that are increasingly responsible, courageous, and compassionate. And that, in turn, requires us to develop the consciousness skills—i.e., the habits and capabilities within the inner world of our psyches—that *enable* us to act lovingly and responsibly, to engage in what Buddhists call "right action," and to live out the perennial wisdom to "first, do no harm," as articulated by the ancient Greeks.

This call to kindness, and to a non-harming life, leads to another major theme that this book explores: the challenge of applying the essentially religious admonition to "love our neighbor as ourselves" (in the phrase of Judaism and Christianity) to the most challenging problems of society. And given that quite a few of my religion-page essays addressed societal themes, writing them occasioned an important new avenue for addressing social issues in the context of my ministry.

As active clergy well know, preaching on sociopolitical issues must be undertaken with great care. But as my religion-page column evolved over the years (while I was serving a succession of churches), it became an unexpected way to address social questions with much more freedom than was readily available from the pulpit alone. For just as my articles were bringing spiritual-religious ideas onto the mental screens of people who were not church-attenders, they also played a role in encouraging at least *some* of my parishioners to consider the social and political implications of their own religious values in new ways.

Some of my church members, of course, didn't want to hear me preach about politics on Sunday mornings because they held views that were quite different from my own. And some others, more generally, didn't want our congregations to be partisan in *any* direction because doing so would, inescapably, become divisive. I understood, and had quite a bit of sympathy for, both viewpoints.

What I learned, though, and came to appreciate, was that most of those same people—including those whose social views differed from mine—fully honored the free expression of my thoughts appearing in print in a secular forum. And some, to my surprise, were more than willing to let my column act as a stimulus for one-on-one discussions with me about those views. And such conversations left a wider berth for rancor-free exchanges, ones that would not have been possible if I had been expressing such social views so directly and so frequently from the pulpit.

This leads me to one final observation that has emerged from the process of reviewing and preparing these articles for publication. As I've worked on them, I've become aware of the marked similarities between the social challenges I was writing about twenty to thirty years ago and those that still greatly beset us today.

The most notable example is our chronic cultural denial about the severity—even the existence—of climate change, and of our systemic human contributions to it. In the past few decades we have progressed remarkably little—and, in fact, have regressed—in dealing with that crucial problem (and with environmental degradation more generally). The psychological denial evident in our unwillingness to meaningfully address this challenge—and our resulting political paralysis about it—is distressing indeed.

The same can be said about America's unwillingness to deal with the growing gap between rich and poor, and the domination of our politics by big money. We see it also in our ongoing resistance to confronting our racial issues; and the failure to face our collective addiction to violence (whether in the form of domestic abuse, gun deaths, or persistent international warfare). The very fact that these all-too-current social challenges were already such clear and present dangers in the 1990s and early 2000s (but have been so little dealt with decades later) shows the depth of denial that has maintained so strong a grip on our national mind in recent decades. And it testifies just as powerfully to the depth of our collective need to face and overcome those patterns of denial.

It is my prayerful and heartfelt hope that these writings might help stimulate a renewed conversation about how to creatively and effectively address these denials and dysfunctions that currently compromise our culture—and have done so for such a long time. Responding to the dysfunctions of our time must start with the simple fact of being willing to see what the dysfunctions are; being willing to move beyond denial about their severity; and being willing to undertake the study, critical thinking, and hard work required for framing an intelligent analysis not only of what those predicaments are, but of how we might go about addressing them.

And here is a crucial point: dealing with those dysfunctions necessarily includes being smart enough to keep drinking at the well of history's greatest wisdom-streams, whether spiritual or religious, philosophical or psychological, aesthetic or scientific. Many of humankind's great articulations of wisdom and truth are ancient. But some are newly unfolding around us right now.

Whether the wisdom is old or new, however, is never the main point. What is decisive is our degree of willingness to put *all* our wisdom-sources to practical use. That starts, as we've seen, with moving beyond our chronic avoidance of confronting the difficulties inherent in the human condition. And such moving forward happens by being willing to see and experience the inescapable pains as well as the liberating potentials of our condition.

But such seeing is incomplete without *doing*. Broadened vision is only meaningful if it engenders a growing commitment to bettering the world through tangible and sustained choices based on love, mutual support, and the pursuit of wisdom. Our future choices will, inevitably, take many forms. Some of those will require the long-term, structured disciplines of spiritual practice, such as committing to regular meditation, and/or working for economic justice; joining a spiritual community, and/or working with a group that focuses on protecting the environment.

Though the specifics will vary, contributing to the betterment of the world in effective ways depends on embracing and embodying humanity's perennial and best wisdom: to offer love when we hear cries for help; and to cultivate trust in that larger divine Force for life and for good that keeps unfolding throughout human history—and indeed, within the universe itself. That Force of divine creational love is the power of life itself that lives and moves from within the very fabric of things, including from within our own beings, despite our chronic (if mostly unconscious) efforts to deny and derail it. And saying "yes" to that perennial wisdom calls us, importantly, to pursue liberty and happiness not just for our *own* lives—as our culture so loudly encourages us—but, more importantly, to serve the common good.

It is that service to the whole global community—and to the Wholeness itself—that is the one endeavor most worth undertaking. Our future depends on it.

BEYOND DENIAL

THE CENTRALITY
OF CONSCIOUSNESS

လာ

MAY 1990

WHEN I ATTENDED a church growth event last month, a notably large number of my fellow clergy were in attendance—not a surprise, given the woes afflicting formal religion these days. The workshop leaders focused on ways our congregations can better appeal to existing and potential members. To that end they emphasized new approaches for worship services such as greater use of contemporary music; sitting in a circle rather than facing forward; allowing time for discussion; sharing personal concerns; and so forth.

Changes like that have significant value, no doubt. And I have used some of those ideas to good effect in my ministry on more than one occasion. But despite that, I came away from that event disappointed. The heavy emphasis on such procedural fixes seemed short-sighted to me because of the lack of attention the presenters gave to a much more urgent topic: clarifying the main mission of the spiritual-religious enterprise more broadly, and developing new articulations of its core purposes—ones that "work" for, and speak to, today's people.

What, then, might we say about that main mission of spirituality and religion? To answer that briefly (fool's errand though that might be), I would say this. The primary function of spirituality and religion starts with promoting the *centrality of consciousness*. Although that might sound abstract or merely theoretical, I think it is, in fact, quite practical. Let's consider some specifics of what the pursuit of consciousness entails in real life.

Greater conscious awareness involves, most essentially, learning to recognize important realities and processes that we haven't previously noticed; especially those that are invisible to our physical senses. One way to wrap our minds around what this can mean in practical life is to look at some of the discoveries of modern science.

Consider, for example, how the physical spaces you and I are inhabiting right now, including our very bodies, are filled with all sorts of unseen things: TV signals and radio waves, electromagnetic fields and microbes—not to mention thoughts, attitudes, and emotions. Despite the fact that such phenomena are invisible, contemporary science and psychology have enabled us to become conscious that those things are all quite real.

Think also of what the astronomer Copernicus saw: that the earth goes around the sun, even though the opposite was "obvious." Think of the pioneers of medicine who opened their mental eyes to the existence of cells and other micro-organisms. Some of them were initially ridiculed for "believing in germs." But who laughs at them now?

Or consider the work of Darwin. Can anyone *see* evolution? Though our physical eyes cannot, we *can* learn to perceive how evolution unfolds as we consciously notice and record its incremental changes. Consider, again, Einstein's perception of the interchangeability of energy and matter. Our five senses couldn't begin to discern that unaided. But it's a fact.

What these thought leaders all had in common was an openness of mind that helped humankind as a whole to become more conscious of, and to map out, previously unseen phenomena.

And they did so through specific and sustained acts of consciously noticing the evidence trail of the processes and entities they studied, even though none of those realities I've cited could be detected immediately or directly.

And here is a key point. That same method of conscious "noticing" that we see in science is—and needs to be—a core methodology of the spiritual-religious enterprise. Just as science proactively probes invisibilities in the realm of reality we label as "physical," a mature spirituality is one by which we commit ourselves to probing the realm of reality traditionally labeled "spiritual," which (like electromagnetism, evolution, etc.) is tangibly real, though not directly visible.

And just as science has greatly advanced by fostering conscious awareness of the subtleties of physical processes, so must the spiritual renewal of our time proceed by peering into—and thus empowering ourselves to better access—the hidden energies of the psycho-spiritual dimensions of existence in and around us.

Although this need to consciously access psycho-spiritual resources is always with us, I would argue that it is especially pressing today, given the many looming challenges humankind now faces in the form of environmental disruption and economic inequality, escalating political and international conflicts, and prevalent worldview breakdowns. These upheavals will need to be addressed in many ways and from many angles. But what they will require of us more than anything else is ongoing growth in awareness. This starts with acknowledging—i.e., becoming *conscious* of—the nature and dynamics of the problems themselves. And that, in turn, will require us to move beyond denial of the severity of these problems—a denial that has become chronic in today's culture.

Such growth in awareness will also call on us to develop within ourselves an expanded repertoire of psycho-spiritual skills, practices, and approaches that can help us creatively address our challenges. This "consciousness project," as we might think of it, will call for developing skills of this kind in three main realms of life.

The first is becoming students of our own psyches: developing a greater working knowledge about—and mastery of—the complex processes that take place within our own minds and beings. Such proactive inner work is the very heart of spiritual practice. This can involve, variously, engaging in a regular contemplative life or meditation practice, working with a spiritual director, doing bodywork, developing our relational skills, and participating in groups for support and recovery. Another important tool along these lines is psychotherapy, which formal religion sometimes fails to recognize as the *spiritual* practice it very much can be. Spiritual practice, to be sure, importantly includes committing ourselves to lives of service and/or activism. But we mustn't forget that the work of social repair around us finds its best and most lasting success if it is grounded, first, in doing the difficult but necessary *inner* work of self-awareness, self-healing, and self-development.

This work of studying—and mastering—our own psyches is an activity for which the analogy to science is especially apt. For us moderns, accepting the reality of invisible, physically objective processes, as I've described above, has become second nature. But we are still mere beginners at seeing how much the unfolding of our own inner processes is correspondingly beyond the reach of ordinary awareness, although those same psycho-spiritual processes are substantively real.

If the truth be known, the great *majority* of what happens within our psyches is quite hidden to us. And what goes on in us behind the scenes of everyday awareness (especially our assumptions and core beliefs, our fears and antagonisms) has a major effect on our choices, and thus on how our own lives unfold—not to mention the lives of those around us. This is where psychotherapy (or working with a spiritual director) can be particularly valuable. It can enable us to see the reality not just of molecules and microbes, but of our own unconscious behavioral patterns and programming—and of the powerful effect those influences have on ourselves and those around us.

This leads to the second benefit of pursuing greater consciousness: gaining greater understanding of what is going on in our society. I would suggest, specifically, that increasing our *societal* consciousness is also a fundamentally *spiritual* undertaking. This side of spiritual practice involves training ourselves to perceive the underlying causes of, and possible solutions for, our social problems—most especially the increasing damage being done by our society's environmental and economic approaches.

Consider how often we overlook the fact that most of the hurt and harm we humans inflict on one another takes place through actions undertaken *collectively*—by the social groupings we take part in and identify with. We tend to be blind, specifically, to how our support for harmful societal patterns provides an outlet for our own unacknowledged fear and aggression.

To cite one stark example, it is easy to see that murder is a terrible thing. Yet the damage done by the human addiction to war and collective violence in this twentieth century has dwarfed the damage done by all individual murders combined. Most people find ways to be in denial about that clear fact. This unconscious denial about collective violence happens through a range of mechanisms: enshrining war as noble; lavishing honor on soldiers and the military; lending enthusiastic support to the war of the moment as "justified"; and supporting economic, racial, sexual, and religious attitudes and agendas that cause hurt and harm, and thus sow the seeds for later social upheavals, including wars.

The third and greatest boon of expanded awareness is the access it gives us to the subtle resources of Spirit at work in things—including within our own beings. This is the main theme of our greatest spiritual exemplars. It is what Jesus and the Buddha, Moses and Mother Teresa, Hildegard of Bingen and Rumi, Lincoln and Gandhi, and countless more keep advising us. "Keep learning more," they are saying in effect, "of how life works—and *can* work—at its most fundamental levels; and let your lives be filled with the compassion and confidence that flow forth from seeing, and feeding on, the beauty and the energies of Being itself—of the truest divine Reality at work in and behind all things."

The spiritual renewal of our time must start with letting go of the ignorance, fear, and adversarial thinking that arises when we remain shackled to what Socrates calls the unexamined life. The better way—i.e., the life that *is* proactively "examined"—is the path by which we embrace the invitation from Life itself to become continually more conscious of the core inner and outer dynamics that move and shape our beings.

BEYOND DENIAL

NOVEMBER 1990

On August 2, 1990, President Saddam Hussein of Iraq attacked and annexed the neighboring nation of Kuwait. In response, US president George H. W. Bush declared, "This will not stand," and organized a coalition of thirty-five nations to retaliate if Iraq did not withdraw. When Iraq refused, coalition forces attacked on January 17, 1991. Hussein's troops suffered horrific losses and were pushed out of Kuwait. Hostilities officially ended on February 28, 1991.[1]

As AMERICA draws closer to attacking Iraq, the US claim that Saddam Hussein is the cause of this conflict doesn't hold up. The impending war is, in my view, less about Iraq's aggression than about America's fixation on oil. Given our economy's unbridled consumerism and heavy dependence on oil, keeping a cheap, plentiful supply of it under US control has preoccupied our power-elites for decades.

Although Saddam Hussein's seizure of Kuwait in August was abhorrent, it needs to be seen in context. For most of the 1980s, America courted this same man as an ally. When Hussein invaded a different neighboring country—Iran—in September of 1980, the United States actively *supported* him in that action.

Let me repeat for emphasis: we didn't just *condone* that military invasion of Iran by Saddam Hussein ten years ago. We fully

---

1 Editor's note.

9

favored it, sending Iraq billions of dollars, supplying arms and intelligence, and offering special-ops training to Iraqi soldiers. In 1982, the Reagan-Bush Administration removed Iraq from its list of states alleged to sponsor terrorism. Why? To make our support for Iraq "legal." More than half a million people died in that Iran–Iraq War. (And more than 10,000 Iranians were killed by Iraq's use of poison gas.)

Given that American "yes" to Hussein's attack on Iran in 1980, why do we say "no" to his attack on Kuwait now in 1990? The answer is obvious—if we are willing to see it. In 1980 America wanted the government of Iran weakened—or removed—and was happy to let Iraq do the dirty work. Saddam's attack on Kuwait this past summer was not different in kind from his earlier aggression against Iran, except for this one key difference: *this* year's invasion threatens America's control over the reliable supply of oil from the Middle East.

The president has said that Iraq's action threatens our way of life. That is a telling statement. And we would do well to ask: Just what is that "way of life" he is referring to? He is clearly referring, most generally, to our economic system. But this economic system he so reveres is one that is based not only on massive consumption, but on overwhelmingly *wasteful* consumption patterns that are perpetuated by an undisciplined American appetite for global resources. Most specifically, this is a system that requires a massive, environmentally destructive burning of the world's oil. And that, in turn, leads back to our ongoing American obsession with controlling the petroleum *supply*.

Put bluntly, we will soon go to war—likely killing many thousands of human beings—so that our country can keep this form of economic system running. What we don't want to hear, though, is that our addictive consumption patterns, and our felt need to control the oil to maintain them, enslaves us to the threat of ongoing warfare to keep our supply lines in place. This soon-to-be war, in other words, will almost certainly not be the last. And so long as America keeps trying to dominate the Middle East and its oil and its politics, there will be pushback from the *peoples* of the Middle East. The best we can hope for in that scenario are some relatively peaceful pauses *between* active conflicts.

In addition to that bleak future of repeated warfare, there is another looming consequence from our oil addiction: the damage we are doing to the environment. Despite our long-standing and continuing denial, global warming is at hand. And its burgeoning effects—rising sea-levels, severe storms, droughts, forest fires, etc.—are potentially catastrophic. When the recent UN Climate Conference proposed new carbon-dioxide-reduction goals, the United States was the *only* major opponent, despite the relative modesty of the suggested targets, including keeping CO_2 emissions at current levels by the year 2000.

This ongoing American resistance—and the attitude of denial that lies behind it—highlights our need to become more conscious of the addictive quality of this "way of life" President Bush so reveres. Our culture's over-consumption is not a blessing to be protected. It is, much more, an addiction to be recovered from. We are like drunks who can't admit their drinking problem. It is a near form of faith for us Americans that more is better. But where is the "better" in more war—and ecological disaster?

Much as we prefer blaming Saddam Hussein for this coming war, there is a deeper root cause for this war that is to be found in ourselves—in our own economic addiction patterns. Instead of blaming Hussein, we would do much better to get on with becoming conscious of, and dealing with, the flaws in our own national character. Our choice is stark: less consumption now, or more war—and ecological catastrophe—later.

The sage from Nazareth once asked, "How can you say to your brother, 'Let me take that splinter from your eye,' while there is a log in your own eye?" (Matthew 7:4). That is a question we would do well to become willing to hear. And then hear still more. And act on. Instead of attacking Iraq, let's move beyond denial by dealing, first, with the dysfunctions of our own house.

SOCIAL LOVE

∽

FEBRUARY 1991

T HE SOCIOLOGIST Robert Bellah, a keen student of religion, has said that when it comes to social policy, "love is not a popular idea" among Americans. We can see this clearly in the broad public support for our attack last month on Iraq. "Sending in the Marines" is almost always supported by our population whenever that happens (which is often). And it should be clear to any honest observer that unleashing a major war is hardly a "loving" approach to international problem solving. Doing so shows how much more faith we place in war and violence than in love-based social policies—including nonviolent approaches to global conflicts. Our trust in force and the fist is clearly much more prevalent among us than any supposed national "faith in God."

We've been hearing a lot recently about religious justifications for war. Saddam Hussein calls his war-making "holy." George Bush calls his "just." But I don't see much evidence that either of those men has any strong interest in either holiness or justice. Each claims God for his side. But neither seems led, like Lincoln, to seek out the divine side. Both are trying to leverage the religious yearnings of their peoples as yet another tool for gaining raw power in the service of personal and national advantage.

The real question this war presents is not whether the war itself is just or holy, but whether our choice to wage it is *loving*. Is it a love-based practice to burn people alive—whether civilian or soldier? Is it loving to blow off people's legs? Is it an expression of love to explode whole truck-loads of human beings and then call it a "clean" strike? Are we following the law of love when we paralyze people or render them terrified to the point of insanity, crippling their minds, often for life?

For anyone whose heart is meaningfully open, and who truly believes in kindness and compassion, the answers to all these questions must be a resounding "no." And if we can allow ourselves to see that love is the sole standard by which war—and all our doings—can rightly be judged, we can see too that the true "enemy" (if we must have an enemy) is not Saddam Hussein (nor, to be sure, George Bush), but rather is, much more so, our own un-thought-through (and thus unconscious) willingness to repeatedly lend support to wars like this.

When the Bible says that "God is love" (1 John 4:8), it is affirming that the core energy of the universe is fundamentally divergent from the kind of energy we see in the approaches based on domination and violence, which our culture reveres with such unthinking and unconscious trust. By contrast, this universal divine Power—this God that is Love—is a force for unity, and for the life-enhancement and growth that unity fosters. That is what love is: a force that creates, unifies, and propels living things to grow and to achieve their fullest possible development.

There is a strong strand in American thought by which many of us think that our country is a notably religious, or a specifically Christian, nation. But it is important to notice that today's American disdain for bringing love to bear in framing social policies is at odds with what its own principal Judeo-Christian traditions actually teach.

The biblical prophets, for example, were quick to condemn ostensibly pious kings for harsh treatment of the poor. A later Jewish prophet, Jesus from Nazareth, also spoke against the powers that be of his era for their hardness of heart toward the poor and the sick, women and children, foreigners and non-Jews. These stances by the Hebrew prophets advocating "social love" were also at the very heart of the mission of Christ. (And they were paralleled, we might also note, in the Buddha's far-ahead-of-his-time condemnation of the unjust and unloving caste system in India). One important theme the Hebrew prophets and Jesus (and the Buddha) all have in common is this: their advocacy for embracing love as a guide not just for individuals, but for *society as a whole.*

But despite our culture's wide disbelief in applying the principles of love to the workings of society (as noted by Robert Bellah), the establishment of love-based social systems keeps advancing nonetheless. Consider how, in much of the world, such practices as slavery, child-labor, and torture have been outlawed. Consider how women are approaching equal status with men in many countries, and how once-hostile races and religions are finding more common ground in many places globally. Consider how, in most of the industrial world, universal health care, education, and suffrage are now considered to be rights, not privileges. And consider how the lessening of pollution, and increases in recycling, are being willingly embraced by millions of people. All these developments can and should be seen for what they are: the growth of a more "loving" stance both toward our fellow humans and toward the biosphere that cradles our common physical life.

I understand fully that such progress in the growth of social love is maddeningly incomplete. And I understand too that when progress of this kind appears, it is often followed by times of regression, as fears about change (and nostalgia for the old ways) inevitably surface. But in the larger arc of history, the development of humane social systems (which means: more *loving* social systems) keeps inching forward.

And here is the key point: advances like the ones I just cited proceed, most essentially, from a commitment to, and a belief in, the introduction of effective expressions of love into the structures of society. The very definition of whether social change is in fact *progress* (and whether it is *humane*) springs precisely from evaluating whether or not it has a loving effect on the actual living people of that society.

As our culture today says "yes" once again to its ancient faith in killing, war, and violence (as evidenced by the wide support for this current war on Iraq), let us be reminded of a better, higher faith that looks to the spirit-based power of love, and the divine Ground from which it springs, as the best and most effective basis for solving our collective problems.

To that end, may we keep working for a world in which compassion is not just a sometime hope, but the emerging norm for how we do the ongoing work of structuring, and healing, human society on all its levels.

HAS GOD FALLEN SILENT?

⤝

FEBRUARY 1994

RECENTLY, I was asked to give a talk on spiritual practice at a conference. After my presentation, someone said to me, "I still pray . . . but is anyone there to hear it?" That comment reminded me of a phrase I've heard often lately in theological circles: the "silence of God" in our time. Has the Divine *actually* fallen silent? My personal experience says "no." But for many moderns, the answer clearly seems to be "yes."

To address this experience of God's seeming silence, we need to start by re-examining our prevailing Western ideas about what God *is*. This begins with focusing on one of the most entrenched assumptions of Western theology: the idea that God is a person, or in some way a person-like being.

In my work as a minister, I hear many people tell me that portraying the Godhead in an anthropomorphic way like this (as if the Ultimate were a person) is a paradigm that no longer speaks to them. Put simply, it is an approach that is no longer anywhere close to being intellectually viable.

But despite the widespread decline of belief in that *traditional* view of the Divinity, there continues to be a large number of people in our culture who nonetheless still "believe in God" (in whatever ways they might conceptualize that God), and who still engage in serious spiritual pursuits. In short, there is no lack of spiritual interest *per se* around us. What mainstream Western religions currently lack, however, are broadly effective articulations—or, more to the point, effective reframings and reinterpretations—of the main themes at the heart of those religions, most especially their prevailing ideas about the nature of the Divine.

Given that ongoing heart-hunger for ultimate things, our religions need to develop new ways of presenting spiritual truth to today's people in ways they can hear and understand, speak about and access. Doing so calls for a broader spiritual vocabulary that "works" for the contemporary mind. And this very much includes moving beyond those outmoded, anthropomorphic God-concepts I mentioned earlier.

Moving in that direction must begin with giving careful thought to the nature of religious language. This means, first, remembering that skillful theological speech must make the distinction between *truth* (what actually exists) and credal statements *about* what exists. And it means, second, understanding that the nature of the Godhead is inherently ineffable; i.e., it cannot be expressed directly through any human words or descriptions. As the philosopher Wittgenstein demonstrated in the first half of this twentieth century, language can at best point *toward* what it tries to describe, but can never reveal it fully or adequately.

All God-concepts, then, are necessarily metaphorical. Metaphor itself is a valid and invaluable tool for pointing toward ineffable things. But over the course of history, the metaphors that various spiritual traditions use—and that their peoples understand and respond to—inevitably change. And when that happens, religious leaders need to be ready to revise, and if necessary replace, their range of metaphors that they use to describe the Divine.

The important implication of all this is not that our theological statements—our creeds and doctrines—*may* change, but that they *must* change. (And, it should be noted, this applies to *all* our cultural, scientific, and philosophical paradigms, not just those of religion.) Like all living things, our ways of understanding the world must continue to find new forms of expression, and to evolve new worldviews. And in the process, we may need to let go of some of our old worldviews entirely, if and when they outlive their usefulness. The nature of the Godhead, then, may be unchanging, but our concepts *about* God—including all specific beliefs and creeds, doctrines and dogmas, terminologies and articulations—are inescapably in flux and subject to the need for change.

At the conference I mentioned earlier, I spoke also with a thoughtful older woman who had been raised to believe in a God that was a literal old man, with an actual white beard, on a physical throne. But even though she has long since let go of such primitive God-concepts, the Divine is still vitally real to her. She has learned that many human ideas about the larger Power are transient. But in the face of that, she has been willing to let her childhood God-pictures shift and grow (and she has let some of them go completely). And our religions as a whole need to be willing to follow exactly that example.

To flesh out what such a post-anthropomorphic paradigm for the Divine might look like in much detail is beyond the scope of a short essay like this. But here is one necessary starting place: to understand that the Ultimate is *not* a person or a person-like being, and consequently does not perform the same functions that human persons do.

In a post-anthropomorphic view, God does not "act" or "decide." God does not "permit" or "prevent" specific events. Nor does God "choose" or "elect" favored groups, or "judge" those who act wrongly. All of those activities—acting, deciding, judging, etc.—are functions specific to human personhood, and can thus only be engaged in by persons. I believe strongly that what human religions are trying to point to when they speak about God has real and actual existence. But since that Reality we are pointing toward is not a person, we need to stop misleading ourselves and our people (partly through outmoded language) into thinking that the Divine chooses to "act" or "make decisions" in the same ways that human persons do.

If the Godhead, then, is *not* a human-like person, what can we say about what God, in fact, *is*? That, again, is a large subject. But here is a quick sketch of some options. We can think, first, of the Godhead as Being itself (a phrase often used by the thirteenth-century Roman Catholic theologian Thomas Aquinas, as borrowed from Greek philosophy). Or we can frame God as the Ground of Being, a term favored by the twentieth-century Protestant writer Paul Tillich. In the writings of an earlier Protestant thinker, Friedrich Schleiermacher (often called "the father of modern liberal theology"), one of his main names for God was "the Universe." Interestingly, although this term has found favor as a "name" for God in today's New Age community, using such terminology is largely ignored by church people today (probably because it is deemed to imply a supposed "pantheism" to which mainstream Christian thinking has remained doggedly opposed).

We can also understand the Divinity, variously, as the world-generating Life Force; as the universal Intelligence operating nature's laws; as the underlying Consciousness and Energy that sustains life; or as the all-connecting Continuum that holds the *uni-verse* together as a *uni-ty*.

The experience of my life tells me that what I am referring to when I speak of "God," or "the Divine," is a real and present power. But the spiritual paradigms—and terminology—about the Ultimate handed down to us from previous times must undergo greatly needed changes and expansion. And for those of us involved in religion today, one of our main jobs is to proactively shape and promote the unfolding of such changes in how we think about the Divine, not ignore or resist them.[2]

---

[2] A number of other essays in this volume grapple with the questions of how to describe the Divine and what metaphors can best serve a growth in our theological understanding. See, for example: "The Continuum of Consciousness (Parts 1–2)," "The Worth of Worship," "Beyond God the Judge," "Finding God in Nature," "The Universal Mind," "Meeting Jesus Again for the First Time," "A God with Some Skin," and "'How Could God Allow . . . ?' (Parts 1–3)".

DEALING WITH THE SHADOW

⌁

JUNE 1994

On June 12, 1994, Nicole Brown Simpson and her friend Ron Goldman were stabbed to death in Los Angeles. The actor, TV commentator, and former football star O. J. Simpson (Nicole's ex-husband) was soon arrested on murder charges. As his trial approached (and before much of the evidence had become public), many Americans formed strong convictions about his guilt or innocence. Simpson was acquitted of both murders after a lengthy criminal trial. But he was found liable for those crimes in a subsequent civil trial.[3]*

THE O. J. SIMPSON SAGA has captivated us this week as have few events in my lifetime. There is much more of this tale to unspool, no doubt. But what intrigues me most right now is not so much Simpson's potential guilt or innocence, as the broad resistance among many Americans to thinking that he *could* be guilty. For many among us, the horror seems less directed at the violence itself than at the idea that this particular celebrity might have perpetrated it.

Here's an example. Simpson's fellow football announcer, Al Michaels, said this week that the likelihood of the O. J. he knows doing this crime is "unthinkable . . . even off the page" of

---

[3*] Editor's note.

possibility. Others in Simpson's professional circle have expressed similar disbelief. In various interviews they have characterized him as a person who is *up, sunny, cheerful, nice, fun, friendly,* and *rarely even irritable.*

Likewise, when we in the general public think of O. J. Simpson, we often think of him in his various screen roles as a charismatic athlete, a well-spoken sports commentator, and the star of several funny movies. We remember him as the man "running through airports" in rent-a-car ads. In those settings, he comes across as amusing, lighthearted, and controlled. That is the image. But what is the reality?

Let's start with the caution not to prejudge Simpson's guilt or innocence regarding these specific murders. But even if we suspend judgment on this current case, there is other disturbing information. Consider that several of these same people (such as Al Michaels) who describe O. J. Simpson as a "good guy" are fully aware that he is, in fact, a *convicted felon*—a man found legally guilty of severe battery of his wife in 1989. These commentators are also fully cognizant that when the police came to the Simpson house on that occasion—finding Nicole Simpson badly bruised from an O.J. beating—it was the ninth time she had summoned the police with allegations of his attacks.

Let that sink in. This was not the first or second time, but the *ninth* time she had called the police. Those cases were all *widely publicized.* But for many of his fellow-celebrity apologists, those incidents—including the battery conviction—don't seem to stick in their consciousness, given that they now describe him so positively, and are incredulous at even the *possibility* of his guilt. Al Michaels and others seem determined to believe in the public screen-image version of O. J. Simpson (and, perhaps, in the congenial way he may have related to them on-set) much more than the extensive, widely available news reports of his actual hostile behaviors.

Consider one more thing. After Mr. Simpson was convicted of that spousal battery in 1989, the Hertz Corporation, for which he did the rental car ads, continued to employ him for three more years. Why would they do that? And why would Al Michaels and others describe someone with such widely publicized anger problems—including that battery conviction—as a man about whom it was "unthinkable" that he might murder his wife?

The answer? It's a form of denial. Those people and companies—along with much of the public—have come to see the Simpson on their TV screens as a celebrity good guy. And because they are comfortably familiar with that image on the "screen" of their consciousness, that image has now become not only how they are accustomed to seeing him, but how they want to *keep* seeing him. This, in turn, has led to a widespread psychological denial of his destructive side. It is well-documented, and there for all to see. But many choose not to see it.

This O. J. Simpson case is a teachable moment for our culture. The American public is confronted, in a certain sense, with a choice between beliefs. People can believe *either* the positive narrative about Mr. Simpson so carefully constructed in his various screen images. *Or*, they can believe the negative facts about him shown in his felony conviction and in many other news reports. For many Americans, their decision seems to be: we'll skip the facts, and stick with the positive narrative that we've already bought into; we'll maintain the image of the O. J. that we like, the one we've seen packaged for our entertainment on our TV and movie screens.

As I watch all this, I find myself wondering more and more if there isn't a kind of trance of denial coming over this culture, one that is heavily fed by this growing syndrome of embracing the various story-lines we see on our TV and movie screens as if they were factually true. We seem to be buying into such screen-narratives more and more passively, and without subjecting them to anything resembling careful study, factual analysis, or critical thinking.

There's no way of knowing how this Simpson murder trial will turn out. Right now, though, many Americans do seem captivated with some form of "belief" in the O.J. they've become entranced with on their electronic screens. What this part of our population enjoys, and seems to want to maintain, is the image of O.J. they've seen on TV running the football so powerfully, and shilling for Hertz so entertainingly. They want the one commentating on the NFL broadcasts, or appearing in comedies with Leslie Nielsen. They want to maintain that friendly screen image that they've trusted to entertain them for years, rather than confront the hard news about O.J.'s battery conviction—and multiple other allegations of violence. This is a segment of our American psyche that tends toward believing the manufactured images on its screens that are comforting, rather than perceiving the actual realities that are unnerving.

In Simon and Garfunkel's old song "The Boxer," there's a line about a man who just "hears what he wants to hear and disregards the rest." That's an apt description of what seems to be going on these days when much of America sits anesthetized and numb in front of the TV and sees what it wants to see in O. J. Simpson.

A CALL TO SPIRITUALITY

✧

*T*he Gnostic Gospels by Princeton historian Elaine Pagels is a remarkable book I've been reading recently that describes a bounty of early Christian writings rediscovered in Egypt in 1945. Nearly sixteen centuries earlier (in 367 CE), officials of the predominant church of the day had ordered all copies of these works burned, including the now much-revered *Gospel of Thomas.* They apparently believed that the portrayal of Christ in those texts diverged from official doctrine in a way that could damage the souls of the faithful—and the church as a whole. Some dedicated monks, though, defied that dictate. And instead of burning their collection they carefully and lovingly buried it, thus preserving it for posterity.

What these rediscovered works all have in common is their advocacy for the value of direct spiritual experience based on *gnosis* (a Greek word meaning "inner knowing"). The knowing in question here goes beyond mere *intellectual* knowledge. Just as, in biblical Hebrew, "knowing" a beloved implies deep union with his or her being, this gnostic idea advocates going beyond mere cognitive thinking *about* God and the spiritual world. And it points instead to a firsthand sensing of the spiritual realm through being

24

joined with it. This involves opening ourselves to the Divine as a palpable, pervasive Presence that exists not just beyond us, but within—and even *as*—our own beings. The core gnostic idea is to encourage committed seekers to develop a spiritual practice that helps them directly experience their inherent connectedness with God.

This gnostic strand of early Christian thinking, based as it was on such immediate experience, de-emphasized the need for organized church structure. Spiritual community, though valued, was seen as a resource more than as a binding authority. And although gnostic Christians revered Jesus, they didn't view him as one who bestowed "salvation" from the outside in. They saw him, instead, as a transformative teacher; a model and mentor; a guide and trailblazer; one who had attained the gnosis himself, and then taught it to others as an act of service. As a result, gnostic Christian views of religion were minimally hierarchical. They tended to locate the transformative, divine Power much more in the inner consciousness of the believer than in the exterior institution of the church.

Some of those gnostic Christian communities (though not all) insisted on the then radical belief in the equality of women. One exquisite discovery from that 1945 trove of documents is the *Gospel of Mary*, which makes clear that Mary Magdalene was a significant leader and teacher in the early Christian movement. Needless to say, the so-called "Fathers" of the church of that era disapproved female equality with males—just as they disapproved the gnostic emphasis on direct, spiritual knowing without much help from the church hierarchy.

By contrast, those early church officials demanded assent to official creeds, and obedience to the (male) clergy. After Christianity won majority status and became the official faith of Rome by the end of the fourth century, its bishops and priests, who had once been victims of the Roman police, had now become their superiors. And they used that newfound power to try to expunge the gnostic texts from history.

For those seeking spiritual renewal today, however, these gnostic viewpoints constitute an invaluable set of resources that, though old in their origins, are powerfully new to the awareness of many of us. One important role they can play today is, first, to highlight the priority of spirituality over religion. For us, these gnostic texts can be a rich seed-source for coming to see that the goal of the spiritual life is not to affiliate with any specific "true religion." The more foundational goal is to develop a repertoire of tools for accessing the spiritual dimensions of reality more generally. And that process of spiritual search and discovery can be sought out through any number of religious and/or spiritual traditions.

But despite the fact that there is no single superior religion, specific religions can nonetheless continue to play a major role in fostering such spiritual awareness. The texts and truths of these great traditions contain many lasting treasures; and our existing churches and other religious meeting-places can—and must—continue to be vital centers of community and connection.

Here is an analogy that I think can help us understand this relationship between traditional religion and the more comprehensive view of spiritual-religious traditions that I'm describing. Just as the thirteen American colonies had to yield their individual primacy in order to constitute a new nation, so too must our historic faiths see beyond the limits of their local beliefs and practices, and move toward membership in a larger, global spiritual community.

In this process, they must learn to move past competition with other traditions, and move toward greater cooperation with them. For only by so doing can they come to create (as those thirteen colonies did) a new "congress" of spiritual seekers and finders—and, crucially, global healers. After the American Revolution (in the terms of my analogy), each state had to yield primacy to an emergent nation of newly "united" states. But as that process unfolded it did not require, for example, my own birth-state of New York to fade out of existence. Quite to the contrary, New

York (or Rhode Island, Virginia, etc.) continues to be a vital and valuable entity that plays an ongoing role in serving and bettering our country and society.

And so it must be with our religions. The fact that they must yield their primacy does not mean that they will lose their significance. Quite to the contrary. The real job of religion has never been about primacy or superiority or dominance. The real role of all religions is to themselves embody the ethic of selfless service that most of them teach their own adherents to embody in daily life. The real role of our religions, in other words, is to become servants—not masters—of new and continually evolving forms of spiritual experience, connection, and community.

Helping our houses of faith grow in *that* direction, through using both traditional and alternative resources, is our best hope for accessing the full range of spiritual riches that are available to—and greatly needed by—the human race going forward.

LOOK TO THE LIGHT

⊷

NOVEMBER 1994

T HE ADVENT AND HANUKKAH observances that start tomorrow can seem quite different on the surface. Advent is Christian, and marks the birth of a heralded baby; while Hanukkah is Jewish, and observes a political rebellion against foreign oppressors. But despite those differences, they have an important common focus: the celebration of light.

On each of the eight nights of Hanukkah, often called the "Festival of Lights," a new candle is lit. This symbolizes how, in 165 BCE, a small store of temple oil is said to have burned miraculously long, and thus signaled hope for the Jewish nation to throw off its conquerors. Likewise in Christianity, on each of the four Sundays of Advent a new candle is also lit, symbolizing the church's belief that the birth of Christ also brings hope for a new birth of light for all.

If we look further back in history, we see that both Advent/ Christmas and Hanukkah have historic roots in—and can be seen as reinterpretations of—solstice celebrations of old, in which people affirmed their faith in the return of light (and warmth) from darkness (and cold). The reappearance of these themes of light and dark in distinct traditions (such as Judaism and Christianity) can help show us that the specific faith we take part in is less important than setting our sights on the Light itself, in *whatever* form or tradition it manifests.

I have a friend whose infant son is entranced, like most babies, by gazing at bright and colorful lights. Those two have a game going—mostly on the side of the dad, to be sure—in which he points to various lights and says, "That's God." And as the wide wonder of the boy's gaze shows, he believes! When the Bible counsels us to "become again as children" (Matthew 18:3), it reminds us to maintain our fascination not just in the lights that illuminate our homes and streets, but in the Light that fills and runs the cosmos; the Light that makes sense of life as a whole. In the early eighties there was a pop song I listened to countless times called "Keep Feeling Fascination" (sung by the Human League). Children don't need to be told to do that. But we adults often need reminders.

How do we keep alive our fascination for things of the Light, and our hope for renewed and better lives? One place to start is by learning what it means to live our lives more and more from our hearts. This means living increasingly from a sense of connectedness and compassion. It means surrendering less and less to fear and its tendency to focus our attention on short-term self-protection and self-advantage. It means letting our cognitive minds function as servants, not masters, when it comes to choosing how we shape our lives. It means having the wisdom to focus on things that feed us on the inside, rather than prioritizing *outer* acquisition, as our culture so loudly urges. It means making room at the inn, so to speak, for ways of life that nourish what Quakers call the "Inner Light." And it means serving the common good more than mere personal promotion.

We must keep in mind also that opening ourselves to the realm of the Light requires choice and practice. A great athlete cannot master her sport just by appearing in official games. High-level performance comes only from much practice before and between the games.

And so it is with the life of the spirit. Looking to the Light means learning to be more aware of the spiritual Presence through a disciplined development of specific spirit-skills. This is why "practicing" such things as meditation, prayer, yoga, psycho-therapy, artistic creativity—and working for social justice—are so essential to a Light-filled life. Those are all forms of spirit-practice that help us claim our capacity to be illuminated by the spiritual energies and values in and around us, values that we can't other-wise see with our physical eyes alone.

Do we wish to let in the Light that helps access life's available spiritual power? Do we hunger for wisdom and joy? Will we choose to make heartening music with this major "instrument" that each of us plays, which is the gift of our life?

In answer to those questions, Hanukkah and Advent, for all their surface differences, both say the same: look to the Light

CHANGES

ᮜ

DECEMBER 1994

A S A NEW YEAR APPROACHES, I'm aware how much has changed for me in in these past months. My sister Bena died last year at fifty-four. Both my mother's brothers died soon after that. And then, in September of this year, my father also died. After that, my mom quickly dismantled our long-standing family home and moved in with my surviving sister, Chris. So when I arrived for our family Christmas last week, even though Chris's place was lovingly prepared and festive, it was not the same "home" I've gone to for many holidays past. Big changes.

Coming to terms with this first Christmas without Dad was hard. Before traveling, I scheduled a massage as a seasonal gift to myself. While lying on the table, a sudden rush of emotion welled up into long, deep weeping. "I miss my dad," I heard myself cry out over and over. A painful change.

During the Christmas visit itself, I took my mother on two "trips." One was a quick swing into town to help her with buying a gift for someone. On the second we picked up a painting in the old house. For her at eighty-four, now barely able to walk after a stroke, those were trips indeed. Navigating the three front steps of my sister's house was noticeably harder than it was for her even last summer. A difficult change.

At visit's end, after smiling and waving goodbye, and when my car was out of sight, I started crying again. "What's wrong?" my ten-year-old daughter asked, puzzled, innocent. I tried to speak my sudden sense that my mom's sweet, sad face on the stoop might be my last sight of her. Probably not. But maybe. Change, again.

The shifts in my life these days aren't all hard. I'm starting a new job next Monday morning (as interim minister of the Congregational Church in Claremont, New Hampshire). That is a happy event which I'm looking forward to, although that move will put me at some distance from my accustomed social ties in southern Vermont. Yet more change.

Through all these transitions, I've been learning to see that even when the changes bring loss, the losses themselves can bring forms of gain. There are aspects, for example, of my love for my father that I didn't know, and couldn't feel, until after I lost him. And there are sides of my love for my mother that I didn't fully feel until I had gone through losing my dad.

In the sixties, the pop singer Donovan had a song with the line, "Caterpillar sheds its skin to find a butterfly within." In the end, I guess, what counts most is how I choose: Will I focus most on the loss of the cocoons—or on each next chance to fly off somewhere new, like the butterfly?

IN SEARCH OF REAL
LEADERSHIP

↔

FEBRUARY 1995

T HIS WEEK's Presidents' Day observance is a good time to think about the nature of leadership. We Americans have been fortunate to have some real leaders in our history, people of principle who have risked failure and political defeat to move the country forward.

Franklin Roosevelt comes to mind. When we consider FDR's initial years as president, we often think first of his work to end the Depression. But his leadership against Nazism and fascism prior to Pearl Harbor was at least as important. These days, we tend to forget the strength of isolationism in America before Pearl Harbor. President Roosevelt's strong voice for Britain, and against Hitler, directly countered the neutralism that was popular in the US during those years. He had to step carefully in support of England and did so with skill. But in that crucial moment he was willing to risk sailing against the wind of popular opinion—a willingness lacking in many of our current public figures. He was reviled by many. But he was right. He was a leader.

And then there is George Washington. To the mass mind, his image is mostly myth and legend. But he was a real person who made hard choices, many of which were both correct and courageous. The desperation of his army in its Valley Forge winter of 1777–78 cannot be overstated. Without Washington's will—and personal charisma—his army could easily have collapsed, and the nation might have gone unborn.

After the war, Washington saw rightly that the nation's first governing framework, the Articles of Confederation, had brought too little central power. And he saw that making him king, as some wanted, would bring too much. He was right on both counts. He was one of our few presidents who would have preferred not to take office at all, but did so from a sense of duty. He was a leader.

And consider Lincoln. It can shock people today to learn how much ridicule he endured. He was called a buffoon—even a baboon. His high-pitched voice and angular face were mocked. He was despised not only by slaveholders but by quite a few abolitionists as well. But he sensed a higher Hand stirring the cauldron of his time. He rightly read the main themes of his era: freedom and unity. And he had both the wisdom and the skill to push for what was possible, *when* it was possible. He was a leader.

And that brings us to today. Where are the leaders? To my eye, they didn't seem much in evidence here in New Hampshire last week among those in Lincoln's party who might compete next year for his presidential chair. But our deficit of current leaders is a good occasion to ask anew what genuine leadership looks like.

I would start with this: leadership begins with a commitment to realness—and a parallel refusal to succumb to denial. The true leader is one who champions honesty and unmasks avoidance. This requires the courage to see and state our real problems as they really are. It's a practical law: finding long-term, workable solutions to complex problems requires a thorough and fearless acknowledgment of what the problems actually are. Anything else is a distraction that leads to false hope and wasted time.

This commitment to realness and truth—and rejection of denial and avoidance—is disturbingly lacking in today's America. And one place it is most conspicuously lacking is in the current mantra of the radical right that our central problem is "too much government." Yes, of course, there are instances of governmental waste, fraud, overregulation, and bad programs. And where those exist, they should be addressed and dealt with.

But what the political and religious right can't—or won't— acknowledge is that there are also many areas in our national life where there is substantially too *little* government. There are some urgent national problems that only the federal government can address. In light of this, the leadership we most need today is not to condemn excess government, but to confront the extent of our deep national denial about the real challenges facing our society that can only be effectively dealt with if our central government plays a significant role.

The list of today's American denials is long. It includes refusing to recognize the degree to which money controls and damages our electoral process; the extent of environmental degradation; the insanely easy accessibility of guns; the tabloidization of journalism; the scourge of homelessness; the growing gap between rich and poor; the strains in our schools. The list could go on. The truth is that although such woes can't be solved by government alone, they also can't be solved without at least some major government role.

Our current president, Bill Clinton, may be right to extol government that is leaner not meaner, one that is a balanced partner in a complex covenant. That's the good news. The bad news, to my ear, is that thus far President Clinton has not seemed to find a leader's clear voice to articulate this truth in a way the people can hear and clearly grasp. I can only hope that he might still find that voice. And if he does, I hope even more that the people will be willing to hear it—and respond.

THE CONTINUUM OF CONSCIOUSNESS (PART 1)

MARCH 1995

I SMILED THIS MORNING when I saw the year's first crocuses. Alongside my quick pleasure at their presence and color, I felt a sense of awe. How do those flowers "know" when to reappear each spring with such precision—and breathtaking beauty?

It amazes me when people can't see the underlying field of intelligence at work within nature. How do butterflies migrate with such accuracy, or ants self-organize in such complex societies? What enables bees to "understand" the millions of steps needed to structure their hives? Is it not self-evident that there is some ordering form of mind, some unifying consciousness at work within things? But what exactly is it?

Sketching out a possible answer to that question must start with considering the nature of consciousness itself. In the case of this morning's crocuses, their ability to reappear with such regularity each year does not arise, clearly, from a mind or intelligence self-contained in any single crocus plant (or in any single butterfly, bee, or ant). The forms of informational processing visible there do their work in and through a larger *field* of mentation. And that field extends far beyond any of the specific individual entities within it.

That might be an unremarkable statement about plant or animal societies. But when it comes to how we humans think about ourselves, many among us (especially in our intellectual elites) would object strenuously to the idea that a human psyche holds its existence in (let alone derives its existence from) a field of consciousness that extends beyond our own brains, or that is larger than humankind itself, or larger than the biosphere.

When most of us think about the nature of our minds (if we ponder that at all) we usually do so with a pre-existing assumption that each psyche is a distinct, separate, and individual entity. And we assume that the inherently individual nature of each mind is, in turn, a key building block necessary for each of us to become a well-functioning person (often referred to in our language, tellingly, as an "individual").

Each of us, then, is shaped by a deep cultural belief in, and a felt sense of, the human mind (and of personhood more generally) as being fundamentally separate from the rest of reality. And indeed, this emphasis on personal individuality can have a near-sacred tinge to it for many people. For many among us, it would be no exaggeration to say that becoming a separate, stand-alone individual person, one characterized by autonomy, freedom, and independence, has become central to the meaning of life itself. This paradigm of the separate self stands at the very core of how our culture teaches us to understand what it means to be and become a full human being.

From this perspective it might seem obvious that the inherent nature of the human psyche is to be (and further become) a separate, individual entity. Because that seeming separateness of things seems so obvious, it should be no surprise that the fundamental separateness of the human self is so widely believed in. But this is one of those cases where we should remind ourselves that although something may seem obvious, it is not necessarily true.

We are offered a daily reminder of this unreality of the obvious when our eyes tell us that the sun "rises" in the morning, and then "goes across the sky" before presumably completing its circle "around the world" and returning to do the same tomorrow. Those events are all quite obvious. But those descriptions are all quite wrong (if believed literally or uncritically).

Over time, we have come to see that the surface impression of the sun "rising" and "moving across the sky" is an optical-mental illusion. But when it comes to our surface impressions about the nature of the human *psyche*, we haven't yet made the analogous shift. We still rely on what seems obvious: that the psyche in each person seems to be inherently distinct and separate from other minds—and from the rest of reality.

What I would suggest, though, is that the seeming separateness of the psyche, like the "rising" of the sun, is quite misleading, even illusory. A more accurate paradigm of mind must include an acknowledgment of the ways in which our individual consciousness is integrally connected with larger fields of consciousness.

We can see this, first, in the tangible interconnectedness between our minds and other human minds. (This, for example, appears in what the psychiatrist Carl Jung sketched out in his writings about the "collective unconscious." And it is what the Christian theologian Teilhard de Chardin depicts in his concept of the "noosphere.")

And then, secondly, we can see evidence of such interconnectedness in those instances when our seemingly separate psyches can sense their radical interconnection with a larger field of consciousness that extends beyond the merely human sphere. That larger field includes heightened connections within the world of nature. (And it also extends beyond that to what, in spiritual and religious circles, is sometimes called "the Mind of God," or "the divine Consciousness.") To exemplify how this phenomenon of trans-individual consciousness can manifest itself, consider two related experiences I've had.

The first was a dream I had a few weeks ago in which an old friend was insistently trying to find me so we could talk. In waking life, I hadn't seen or spoken with this man for several years. But only hours after waking up from that dream, my phone rang, and the caller was this same friend who had appeared in the dream. He said it had just popped into his mind to get in touch and catch up, so he picked up the phone to do so.

Was that a mere coincidence? I strongly doubt it. I've had several predictive dreams like that in my life. And their repeated occurrence seems to indicate some larger field of communication, and some process more meaningful than simple coincidence.

The second of my experiences happened several years ago. One day, as I was driving on an interstate highway, a song popped into my mind. (It was "Three Times a Lady," by the Commodores.) After the chorus of the song had been running through my mind for a few moments, I reached absentmindedly to turn on the car radio so I could listen to some real music. But when the sound came on, the song that was playing was that exact same Commodores song that "just happened" to have been in my mind seconds earlier. That also did not seem coincidental to me. What might be at work when things like that take place?

When I had that experience in the car, my immediate sense was that my mind had accessed a larger field of awareness, one in which the electronic "signal" of the music, which was active around me, was available to be "picked up" not just by the radio, but by my psyche as well. In the same way, with my more recent dream, it seemed as if a part of my mind had registered my friend's wish to talk; and that his wish to be in touch had been transmitted "over the air," so to speak, in a way analogous to a radio signal. I can't prove any of that, of course. But these are legitimate ways to sketch an outline of what *might have* being going on in those occurrences.

As for my musical experience in the car, even if (for the sake of argument) what happened there was, in fact, "just a coincidence," and even if you don't buy the idea that a human brain might be able to decode the same energetic pulses that a radio can, still, the phenomenon of radio technology itself has something important to teach us. Radio—and all forms of telecommunications—demonstrates an inherent interconnectedness that is fundamental to the natural world itself. And this inherent interconnectedness in nature is so prevalent that we tend not to notice it at all—just as the fish, in a Zen story, has no awareness of water.

It is important for today's people to understand the degree to which our thinking has come under the thumb of the mechanistic-materialistic paradigm that is promoted by many (but not all) of our scientists. And that version of scientific belief has resulted in many among us being programmed to disbelieve in things like telepathy and predictive dreams (and in spiritual experiences more generally). Further, such thinking certainly encourages many people to automatically assume that the kind of musical experience I had in the car must have been a coincidence, and not the result of an actual mental apprehension.

But I have yet to meet someone who disbelieves in the possibility of a mechanical radio picking up music through the airwaves electronically. (And such radio transmissions are all created by, and are far less complex than, the human mind itself.) In my view, we can learn some important things from this inherent nature of the natural world, not just from the fact that such radio transmissions do happen, but also from the *way* they happen.

Think of the various elements required for a radio broadcast. There is the specific radio receiver as well as the studio from which a broadcast is sent out. There is the transmitter tower, the electronic frequency of the signal itself, and the physical airspace through which the radio signal moves. To ordinary perception, all these elements, if looked at in isolation, can seem distinctly separate.

On closer inspection, however, it is clear that when all those elements of radio technology are working to play music, or deliver the news, they are able to do so only because they are all conjoined in a radically unified field. Is the atmosphere separate from the signal that passes through it? Not at all. Nor is the signal separate from the tower that broadcasts it; nor is that same signal separate from the particular radio unit that decodes and plays the song.

All those components that link up to allow a "simple" radio broadcast must be seen for what they are: elements of an intercon-nected continuum. And here is the key point: the interconnected continuum that I'm describing is not just a feature of certain specific phenomena such as radio transmissions. Rather, it is intrinsic to the nature of reality *as a whole*. Interconnectedness is a fundamental aspect of the core structure of the universe itself.

And I would suggest further that just as there is a unitive, material continuum-field through which human cultural information (such as music on the radio) can be transmitted, so too there is a larger informational continuum—a larger field of conscious intelligence—in the universe at large, through which many dimensions of information and awareness can be and are transmitted throughout the physical world.

And that includes, while we're at it, "informing" those crocuses I mentioned at the start about when to resurrect themselves every spring, and about how to "know" just exactly how to do so.

THE CONTINUUM OF
CONSCIOUSNESS
(PART 2)

⊸

MARCH 1995

IN OUR CULTURE there is a broadly accepted assumption that what any of us thinks of as "my own mind" is essentially separate from any other mind (or from the rest of reality). In several spiritual traditions, however, we hear an alternate view—one that I find more convincing: that a human psyche is integrally connected to a larger *field* of consciousness, one that is pervasive throughout reality as a whole.

In line with this perspective, I believe that reclaiming awareness of this "membership" of the psyche in a larger field of mentation is an important part of the spiritual endeavor. I say this for several reasons, not the least of which is the help this understanding can give us in claiming a greater access to the mental-spiritual powers that are present there in that larger spiritual field. But gaining the benefits of that access comes with a price. It requires transcending the merely cognitive and sensory modes of knowing that a heavily separational worldview limits us to. It requires moving beyond our culture's chronic overfocusing on the aspects of the human psyche—and of human selfhood more generally—that are commonly conceptualized through the categories of distinctness, separateness, and individuality.

Before proceeding, let me be clear that I am *not* suggesting at all that our human minds (or bodies or personalities) lack real, ontological distinctness. Nor do I think we should neglect developing our distinct individuality, or the capabilities of our unique personhood. But what I do want to stress at the outset is that being *distinct* is not the same as being *separate*. To that end consider this analogy.

When I look at my hand, I can see the real distinctness there. That hand is legitimately distinct from my elbow and shoulder, etc. But my hand is also fully "at one" with my arm, as my arm is with my shoulder, my shoulder with my torso, and so forth. That hand, in other words, exists in a continuum with the rest of my being as a whole. Seeing it as distinct has a clear, operational (and ontological) legitimacy in that my hand can learn to engage in actions and tasks that are different from what my elbow can perform, and whatnot.

But here is a key point. Just as this hand aspect of my being is simultaneously both distinct *and* non-separate, so is my being as a whole simultaneously distinct from, but also not separate from the rest of reality as a whole. And in like manner, what we usually think of as my separate "individual" psyche is not only distinct from, but also connected to (and not separate from), the larger consciousness-field at work in all things—and thus, in each person.

This understanding has major implications for questions of identity. When we ask, *Who am I?*, a comprehensive answer must include two contrasting poles. One pole of the answer (acknowledging distinctness) must say: *What I am includes the unique mix of traits based on my abilities (nature), my history (nurture), and the sets of choices I have made and continue to make (responsibility).* But there is also a second, equally important pole of the answer (acknowledging connectedness) that must say: *What I am also includes a mix of traits that spring from the state of oneness my being holds with reality more generally.* (We might also refer to this as being a state of full *communion* with reality itself.) Just as my hand is distinct but not separate from my body, so are *all* aspects of my being and existence—including my psyche—distinct within, but not separate from, the universe as a whole—from what we might call the divine Totality.

As we consider this interplay between distinctness and oneness, it is crucial to emphasize that the oneness aspect of our being is both more ontologically fundamental and of a higher level of *importance* than the distinctness aspect. This is clear from the fact that if a hand (in our analogy) is *actually* cut off and separated from the whole body, it immediately loses its capacity to *be* a functioning hand at all. And what worth is there to its distinctness as a (seemingly separate) hand, then?

As we further study this distinctness/continuum polarity, it is important to notice how the prevailing separateness-focused paradigm in our culture conditions us to focus overwhelmingly on the distinctness *aspect* of existing things. And that overfocusing heavily programs us to see reality as if its fundamental nature consists of individual, distinct entities. And that, in turn, includes shaping our thinking to see ourselves as beings who are, most essentially, separate from other beings and from reality as a whole.

Giving attention to the distinctness side of things is not wrong in itself (and is, in fact, essential to functioning as a responsible member of society). But it is only *partial*; i.e., it only gives us a partial view of the actual nature of reality. Yes, distinctness is real, and must be developed. But when we make that side of reality the main story, the equally real oneness-in-continuum aspect of things becomes chronically underemphasized. And as a result, it also becomes chronically unseen. Overfocusing on distinctness, as urged on us by the mechanistic-reductionist paradigm of orthodox science, fosters the very real tendency to lose sight of the inherent and ongoing oneness that prevails *between* each distinguishable entity, and that *unites* every existing thing with the dynamic field of existence in which it sits, and from which it derives its being.

One obvious place to see this cultural over-focus on distinctness is in the ways we teach our young to view the world through the lens of language. When we teach our children, for example, to say "Mama" or "Dada," "spoon" or "fork," we aren't just teaching them words. We are, more foundationally (and mostly unconsciously), programming them to frame their view of the world through this interpretive lens I'm describing, which assumes that what is most real (and, certainly, what is most important) is to see the world as being divided into fundamentally separate parts: this here versus that there.

This cultural worldview leads us to invest enormous effort, and offer much positive reinforcement, in the service of teaching our kids how to register and label such distinctions (not to mention how to manipulate those distinct things through sensorimotor skills and—eventually—ever more complex technologies). But no matter how hard we work to inculcate that belief in the essential dividedness of things, it is nonetheless the *oneness* aspect of reality—and of our own personal and societal lives—that holds a much higher level of importance and utility than the separateness/distinctness aspect.

Why does the oneness side of things hold primacy? It does so, first, because oneness (think: continuum) always precedes distinctness. The human body, for instance, starts in the womb as a small functional unity before it elaborates ever more "distinct" limbs and organs, fingers and toes, and so forth. Consider again our analogy of the hand and arm. The hand can potentially get cut off and be made actually separate *only* if it first comes into existence as a conjoined part. An arm doesn't come into being by taking a pre-existing separate hand and joining it to a pre-existing shoulder, etc. Rather, the various, distinct parts emerge simultaneously as part of a unified continuum. And all the distinct parts of that continuum develop, over time, from within that state of pre-existing unity.

Distinctness, then (which we commonly think of as separateness), is only possible because there was an original unity that preceded it. There is, in other words, an inherently sequential element in the way finite things unfold. The differentiation we see in complex systems in the universe is only possible because of an earlier, prior oneness. This is a pivotal point. Complex systems do not come into existence by many separate, small things being joined together to form larger, more complex things.[4*] Rather, the unified field of existence (which we could also describe as Being itself) comes first (in its inherent, original nature as a continuum), and only later actualizes its potential to evolve and extend outward, complexify and differentiate.

Because continuum precedes differentiation, any working paradigm for the nature of Being itself must include, first, a recognition that the oneness side of things holds a certain kind of ontological importance and priority that derives, at least in part, from the fact that the oneness was sequentially first.[5†]

And then, second, the oneness aspect also holds major importance and priority because the functional capacities of all differentiated things *require* the oneness in order to sustain their existence, and to continue functioning *as* distinct entities. The pre-existing oneness was not *only* necessary in its role of allowing for an earlier developmental stage to bring something *into* existence. That ontological oneness continues to be important

---

[4*] Many of our scientists, of course, would say that this is *exactly* how higher-order complexity comes into being. But the materialist-reductionist paradigm on which that view rests is an arbitrary, pre-existing assumption. It has never come close to being empirically proven and is, in fact, unprovable. But despite that, this paradigm has hardened into a kind of ideological dogma among many in the scientific world—one that, ironically, resembles some forms of the religious dogma that many mainstream scientists strongly reject.

[5†] Before proceeding, a clarification may be helpful. I am not suggesting that importance (or value more generally) is determined by chronological sequence per se; i.e., something is not inherently better or worse, more or less important, just because it came earlier (or later). But that being said, there is one specific form of importance that *does* derive inherently from sequence. And this is found in factors that are required for development, or evolutionary progression. I'm referring here to the aspect of how finite things emerge whereby complex development is fully dependent on earlier levels having been successfully achieved. As an example, before a baby can run she must walk; and before she can walk she must crawl. That doesn't mean that walking is more important than running (or that walking is less important than crawling). Clearly, walking and running have no inherent scale of ranking or importance relative to each other. But in order for those functions to become actualized, there is a *high* degree of importance in the developmental process happening in the right sequence. Running is not more important than crawling (i.e., it does not have any higher inherent value). But if that baby is to walk and eventually run, it is crucially important that she successfully achieve earlier stages—leg-strengthening, crawling, etc.—up to certain functionally acceptable developmental levels.

in present time as a kind of ground-source that allows things to *continue* to exist.

This is so because the oneness aspect of things is the permanent and essential "home base" of each distinct, differentiated thing. Returning to the example cited earlier, a hand needs to *remain connected* to the larger oneness of the total body in order to continue functioning. That hand is unalterably dependent on the aliveness and health of the organism's unified *wholeness* in order for it to sustain itself and its differentiated structure, as well as its functioning *as* a hand.

And just as that is so with our example of the hand, the same principle applies to all aspects of our being, including our psyches. Our mind—the consciousness and intelligence within each of us—is able to exist *only because* it holds its existence in, and is a local expression of, a larger field of mentation/consciousness/intelligence. And that larger consciousness-field is, in fact, a core component of the nature of Being itself.

This indivisible continuum of Consciousness I'm describing here is the aspect of reality that one stream of ancient Greek philosophy called the *Logos*: a fundamental, pre-existing field of creative Intelligence that generates and structures, permeates and unites the universe. (This Logos concept was later incorporated into Christianity, as can be seen at the start of John's gospel in the New Testament.)

In my view, this underlying consciousness-continuum is, in a very real sense, the core nature of each individual, sentient being. And as such, that universal Mind must be seen as the essential substance, the raw source-material as it were, of which each individual psyche (and all else that exists) is composed and from which it draws its capabilities. It is the unifying, conscious Force through which all our individual minds and beings are joined and are empowered to function and cooperate.

This consciousness-field, as I see it, is the vital reality that has traditionally been called God: the radically intelligent, creative, and life-giving Power that is both larger than, and unitive of, the seemingly separate things that comprise existence. And coming into an awareness of this, not just with our cognitive minds but with our whole beings, is basically the same as what traditional religion has called, more simply, "reconnecting with God." But for those of us engaged in the spiritual-religious enterprise, it is important that we not be fully bound by such traditional or already established language. (Nor would we be wise to fully dispense with such existing language-systems.)

But the emerging spirituality of our time presents us with an urgent need to develop new terminologies for describing the God-Force, ones that are comprehensible within the conceptual paradigms of the era in which we live. This includes turning to some of the God-concepts we have been using here that are, most specifically, non-personalistic and non-anthropomorphic in nature. There is an urgent need these days to develop new forms of religious and theological thinking that are more cogent, and more intellectually viable, than those offered by many of the familiar and traditional theologies in our Western religions. Who can doubt that much of our traditional religious language has become outmoded, and lost its effective power to communicate spiritual realities to today's people?

One of humankind's greatest wisdom-voices, the Roman-era rabbi Jesus, put it like this: "No one would deny that old wine is good. But when the wine is new, it must be poured into skins that are new" (Luke 5:37–39).

We could learn a great deal from that. And we would be wise to give that ancient rabbi a respected place in our pantheon of voices we choose to listen to.

THE LESSONS OF
OKLAHOMA CITY

∽

MAY 1995

A FTER THE OKLAHOMA CITY bombing last month, who
will soon forget that limp, dead baby being carried from
the rubble—and the parents' anguish? In such times of
hurt, our hearts can tell us—if we'll hear them—that we are all
interconnected members of a single human family.

For those of us watching from a distance, the shock of this
bombing has much to teach us about our habitual collective
thinking, especially how we react to threat. In that regard, two
things seem clear.

First, the voices in our country saying that the federal government is all bad are dead wrong. For several years, America's
prevailing politics have fed on the repetitive mantra that "government can't solve our problems; government *is* the problem."
Such nonsense is evident in the remarkable investigation that
has followed this bombing.

Consider the stunning speed with which investigators identified and arrested two principal suspects, and traced the truck that
carried the bombs. Much of that work was done by employees
of—yes—the federal government. Thank goodness they are in
place, and their jobs didn't disappear in some foolish budget cuts.
Their efforts show clearly that some jobs can only be done at the

national, federal level. And that is not just true for confronting terrorist acts, but for addressing many other social ills as well.

Second, this tragedy reminds us how quick we are, when threats come, to assign blame based on pre-existing fears rather than verified facts. In the hours after the bombing, for example, the airwaves—and many conversations—were filled with talk of Muslim jihad. One news network ran a long piece on the large number of Arabs living near Oklahoma City. There were detailed descriptions of a Muslim convention held there last year, reports that were paired on TV with grainy footage of possible "extremists" in attendance. This was an American version of "round up the usual suspects."

The only problem is: those usual suspects (Arab Muslims) were not involved in the bombing at all. The *actual* suspects are white, right-wing, American super-nationalists! This is a stark reminder of the damage that can be done by our all-too-human tilt toward blaming the villain of the moment, the group that our predominant social attitudes "frame" as the most likely threat, without bothering to find the facts. It's called prejudice. That's what the word *pre-jud-ice* means: *pre-jud-ging*.

To their credit, federal officials, from President Clinton on down, did *not* do that. They let the facts lead where they led. This is an object lesson about the "commitment to truth" our great spiritual traditions advocate. The teaching of Jesus that only the "truth can set (us) free" (John 8:32) is one we would do well to remind ourselves of in cases like this.

Truth is what actually is the case, regardless of what we humans may think, or what explanatory narratives we may concoct. Prejudice, by contrast, is believing in a story-line we have created or embraced in advance, because we *want* it to be the case, and then enshrine as one of our "convictions," regardless of any new information—and sometimes regardless of any information at all. Truth is accurate and now-based. Prejudice is fictitious and past-based (i.e., it is based on story-lines we heard and adopted in the past and are now unwilling to rethink or un-think).

Truth is always important, but when complex and dangerous social problems arise, commitment to truth is especially crucial. In the Oklahoma bombing case, that includes protecting the public from future violence by finding and confining those who committed the murders. But it also includes the even harder work of addressing and healing the larger social patterns of divisiveness and fear—including fear-based us versus them mentalities—ones that are embedded and prevalent in American culture. And commitment to truth includes facing and overcoming our chronic denial of our own national dysfunctions. The healing we need in this country requires the courage to see what we need to be healed *from*. And such healing, and the prerequisite seeing, begins—like charity—at home.

That scar in downtown Oklahoma City is a wake-up call to heal such dysfunctions in our national mind and social fabric before we reach a tipping point after which the consequences of failing to deal with them may well become needlessly severe.

A WEEKEND FOR MEMORIALS

✧

MAY 1995

MOST AMERICANS think of Memorial Day as a time for remembering our wartime dead. To the people (and their families) who lost lives in America's wars (regardless of the wisdom of entering them) we certainly owe major thanks. And whatever we might think about the justifiability of war, we can all be grateful that slavery ended after the Civil War, and that a century later Nazism was defeated—to cite two rare examples where war *might* be seen as just.

Beyond that usual meaning of Memorial Day, though, there is another side to it we usually forget. Military holidays have a seductive quality. Through glorifying smartly pressed uniforms, stirring music, and the synchronized motions of marching, these observances tend to lull us into romanticizing martial life as a source of power and safety.

But beneath the fun of such parades, and behind the fireworks we may watch with our kids at night, most of us usually lapse into a habitual forgetting of—and resulting denial about—the reality of human war. For every name we see on a military memorial, there was, first, the agony of a human death. This the realm of lost limbs and prison camps, forced labor and torture. It is the realm not only of ripped flesh but of fractured minds that foster the addictions, mental illness, and even insanity (as caused by the terrors of combat) such as we see among so many veterans and other war survivors.

On Memorial Day we don't want such things anywhere near the forefront of our consciousness, do we? And the reason we are so ready to forget those harsh realities is not at all because we want to honor the dead, but because of our felt need to shield our own minds from the discomfort of such awareness. Denial is a strong force. But if we wish to do justice to this time of remembrance, we owe it to ourselves, and our children's future safety, to remember war's harshest realities as much as we focus on who won, who lost and who was or wasn't justified—let alone who died.

Most of all, we need to recast our mental priorities toward remembering not just our soldiers but also those rare jewels of the human race who devoted their lives to finding practical solutions for society's problems through peaceful methods—instead of turning to the violence of war.

With this in mind, let us also remember this weekend a man such as Martin Luther King, who championed hope against great odds by affirming that love and courage are powers superior to antipathy and violence. Let us remember President Lincoln, who even in the midst of a war he hated, planned for a peace with the South based on forgiveness. Let us remember Mohandas Gandhi, who succeeded in freeing a major nation from oppression *without* war, by holding up truth as stronger than force, and love as a greater vehicle than violence.

And we would also do well to remember the sage of Galilee, the one some call Prince of Peace, who said, "Blessed are the *makers* of peace, for they shall be called children of God" (Matthew 5:9).

On this weekend for memorials, these are the forms of remembrance that best fit the day. And they are the ones we truly need to activate the most, even though only a small minority of us may be so inclined.

SUMMERTIME

⌒

JULY 1995

WHEN SUMMER COMES, not much makes me happier than my eleven-year-old daughter's smiles as she rides a wave at the beach, or tends to part of the garden, or says, as she did recently, "Summers are great. Sometimes I get ice cream a couple of times a day." How could you not love that?

We adults put great focus on teaching our children well—as well we should. But the process of teaching and learning is a two-way street. Our young have every bit as much to show us as we have to show them. The prophet Isaiah saw this in his vision of a coming time in which "a little child shall lead them" (Isaiah 11:6).

How can our kids lead us? And what can we adults learn from them? For a start, they can remind us of the capacity we were all born with for direct, ecstatic joy. The simple delight of splashing in a wave or devouring a chocolate-chip cone are enough to remind them that life is good. Would that I could remember that so readily. Kids can teach us a lot about joy and wonder.

A second thing the young help us see is the power of curiosity and experimentation. For children, every day is a constant, ceaseless variation on the theme of trying new things, going where they once couldn't go, or adventuring "where no one has gone before," to paraphrase *Star Trek*. Every day affords them the delight of handling new objects they've never seen, and using familiar things with new levels of skill and fascination.

Many of us lose this tilt toward exploration and adventure when we "grow up." But it is precisely these qualities that make the example of history's trailblazers so valuable. This is Benjamin Franklin with that damn kite, risking a shock—but helping to light the world. This is Magellan and da Gama sailing to sea; Alexander Graham Bell with his talking box; Gandhi with his truth-force; and Dr. King with his marches. We see the same energy of experimentation in Pasteur with his microscope, and Salk and Sabin with their vaccines. This is JFK saying in 1961, "We will put a man on the moon by the end of this decade." And we did.

Our young still know by nature the core advice at the heart of the spiritual endeavor: Surrender to aliveness! When an infant enters the world, you don't have to teach her to grow. She just does, imperceptibly like a flower, or like the moon crossing the sky as we scarcely notice its moving. Children don't have to learn to sprout hair, or grow teeth. It all just happens, proceeding from the energies of Life itself, the powers of Being itself. It flows out from the divine Mind, which is as we might say, the operating system of all that is.

The full arc of human growth is, of course, more complex than the emergence of hair or teeth. But the new life and growth that "just happens" in children is available to all of us throughout life, regardless of age or stage. We do well to remember that the same natural-spiritual power that grows children's teeth and hair is still present and operative in you and me right now. That same divine Power remains at hand to grow all of us at all ages toward higher levels of love and empathy; toward greater relational skill; toward more conscious awareness; toward more-responsible choice-making.

That divine Power is always "right there." And it is always right *here*—because it is everywhere. The key is to let it grasp and claim us; to have a willingness to surrender to it; and to offer ourselves up as living channels by which the blessings of the divine Life can flow to us—and then through and from us—as blessings to the common good.

ASKING THE RIGHT QUESTIONS

SEPTEMBER 1995

T HIS WEEK I saw an ad for a clergy seminar on "Christian
Baptism." The description listed some questions to be
addressed: Should baptism be for adults or infants? What
actually happens when baptismal water touches the body? And
what are good readings and liturgies for such occasions?

To me, that ad gives a snapshot of the predicament facing
religion these days. Although questions like that about religious
rites felt relevant to many people in centuries past, the number
of those with real interest in such practices is small indeed today.
I see the content mentioned on that ad as an instance of today's
church asking *yesterday's* questions, while contemporary people
are struggling with pressingly different ones.

As a working minister, I feel pained and torn about church life
these days, and I'm often discouraged by its out-of-touch ways.
But I also remain convinced that our society has an ongoing need
for strong religious institutions. I say that because today's major
social and technological changes, despite the many blessings they
bring, also have the potential to trigger a major destabilization of
our society, even to the point of challenging whether our cultural
center can hold firm long-term. But for our civilization to have

56

the best possible chance to stand strong, and to sustain ongoing progress, healthy religious communities among all the faiths will be a greatly needed resource.

What can help keep our faith communities healthy? One important starting place is for religious leaders to offer answers to the questions real people are really asking. And let's be blunt: not many people today are asking about the nature or procedures of baptism (or of comparable rites in other religions). To be sure, today's people *are* asking religious-spiritual questions. The ones they're asking may not be about traditional rites and procedures, but the hunger for spiritual experience and awareness in our population is as strong as ever and, if anything, is growing.

As evidence for that, consider how many recent best-selling books address spiritual concerns: *Care of the Soul* and *Soul Mates*; *The Book of Virtues* and *Embraced by the Light*; *Chicken Soup for the Soul* and *The History of God*; the various offerings from Robert Fulghum, Marianne Williamson, Joseph Campbell, and Deepak Chopra.

The fact that such books are being so widely read reflects the high level of spiritual seeking around us. But notice how few of the books on that list are written by mainstream religious leaders. (And, sadly, many mainstream clergy tend to be quite dismissive about the kinds of titles on that list.)

In response to today's surge of spiritual interest, it is essential that our faith communities at least be asking the right questions, ones that today's people are vitally interested in. These include: What is the nature of Reality—both around us and within us? What are the core principles by which Life itself operates? How can we live our lives in a humane way? How can we best feed our common spiritual hungers? What helps us find meaning? How can we grow and develop individually? How can we restructure our society around principles of love? How can we promote the common good, not just individual liberty and self-satisfaction? And how can we raise children who are not just spiritually wise but also emotionally intelligent (not to mention ensuring that the basic material and psychological needs of *all* our society's children are being met)?

Those are much, *much* more important questions than pondering what may or may not happen in baptism, or in other religious rites. And they are the actual spiritual questions of today's people, ones that need to be answered in ways that are understandable, practically effective, and experientially meaningful.

The renewal of our spiritual institutions is one of our greatest needs for a collectively healthy future. This starts with a commitment to being *real*, both in the questions we ask and in the practical week-to-week offerings we make available.

We need to start—always—with where and how people are currently living, and with the questions they are actually asking.

RELIGIONS MUST ALSO GROW

⌘

JANUARY 1996

T HE ANCIENT GREEK philosopher Heraclitus once said, "You can't step into the same river twice; for all things change, and nothing stays as it was." The truth of that is highlighted by the mind-numbing changes we've seen in the last century. In a historical eye-blink, we've jumped from horse and buggy to the close-up photos from Jupiter we've seen splashed on our TV screens and newspapers this past week.

Alongside those technological changes are the equally major shifts in the worldviews by which we structure our thinking about the nature of reality. When my parents grew up, there were prevalent culture-wide "certainties": a clear sense of right and wrong; a God in heaven overseeing "man" on earth; accepted authority figures and authoritative texts; and defined social roles for races, classes, and genders. But those certitudes that "worked" for centuries (for *some* of our people) are now adrift in the choppy waters of the relativism and deconstruction that currently rule our intellectual circles. How can our culture keep its footing amid such dizzying change?

One part of a possible answer can lie in affiliating with strong spiritual communities that offer human connection and spiritual nourishment, inner healing and moral guidance—but do so in an intellectually open and non-dogmatic way. Today's mainline faiths, though, are clearly falling short in providing attractive vehicles to meet those needs. What can we do to repair that? Here are three suggestions.

The first is to allocate meditative time for silence and stillness into the formal spiritual gatherings of our churches, synagogues, and meetinghouses (whether we call such gatherings "worship," "services," "sangha," or something else). We need to shape our communal meetings in ways that allow for genuine spiritual experience to emerge and be enjoyed. (Doing just this is a key reason that Buddhist meditation groups and Quaker meetings, for example, are appealing to so many people these days.) Our faith traditions, then, need to be teaching people the priority of such stillness practices as a part of our regular meeting times. And to that end we need to be teaching specific and effective methodologies for engaging in those practices.

Second, when we do assemble, we need opportunities for expressing some meaningful level of *emotional* intimacy, including ways to tell each other our personal stories, including speaking about our hard times and struggles as well as our hopes and joys. In that regard it is worth noting that there are a large number of people among us who have come to consider twelve-step recovery groups to be among the most powerful spiritual movements of the twentieth century. I think there is a lot to that. And although there are many factors at work, one of the core attractions of A.A. meetings (and other twelve-step formats) is the opportunity for people who attend to be *real* as human beings, and to do so in what they experience as real community, one that allows for emotional candor, and the expression and release of feelings in a safe and nonjudgmental context.

When people do go to twelve-step meetings they can tell their stories, be honest about their failures and weaknesses—and their successes—as well as seek out spiritual and human help for *specific* struggles. They can voice those things out loud, free of the usual cultural pressure to appear always positive and in control. And those opportunities lead to specific relationships for giving and receiving support. I believe that our houses of worship need to find some working equivalents of such emotional and relational realness in our regular meetings. To the degree that this happens, our spiritual communities can be just that: real *communities* of help, aliveness, and growth for those who take part.

And then finally, we need to proactively embrace the distinction between religion and spirituality. Our traditional religions have become spiritually impoverished in significant part because they often give so much more attention to religiousness (the beliefs and practices in which the religions differ) than to spirituality (primal connectedness to the Ultimate, a goal which virtually all the religions have in common).

The main opportunity of the spiritual life is *not* to adopt any particular religion, but to experience Spirit directly. Jesus, for example, clearly did not set out to found a new religion. But he also did not urge people to "settle" for the existing religion of that day. Rather, he taught them to embrace *some* parts of the religion they'd been raised in—but, importantly, to *reject* other parts. He taught them, in other words, to *sift* the religious traditions of their day—to separate the good from the bad, the wheat from the chaff, the tried-and-true from the tried-and-outmoded. He wanted people to unearth what could renew them from the inside out, rather than submit blindly to rules or formats imposed from the outside in.

Lincoln said, "As our case is new we must think anew." That applies to religion as much as society or politics. As the changes of our culture proliferate, our religions must also change. The great faiths will continue to be needed, but they must learn to shift away from presenting religion mainly as a binding authority, and move toward framing it, more essentially, as a life-affirming resource.

It is helpful to think of religions as living organisms. As such, they must not only articulate the laws of life, they must also *obey* those laws. And the more we see that one of the "laws" of life is transformative change, the more we see that the religions must themselves obey that law by being nimble on their feet and engaging in periodic self-reinvention. That has, in fact, already happened many times in the history of religions. It must happen again now.

Like other healthy life-forms, the best version of all religion lies in being a servant, not a master, and being a way-station, not a destination. It must offer settings for catalyzing real experience of the Divine. Is that not what first birthed each of the religions themselves, in centuries past?

THE WORTH OF WORSHIP

❧

FEBRUARY 1996

O NE OF MY MAIN TASKS as a minister is to prepare and
lead services of "worship." The Old English root of that
word is "worth-ship," i.e., the "shape" in which "worth"
appears. As that early form of the word suggests, a core function
behind what we now commonly refer to as religious worship lies
in its potential as a tool for clarifying value.

Worship, then, must not be thought of as simply a type of
public religious gathering. And it is important to note that this
deeper function, focusing on value and worth, is something we
humans need inherently, regardless of whether or not we consider ourselves religious. And because we have this intrinsic
need to evaluate what is good, valuable, and worthwhile, our
search to meet that need is, in fact, already taking place within
each of us on a moment-by-moment basis. And it is *always*
taking place in us.

Throughout daily life, after all, our psyches are relentlessly
framing positive or negative evaluations through which we say
"yes" or "no" to this or that situation or object: Should I have this
doughnut or not? Should I continue this relationship I'm in, or
not? Should I apply to medical school, or start a family? Should
I buy a new car, or maybe put more money into my retirement

account instead? Such ponderings are, each and all, calculations of *worth*. Our inner minds are constantly calibrating whether there is more value in enjoying the new car this week or having a secure-feeling retirement years ahead. The particulars, of course, change and vary greatly. But what doesn't change is that ongoing inner gauging of worth, which is going on in us all the time.

We are continually leading our lives, in other words, based on engaging in some form of calculating priorities. It is important to note that we are usually quite unaware of the mental processes that are *determining* those priorities. But despite that, the fact that such value-discernment is always going on in us means we are, in a very real sense, "worth-shipping" all the time, whether we are conscious of it or not (or whether we take part in religious services or not).

Noticing this—i.e., being *mindful* about such often uncon- scious inner processes—is an important first step. It can help us see that a key function of engaging in worship (both in the outer, liturgical sense and in the inner, psychological sense) is one way of choosing to engage in the asking of worth-questions more *consciously*. Well-crafted tools and formats that can help us determine value are opportunities to bring such questions to the surface of conscious awareness; to focus on them in a sustained way; and to make increasingly intentional choices about how to best embody good, *worth*-y values in tangible life.

This leads to a core question. What might we say about what is of *most* worth? Although the specifics of our answers will vary, a close look at our responses will reveal some important common- alities for all of us. For just as food, air, and touch are material needs we all have in common, so also there is a common, uni- versal human need to be connected with something larger than ourselves; to experience communion with some valued—and inherently valuable—Higher Power, one that is greater than both our isolated individuality and our short-term self-interest.

Connecting with such a larger value-generating sphere can be seen, more specifically, as cultivating a connection with our original, underlying Source. We humans have an inbuilt common need to find and to sustain a sense of oneness with the ultimate life-giving Ground of our being from which we all equally arose, however we may conceptualize the name or nature of that Ground.

And ... what is that "Source," that "Ground of Being"? Deepak Chopra, a Hindu, refers to it as ". . . an Intelligence, an unseen cosmic force, completely without form, but the source of everything in the world of form." Whether we label this reality "God" or use some other terminology is of secondary importance. What *is* important, though, is to recognize that whatever it is in this universe that generates us, energizes us, and sustains us, that "something" is inherently what is of greatest worth to us.

We humans have developed a wide range of forms—including the world's great religions and philosophies, art forms and psychological systems—to conceptualize and express that core insight. But behind all those forms of expression, the psyche within each of us holds this one common trait: an indwelling sense of dependency on this Source and Ground of our very existence. And because of that we have an inbuilt need to maintain a working connection to this Power that generates life, that structures it and makes it all "work," and that keeps the universe in a state of unity within itself.

The names we give this Source-Stream are legion. We may call it God, the Divine, the Godhead; Yahweh, Spirit, or Holy Ghost. It is described as Light and Love, Great Spirit and Prince of Peace. Some name it the All or the One, Being itself, Life itself, or the What Is. People think of it as the Force, the Way, the Truth, as Energy, Mystery, Consciousness. We hear its voice through Christ and the Buddha, Moses and Muhammad, and through the witness of the natural world. In Shakespeare's words, we see its "tongues in trees and books in running brooks." This Intelligence, this divine Ground of all Being, is the Within of All Things. And it is the Substance of all things, seen and unseen.

If worship, then, can be thought of as worth-ship, and if life holds inherent worth and value, surely the Source of life is, in itself, the *highest* Worth and Value. Some forms of religion can sometimes get derailed by imagining they have found the privileged or superior ways by which to name and describe this highest Good, or to serve its purposes. But although there is no single right way, there is a rich mosaic of ways to speak about the Divine, many of which are valid and valuable. Words are never adequate to fully describe the Ultimate. But we humans need them nonetheless to help shape and sustain our communities, and to help share what we learn there, along with our companions within those communities.

The important thing is this: that each of us finds our *own* way to think about, seek out, and honor the Ultimate. Whenever we engage in acts that help us see the worthiness, or the "worth-ship," of things—including when we might be taking part in services of religious worship—we are doing a good thing for ourselves. We need to embrace all the tools we can find to help guide us forward on our life-journeys in ways that are wise and life-enhancing.

And God knows we all need that.

HANDLING THE HOLIDAY BLUES

⌒⊃

DECEMBER 1997

I F YOU CAN BELIEVE the cultural Christmas hype, this should be "the *most* wonderful time of the year." But is it? There are many of us for whom this is the most painful time of the year, one that brings much more stress than rest. Preachers like me can quote lovely Bible verses about peace and hope. But Woody Allen was onto something when he, too, cited the Bible and said, "The lion and the lamb may lie down together, but I'll tell you one thing—that lamb won't get much sleep."

Here are some examples of the underside of this season that have come across my screen in recent days.

Item: My school principal friend in Western Massachusetts has told me how tense things have been in her school in recent days. The kids are unruly; bad language has increased; one student assaulted a teacher last week; the rate of teachers calling in sick has risen, and finding substitutes is hard. This week she herself came down sick.

Item: A therapist friend has been telling me how much the emotional intensity of his clients increases before and after the holidays, how their distress skyrockets, including increased depression, and greater anxiety about family interactions.

Item: A woman I know in New Hampshire was divorced last spring and is now adjusting to life as a single parent (during most of each week). Because of her suddenly reduced income she can't afford to give her three kids the kind of gifts she's used to giving them, but their father still can. All the Christmas decorations were stored in his attic, and she doesn't feel comfortable claiming them but can't afford a whole new batch.

Item: Another friend of mine, who is active in a twelve-step program, told me this week of recent meetings dominated by people trying to handle family gatherings where alcoholism, abuse, and other dysfunctions abound.

The list of such stories I've heard could be much longer. It's a hard season for many people. But what might we do to shift the reality of this season closer to its promise?

Based on both my personal and professional experience, here are one pastor's tried-and-tested tips that I've found can help.

First, disengage as much as you can from unrealistically positive expectations. Our culture tends to depict this as a time when everyone is—or should be—smiling and having fun. But here's something we often miss. The biblical Christmas story itself depicts a substantially *difficult* time for all involved. The story of Jesus's arrival into the world involved, first, the pain of physical birth itself. His parents were off on a long journey, hardly the time anyone would pick to go into labor. And that birth then took place in some farmer's barn because those traveling parents couldn't find decent lodging. Still later they faced persecution. (Along those same lines, the parallel Hanukkah story of this season celebrates what was only a brief respite between periods of intense political oppression for the Hebrew people.) None of those times, as those stories make clear, were occasions of ease and comfort. And I think that remembering the harsh conditions implied in those source-stories that stand behind these holidays can help free us from thinking we "should" be consistently happy or at ease throughout these weeks.

My second suggestion is: do less—*substantially* less. (And whatever tasks you *do* take on, finish them early.) We reduce the potential beauty of these weeks by chronically trying to fill them too full. But if we give ourselves permission to do less, we have a greater chance to do better with the tasks that we do in fact undertake—and to enjoy them more.

There is no real need, for example, to send out a full bushel basket of Christmas cards this year. (Or any at all, for that matter.) Nor do you need to attend every last party you are invited to; or host every last gathering you think you *should*, with all the cleaning and cooking involved. The reality is that if we let these holiday weeks get frantically busy, when we get to the end of them what most of us end up needing is: a holiday *from* the holidays.

Third, liberate yourself from captivity to "the gift game" of our cultural Christmas; from the pressure to give bullseye gifts that make the recipients light up when they get them. It is not necessary to give a gift to every last aunt or uncle, friend or work colleague. I know a few families in which, among the adults, each draws the name of one other adult at random, and gives a gift to just that one person. That provides the dual benefit of making the gifts we *do* give more thoughtful—while making the season itself less frantic.

I also know one young man who had the guts to tell his family that he wasn't buying any presents at all this year because of the psychological distress that causes him. I see that choice of his as being a gift in itself. At the very least, it showed a willingness to display honesty and vulnerability, both to his family and himself.

Fourth and finally, tend to your own needs and nourish your own spirit. Remind yourself from time to time to move more slowly and take longer, slower breaths. Leave some time each day to be still and quiet. Make space for meditation, contemplation, or prayer. Read a good spiritual book, and talk with friends about what you value most and what makes those valuable things more real to you. The more you disengage from our culture's over-busy pace, the more you can reclaim the freedom to cultivate such spirit-times.

The core boon of this season is not busyness but spiritual consciousness. This is why both Christmas and Hanukkah focus on rituals of light, the universal symbol for becoming more consciously aware. And it is why the stories of those two celebrations are sprinkled with admonitions to "Watch" and "Be awake." What those phrases mean, most essentially, is: Be conscious! Be aware!

Scaling the holidays back from too much culture-induced doing can help us claim the necessary time to proactively seek and find the unseen world of the Spirit. When we do this, we can give ourselves the gift of allowing these holidays to be not only holy, but also occasions that are healthy and energizing.

And who knows: if we have the courage to do less, we might find these days and weeks to be even more joyful and fun than they are when we let ourselves get overtaken by our cultural addiction to frantic busyness.

BETWEEN CLINTON AND STARR,
NO WHITE HATS

⌖

AUGUST 1998

Even before becoming America's forty-second president in 1992, Bill Clinton's campaign was dogged by accusations of "womanizing," and his political opponents dubbed him "Slick Willie" for his skill in handling the scandals that surrounded him. Just one year into his presidency, the Republican-dominated Congress demanded an investigation into Clinton's involvement, years earlier, in a failed Arkansas real estate venture known as Whitewater. That investigation, led by an independent counsel, Kenneth Starr, dragged on for six years. Although no evidence of criminal wrongdoing in Whitewater emerged, the probe led eventually to Clinton's sexual misconduct with a White House intern, Monica Lewinsky.

Charging that President Clinton had committed perjury and obstruction of justice in that matter, the US House of Representatives brought impeachment charges against the president in December of 1998. But in his Senate trial Clinton was acquitted of both charges.[6*]

P RESIDENT CLINTON's increased forthrightness in recent days about his misadventures with Monica Lewinsky was a good step forward. The ambiguities of this story, though, continue to abound. The president's sex-capades are sad to see and he seems a clear candidate for Sex Addicts Anonymous. Beyond his personal self-indulgence with this young intern, his

---

6* Editor's note.

behavior with her has been reprehensible and manipulative given the overwhelming gap in age, status, and power between them.

The case made by conservatives against Mr. Clinton, however, seems equally troublesome to me. Their current talking points about possibly impeaching him are focusing mainly on his lack of candor about this case. He was, of course, wrong to lie about that dalliance. That can't be argued away, and it shouldn't be minimized. But I also can't help but be aware that if someone had asked any of us pointed questions in a public setting about our sexual histories, we might well have succumbed to the temptation to withhold some facts, shade the story, or tell some fibs in the process. Doing so might be wrong. But on the scale of possible sins, such public fibbing about sex would sit at the relatively tame end of wrongdoing.

This whole case is a hard one. On talk radio a few days ago I heard someone say, "But this is the *president*. How do I explain this to my teenage son?" I understand that question. I too have a teenager, a daughter. While driving with her on vacation last week, she asked me all the hard questions about this scandal. I told her that high-profile leaders are nowhere near flawless, but are human and fallible like the rest of us. I shared my belief that you don't have to be a saint to be a legitimate leader. I believe all that. But is that letting the man off too easy for his bad sexual behaviors themselves?

The case that conservatives are currently talking up for impeachment, however, is not a case about inappropriate sex, but about presidential lying. And in that one regard, at least, I think this conservative case doesn't hold much water. It's easy to condemn a current president for dishonesty. But there has been a great deal of earlier presidential lying that we now tend to forget. There are numerous instances of this.

George Bush, for example,[7†] lied about being "out of the loop" on the Iran-Contra affair, when he was running for president in

---

7† That is, George H. W. Bush (b. 1924), forty-first president of the United States and father of George W. Bush (b. 1946), the forty-third president.

1988.[8‡] And he certainly lied about sincerely "converting" to the pro-life position midstream in the 1980 Republican primary season. Although I was not a George Bush voter, I didn't believe he should be impeached for having engaged in those lies. But lies they were.

How about President Johnson lying about the non-existent Gulf of Tonkin "attack" in order to manipulate Congress into approving war action against Vietnam.[9§] How about John F. Kennedy arranging for his doctor to lie about his Addison's disease, or Ronald Reagan lying about how we could cut taxes, raise spending on arms, and balance the budget at the same time? Are Clinton's lies wrong? Yes, they are. But are they fundamentally *more* wrong than those other presidential lies? Not to my eye. None of those leaders came close to being impeached—let alone humiliated—for his dishonesty.

And, much more importantly, if we were willing to calculate the harm done to actual flesh-and-blood people, as caused by some of those earlier presidential lies, the actual damage done would, in several cases, far outweigh any fallout from Clinton's misdeeds. What has caused more actual human suffering: Clinton lying about Monica Lewinsky, or Johnson lying to get America into a ground war in Vietnam? Compared to Johnson's lie (and the devastation that resulted), Clinton's evasions must be seen for what they are: relative blips on the screen of history.

8‡ Major American political scandal of the 1980s. President Ronald Reagan secretly authorized the sale of American-made weapons to Iran, a hostile power then officially under an arms embargo. Reagan administration officials hoped that this would facilitate the release of American hostages held in Iran at the time; they also secretly directed the proceeds of these illegal sales to fund the Contras, an insurgent group battling the left-wing government of Nicaragua. (Such support was prohibited by Congress.) Reagan's vice president, George H. W. Bush, denied any knowledge of the scheme and, when he succeeded Reagan as president, pardoned all of those convicted for participating in it.

9§ In 1964, President Lyndon Johnson asserted to Congress that the USS *Maddox*, a US Navy destroyer, had twice been attacked in the Gulf of Tonkin by torpedo boats of the navy of North Vietnam; Congress responded by passing the Gulf of Tonkin Resolution, authorizing the president to order the use of military force against North Vietnam, then at war with South Vietnam, an American ally.

So how will this all play out? The human psyche loves to think in terms of clear good versus bad. But in this high noon show-down between the sinner Bill Clinton and the inquisitor Kenneth Starr, who's the good guy? As for Clinton, the ordained minister in me can't forget the ancient Hebrew wisdom to avoid bearing "false witness" (Exodus 20:16). Nor can I overlook Jesus's admonition to "Let your 'yes' be 'yes' and your 'no' be 'no'" (Matthew 5:37). When measured against those standards, this president falls far short.

But if Clinton can't ride high with a white hat, neither can Starr. It is precisely his born-again righteousness that gives religion such a bad name these days. Christ comes to mind again. The people he condemned the most were the self-righteous religionists. But in every instance—without exception—his stance toward the sexually errant was largely gentle and tender. (As the baseball manager Casey Stengel used to say, "You could look it up.")

This face-off between Clinton and Starr, then, is utterly lacking in the psychologically satisfying white and black hats given to us in the old Westerns like *Shane* or *Stagecoach*. In an ideal world people like Kenneth Starr would never get appointed, and people like Bill Clinton would never get elected. But this is not an ideal world. As for me, if you press me, I'll take the flawed-but-human Bill Clintons of this world over the religiously prim-and-proper Ken Starrs. But that's not a very appealing choice.

A STUNNING INSTANCE
OF DENIAL

⟡

AUGUST 1998

On August 7, 1998, the two US embassies in Dar es Salaam, Tanzania, and Nairobi, Kenya, were attacked simultaneously by truck bombs, killing more than 200 people. The attacks were found to have been perpetrated by members of the Egyptian Islamic Jihad, an anti-American extremist group affiliated with al-Qaeda, the terrorist organization led by Osama bin Laden.[10*]

I N RESPONSE to the August 7 attacks on two US embassies in Africa, President Clinton has now ordered several "terrorist" targets bombed. I think that was a bad idea, for two reasons.

The first has to do with fairness. Our attacks produced many casualties among innocent noncombatants. We Americans are well practiced at righteous indignation when terrorists kill civilians. But when our attacks do the same, where is the outrage then? Do we really want to be the ones who say: When they do it, it's evil; when we do—oops?

In addition, reports indicate that the Sudanese pharmaceutical plant we destroyed in our "righteous" retaliation produced much of the medicine available to that *entire* country, which is grindingly impoverished. Even if that plant had a nefarious

---

10* Editor's note.

side-business (as some allege), the main losers after our attack will now be Sudan's sickest people. What wrongs did they commit to incur such suffering?

The second source of my doubts has to do with long-term consequences—and not just for others, but for us. How easily we forget, for example, that the downing of Pan Am 103 in 1988 was retaliation for multiple US military attacks on Libya.[11†] And that, in turn, was revenge for an attack on an American nightclub. And that, in turn, was . . . etc., etc. Most of us, when we look at, say, Northern Ireland, can see the insanity of the tit for tat that has beset that land for generations. Do we Americans really want to perpetuate a similar cycle of attacks, followed by retaliatory counterattacks against ourselves, during the decades ahead?

The spiritual traditions of both East and West counsel the greatest of caution about turning to arms, and about retaliatory violence. The *Tao Te Ching*, for example, says that "weapons are loathed by those on the spiritual path." The Bible likewise urges, "Do not repay evil for evil or abuse for abuse" (1 Peter 3:9). And the prophetic voice of Jesus reminds us starkly that "those that live by the sword will die by the sword" (Matthew 26:52). Our minds may try to tell us that such strikes as President Clinton ordered this week will make us safer. But here's a deeper truth: every attack we make, each escalation we indulge in, inevitably invites a next wave of retaliatory responses, most likely *reducing* our future safety, not enhancing it.

The wide domestic support for these attacks mirrors an assumption that the only two options when attacked are remaining passive (seen as weakness), or seeking revenge (seen as strength). Doing nothing may, in fact, be foolish, but doing violence is not the only way of doing something. What could we do, then, that

---

11† Pan Am Flight 103 was a regularly scheduled transatlantic commercial flight between Frankfurt, Germany, and Detroit, operated by Pan American World Airways. On December 21, 1988, a Pan Am Boeing 747 airliner, then flying the Flight 103 route over Lockerbie, Scotland, was destroyed in midair by a bomb that had been planted in the plane's baggage compartment, killing 243 passengers, 16 crew members, and 11 people on the ground. The bombing was subsequently found to be the work of agents of the Libyan government.

might be meaningfully effective, while also nonviolent? Here are three possibilities.

The first is proactively turning our society's attention toward identifying policy options for long-term peaceful solutions, even for terrorism. This could include, for example, creating a national Peace Academy to develop for our leaders a broad and well thought-through range of nonviolent choices for times when foreign crises erupt.

Second, we need to be willing to study and learn both the past origins and current dynamics of global conflicts. Such willingness is strikingly absent in today's America. We live in a society that relentlessly refuses to ask long-term historical questions, such as: Why did militant movements arise in the first place? What generates their adherents' anger? What might help defuse such anger? And what options are available to help re-channel the energies of aggrieved people in more positive directions?

Last week President Clinton said, "They have made (us) their adversary because of what we stand for." That is pure nonsense. The truth is that although the tactics of our opponents are tragically wrong, so are some of ours. But they are *not* opposing us because we are noble and they are evil. Terrorism exists for identifiable historic reasons, some of which are to be found in past actions taken by our own country and its allies. Many of those actions were quite unwise, and we Americans need to move beyond our collective denial of that undeniable fact.

What we now casually call "terrorism" is, in large part, a long-term historical backlash against Euro-American colonialism. Arab-Muslim terrorism specifically is, in the main, a reaction against the attempts by the United States—and the West more generally—to dominate Middle Eastern politics over the course of many years.

Examples of this abound. Since World War II especially, the US has tilted excessively toward blindingly supporting Israel and cruelly disenfranchising the Palestinians. In 1953, America (along with the United Kingdom) overthrew the Iranian government and installed Reza Pahlavi (the Shah, an old Persian term for "king") as dictator. We have tried for decades, with mixed success, to control the flow of Mideast oil. And since the first oil boycott of 1973, we have lacked both the wisdom and the will to become energy-independent.

These American policies were major causes for the emergence of much of today's terrorism. The hard truth is that terrorism will not cease until we give up our addiction to these global power plays. We need to let go of our fantasy that we can coerce various parts of the world to bend to our will without suffering an eventual backlash against our own attempts at domination. Our refusal to see that obvious fact is a stunning instance of denial.

Third, we need to shift toward solutions that are less unilateral and more cooperative. Americans are not the only ones hurt by terrorism. Most of the casualties at our bombed embassies were Africans. Several Arab governments are as threatened by the militants as we are. Many victims of the Pan Am 103 bombing were non-American. And an increased willingness to work with other nations also hurt by terrorism would greatly increase the chances of effective cooperation that focuses on nonviolent actions such as coordinated economic and diplomatic sanctions.

Shakespeare wrote that "bloody instructions, being taught, return to plague th' inventor." We Americans like to think that it is only the terrorists whose "bloody instructions" should or will bounce back on them. But when the next Pan Am 103 goes down, will we recognize it as a possible "return" on such violent retaliations as our military undertook this month? Or will we blindly and simplistically interpret that next attack—yet again—as merely an instance of evil people doing evil things?

Dealing with terrorism in the years ahead will be as complex as its causes. The time has come to begin the hard work of seeking to break its cycles, not extend them.

SPIRITUAL DEMOCRACY

⋖⋗

SEPTEMBER 1998

I LOVED the Sunday service I attended last weekend at the
Weston Priory, a Benedictine retreat center in Vermont. The
priory has become a laboratory for religious renewal among
Catholics and other spiritual seekers. The brothers there have
undertaken the work of transmitting their ancient church tradition in forms that speak to today's people. That's no easy job, but
what they offer seems to be working.

I felt warmly welcomed at that Catholic service, even though
I am a Protestant minister (with doses of Buddhism and other
approaches eclectically woven in). But the ethos at the priory
transcends the divide between denominations that is so often
a hallmark of organized religion. I have several non-Christian
friends who love those services too, and feel equally welcome.

I was also struck by the brothers' blend of informality and
solemnity. The words of the Mass and biblical texts were offered
with the same reverence one might find in a cathedral. But when
two sandy-haired boys—all of five or six—came marching into
that service to show Mom their haul of green apples, the priests
smiled benignly and chuckled with the rest of us. I've been in
more than one church where children were nervously hushed.
Thankfully, not there.

79

That coupling of reverence and spontaneity was reinforced by the brothers' approach to preaching. After the gospel text was read, there was a long Quaker-style pause. But then, instead of the customary format in which just one priest would preach, several of them spoke up as they felt led in the moment. A couple of people from the congregation spoke, too. It was a group sermon, a brazen display of spiritual democracy, and all the more poignant for its contrast with the more hierarchical signals so often sent from Rome.

What made this hour especially rich for me was the music. The songs were easy to learn and were set in a singable range. There were no paper sheets to shuffle, or hymnbooks to get lost in. And these were songs written in this century that sounded fresh and alive, and they were accompanied by well-played guitars.

This is a hard time for mainline churches. Attendance and income have shrunk in recent years as so many people question old dogmas, and find many religious gatherings less than compelling. But those brothers have no problem drawing crowds. Church leaders in other traditions would be wise to study what they're up to. If there were more churches like the Weston Priory, there might be more pews that were full—if not overflowing.

BLESSINGS, MY SON

↭

SEPTEMBER 1998

A S A LIFELONG BASEBALL FAN, I've been watching with interest as Mark McGwire has zeroed in on Roger Maris's single-season home run record. Growing up near New York, I was a Yankees fan in 1961 when Maris set the record. (And I saw one of his sixty-one homers that summer in Yankee Stadium.) Viewing McGwire's sixty-second on TV the other night was electric and unforgettable.

Although hitting those sixty-two (and counting) is a feat that I admire, I am even more impressed with the way he has handled this chase personally. Since early August the pressure to perform has been immense. But after some initial irritability with the press, McGwire has stepped up to the glare with as much poise as he's shown at the plate. Even more remarkably, when his run for the record was being scrutinized most, he got there with a sensational burst of fifteen homers in twenty-one games. McGwire, to use Hemingway's phrase, is showing a lot of grace under pressure.

If Mark McGwire has done well handling that pressure, he's also shown us a lot about handling success. Though never falsely modest ("What I've done is fabulous," he said upon breaking the record), he has shown a generous touch in sharing credit with those around him. He has treated Sammy Sosa, his fellow record-chaser, more as respected colleague than competitor. He has acknowledged his own good fortune to follow teammate Ray Lankford in the Cardinal's batting order. And he has said several times that the real winner in this drama has been the game of baseball itself. In all of this he has struck a nice balance between self-affirmation and self-effacement.

The one thing, though, that has touched me most about McGwire has been his genuine love for his ten-year-old son, Matt. Last spring, *Sports Illustrated* ran a cover story on male athletes who have abandoned or neglected their children, often born out of wedlock or to multiple mothers. Many of these men, making millions, try to keep their child-support payments as low as possible.

It's a happy contrast to see this massive first baseman hoisting and kissing his beaming son after homers sixty-one and sixty-two. When interviewed after the game, some of the first words from his mouth were, "I can't imagine a father being prouder than this." What a great way to interpret the significance of your own success.

McGwire is not perfect, to be sure. He's been criticized for his questionable use of androstenedione (a steroidal hormone). And we would serve him and ourselves badly to try to make a saint of him. But he is a brilliant athlete who also appears to be a good and caring father.

In a culture filled with weak male role models, we could use a lot more examples of good fathering such as we seem to be seeing in him.

SCAPEGOATING,
AMERICAN STYLE

⌒

SEPTEMBER 1998

I N ANCIENT JUDAISM, the killing of animals (in ritual sacrifice) was a central religious act. The idea was this: instead of
God's (supposed) punishment falling on us humans when we
had sinned, we could "escape" that fate by having the penalty fall
instead on a designated animal (often a goat, hence, a "scape"-
goat), which would be killed on an altar during worship.

Judaism was wise enough to progressively phase out this
primitive practice by the late first century CE. But just as Judaism
was doing so, some early Christians chose—unwisely in my
view—to re-legitimize this scapegoat metaphor as a way to
explain Christ's death.

According to that early Christian concept of salvation, just as
God's supposed wrath for human guilt had once been diverted
onto goats, so now, in the crucifixion, it had been diverted onto
Christ to pay the penalty for the sins of you and me. This way of
interpreting the cross of Christ was, in effect, a regression to the
older, barbarous practice of punitive sacrifice, even as Judaism
was largely outgrowing it.

Remarkably, this view of substitutionary judgment, punishment, and atonement continues to be espoused even today by
conservative Christians, quite a few of whom, significantly, are

also conservative American politicians. That is relevant because, as the Clinton impeachment crisis proceeds, it seems increasingly clear that the attempt to push him out of office needs to be seen and named for what it fundamentally is: a scapegoating event in its core psychological roots.

Consider how in the Jewish and Christian scapegoat versions, as we've noted, one solitary creature would, in effect, take the fall for the larger group. This was a blatant mechanism of psychological denial and avoidance insofar as it was a way by which people could evade taking full responsibility for their own bad actions. Instead of directly facing up to negative consequences for their own hurtful or harmful behavior, they collectively convinced themselves that God would accept that these animals could be substituted to receive the penalty instead.

I see a similar psychological dynamic at work in this Clinton crisis. And for those of us who want to move toward a more psychologically healthy approach, I think we need to reframe this drama in two important ways.

The first is to unmask the hypocrisy of Clinton's critics. Their mantra—impeachment is not about the sex, but about the lying—is itself, plainly, a form of lying. What these right-wing extremists are most exercised about on an emotional level is, in fact, very much the sex story—much more so than the lying story. But even with respect to the president's undeniable dishonesty, consider the dishonesty of some of these same critics themselves. In a long list of examples, two stand out.

The first comes from Congressman Dan Burton of Indiana. He called President Clinton a "scumbag" because of his affair with Monica Lewinsky. But now we learn that he himself had an extramarital affair. And, yes, he too lied in his campaign about the existence of the child that he had, in fact, fathered from that affair.

Or, consider also Idaho Congresswoman Helen Chenoweth, who also called on Clinton to quit. She got herself elected on a family values plank in 1994, in part by decrying an extramarital affair by her opponent. But guess what? Yup. She had had an affair too!

What makes this story even more bizarre is that Chenoweth and Burton are not only conservative politicians. They are also conservative Christians. They have both publicly told their constituents how they have asked for and received "God's forgiveness." But they don't offer any forgiveness or gracious understanding to Mr. Clinton for his weaknesses of the flesh. And although they want *him* out of office because of his dishonesty and self-indulgence, they feel no compunction to resign from office themselves—for quite similar misbehaviors.

This is classic scapegoating. Burton and Chenoweth undoubtedly have a sincere belief somewhere in their psyches that dysfunctional behavior should be dealt with, presumably through the acceptance of negative consequences. But here's the catch: they want those negative consequences to fall on someone *else*— not on themselves.

Do you notice something? That is precisely the same mental mechanism underlying the animal sacrifice theology of old. And it's the same idea behind the conservative Christian theology about Christ on the cross. It says: let's honor, and even advocate for, the legitimacy of harsh divine punishment—as long as it falls on someone, or some group, or some substitute other than us. In holding that point of view, they display a clear belief that they themselves are, and should be, a privileged elect.

Here, then, is a question for Americans: Will we let people like Burton and Chenoweth scapegoat the president for flaws (and, yes, they *are* serious flaws) that they themselves—and many others in Congress—also embody? And will we let them enforce a consequence on others they are unwilling to take on themselves?

Presidential dishonesty—and bad sexual behavior—is, to be sure, no small matter. But there is an opportunity in this crisis to unmask the rampant dishonesty and denial that pervades our culture as a whole. How much better it would be to admit: we all lie sometimes, and we all struggle mightily to get our relational lives right. There are few exceptions. The comedian Jerry Seinfeld has a pretty good read on the psyche of our culture. In his "farewell" stand-up tour he quips, "Everyone lies about sex. In fact, everyone lies *during* sex." That's funny because it helps remind us to lighten up a bit about our flaws and foibles.

Yes, Bill Clinton made some big mistakes. But let's not pile on by making the even bigger mistake of killing the king for the crime of resembling his people—and in this case, some of his most vocal accusers. Let's not scapegoat him for the flaws we haven't faced, and are in denial about, elsewhere in our national life—including within our own selves. How much better to do the hard work of inching our own lives toward a more gracious mix of candor, self-examination, and mercy.

Honesty, like charity, begins in the "home" of our day-to-day relationships—both with others, and with our own selves.

TRUTH IN FOCUSING

৩

HERE IN AMERICA, soap opera continues to triumph over substance. Though most Americans want "Monica-gate" ended, our media, with much help from Republicans, keep recycling it in overdrive. Meanwhile, though, there are other, much more important issues needing to be faced.

Consider race, for example. Last week, on the same day that a congressional committee voted to release Bill Clinton's grand jury video, the White House received the report of the Advisory Board on American Race Relations. This report had several good ideas about how to nudge racial harmony forward, including ways to increase educational equality.

Can any sane person hold that White House sex or its hushing (long-standing American traditions both) are anywhere close in importance to American race relations? But our media gave this race report only minimal attention. Even the *New York Times* ran the race story on page 7—and near the bottom to boot—with a mere 500 words. By contrast, the Clinton video story was on page 1—at the top—and was much longer.

The same was the case on TV. On that Friday of the race report and video vote, the scandal dominated the networks. But the race story was late in their broadcasts, and short. The networks' editors devoted what scant coverage they *did* give the race report to their own speculations about how the president's response to it reflected his attempts to appear in charge, not besieged. That may be true. But it is not what is most important. The race issues themselves are much more important than any presidential posturing.

One network anchor spoke about how that report about race relations had been "overshadowed" by the video release. The use of that word *overshadowed* has some real inaccuracy—if not dishonesty—to it. Notice the use of the passive voice, as if the overshadowing happened *to* the networks as the inexorable result of an external event.

But the truth is that the race report was not overshadowed by the video release. Rather, it was the networks *themselves* that chose to overshadow the report by their own coverage priorities, including their editorial decision not to make it a major story, or cover it thoroughly. The video release was important, too. But the networks (and print outlets) could have covered the two stories at least equally.

The neglect of that race report is just one example of how the public's ongoing need for knowledge about important policy issues (race, education, the environment, and poverty, to name a few) is being compromised by our media fixation on circus rather than substance.

Jesus's teaching that "the truth shall set (us) free" (John 8:32) can help remind us that the core mission of journalism is only that: to uncover and portray the truth. But one of the most important aspects of what in fact constitutes "truth" in the field of journalism lies in the significance of what journalists choose to focus on. Good prioritization is at least as important as factual accuracy. Journalistic truth also means making sure that the stories journalists choose to *focus* on are truly the most important. If a major newspaper puts an important story on the bottom of page 7, and a less important one on the top of page 1, it is failing in a key part of its mission: to highlight *relevance* in a well-evaluated way. And such a failure is, in itself, a form of inaccuracy.

Good journalism involves sifting the significant from the sensational. Our fellow citizens would be wise to learn the skills of making that distinction themselves—and insisting on it from their media.

FROM GRACE SLICK
TO SLICK BILL

October 1998

T HE MUSIC LOVER in me has been reading the new auto-
biography by Grace Slick, former lead singer of the rock
group Jefferson Airplane. Her book, *Somebody to Love?*, is
named after that band's biggest hit.

Slick embodies the 1960s. She was a prep-school Wasp turned
rock star, who was soon sexing and drugging with the best of
them. She writes, "Most people, if they think about doing something, there's a counter-thought: 'Maybe I shouldn't because . . .';
but with me: if I want the marshmallow, I take the marshmallow."

That says a lot about the attitudinal shifts that were taking place
in the sixties. Before then, the operative ethic was selflessness—an
expectation that we should serve others external to ourselves and
conform to externally given values. But in the sixties that ethic
underwent a reversal. Instead of meeting the needs of others, the
"job" of the independent self was radically redefined as meeting
its *own* needs. "Doing the right thing" was replaced by "Doing
what's right for me." What are we to make of that shift?

I would start by saying that the easy assumption that those
two views are inherently opposed presents a false dichotomy and
an oversimplification. Our task is not always to choose between

other-orientation or self-orientation, but, in many instances, to balance and integrate them, and discern: Which approach is the most appropriate when, and in relationship to what circumstances? Let's look at the benefits and corresponding flaws of each approach.

The older, more traditional view espousing selflessness holds—rightly, I think—that human beings need codes of behavior that point us beyond narcissism and self-centeredness. We need codes of conduct that are outward and tangible expressions of the spiritual reality inherent in things, and of the inherent spiritual wisdom that life is best when we act lovingly and responsibly. Such codes need to be transmitted from generation to generation through life-affirming texts and traditions, paradigms and institutions.

By contrast, the more recent ethic that came to the fore in the sixties asserts—also rightly, I think—the necessity of self-tending. Yes, we need to learn and practice the skills of unselfish action, as traditional religion highlights. But in order to love others, we also need to love ourselves. And authentic self-love includes turning significant attention inward, and doing the work of achieving self-awareness and self-actualization. In so doing, we need to avoid the excessive outer-directedness in which we often lose our deepest selves in mere doing, even the doing of serving others. (We might say that there is, at times, a paradoxical "responsibility" not to be *too* responsible.) So, yes, there is an important place for the traditional ethic of self-sacrifice and service as prescribed in life-enhancing moral codes. But it is equally important not to pursue that principle to the point of rigidity. As the New Testament says, we must enact "the spirit (of the law) but not the letter (of the law)" (2 Corinthians 3:6).

Spiritual wisdom, then, includes drawing from the wisdom that we find within developed traditions. But it also includes activating the divine Intelligence we find within our own beings. I take that to be the inner kernel of the Judeo-Christian insight that we are all born with the "image of God" implanted in us as the central template of authentic "human" being. And here is an important point: cultivating such inner-focus can help generate within us the spiritual and psychic independence that enables us to serve society through a respectful questioning of (and correction of) the inevitable mistakes and abuses of external authority.

It can be helpful to take note that both the other-focus *and* the self-focus approaches are conjoined in the central teaching of the Hebrew scriptures that we love *both* our neighbor *and* ourselves (Leviticus 19:18). That is one of the greatest wisdom statements in human history. We mustn't forget the both/and of it: loving neighbor *and* self. Jesus later identified and highlighted that wisdom as the core kernel of his birth tradition in his own re-articulation and summation of its meaning.

What these two orientations require of us is balance. The value shift of the sixties was, in itself, a form of rebalancing. It provided a correction against the suffocation of an earlier conformity ethic in which there was too much law and too little grace, too much expectation and too little acceptance. But over time, the "me first" meme of the sixties became its own kind of cultural and psychological "law," with its own rigidities, suffocations, and limitations.

As we look at society today, I would suggest that the current crisis surrounding President Clinton's impeachment process can be seen (from one perspective) as a morality play on precisely these themes. As such, it offers an opportunity to help us outgrow the inadequacies of both the "liberation" of the sixties and the conventionalism of the previous era. Yes, we need to reject the "me first" self-indulgence of Slick Willy (who, like Grace Slick, can't pass up the marshmallows). But we also need to reject the legalistic rigidity of his critics that is a throwback to the norms of the fifties and before. If Bill Clinton, the self-indulger, is the poster child of the sixties, then Ken Starr, the prosecutor, is a reincarnation of the harsher ways of the prior era.

What is the best-balanced approach in this Clinton drama? To me, impeachment seems overweening—but doing nothing seems irresponsible. To my eye, a "censure" of the president by Congress seems the most balanced choice among currently available options.

In the end, the deeper issues fall back on each of us, and on how we ourselves live *our* lives. The task for us all is to become both more responsible *and* more graciously loving than what we see in either Clinton *or* his critics.

IN PRAISE OF FALLING LEAVES

OCTOBER 1998

L OVELY AS SUMMER IS, I greatly love autumn in Vermont. Looking at this week's stunning foliage, I've been struck by the fact that even as the leaves are blazing forth with such beauty, they are simultaneously fading from life. But conversely, as each leaf dies, it is also part of a larger *coming* to life: the leaves will eventually become mulch, which in time turns to soil, which helps grow new trees, which in turn splay out a resurrection of new leaves and life. In this "gospel according to nature," even loss gets its due, along with gain, in the total package that life is.

The culture we live in emphasizes a greatly different view from that, prodding us relentlessly to chase the gaining, springing-up side of things. We are told again and again to get that new car or house; to get the better, more stylish clothes, or cosmetics or computers. In lockstep, our politicians ask: Are you better off than you were . . . ? (Translation: Are you able to acquire, and accumulate, more and more stuff?)

The perennial wisdom of our great faiths, however, offers advice that is much closer to the processes of nature than the seductions of our culture. Both spirituality and nature remind us that real life is flow *and* ebb, high tide *and* low, feast *and* fast, easy *and* hard, life *and* death.

Our culture's relentless tilt toward gain may seem life-affirming on certain sunny days. But looking deeper we see that this bias holds a strong, if hidden, anti-life element, because it seduces us to sustain an ongoing denial of those fundamental life rhythms. It conceals the fact that life in finite form is not a gain–gain game. It is, much more accurately, a *lose–gain* game.

Yes, of course, acquisition has its place. But so does letting go. Abundance *is* good. But so is spare-ness. Greater awareness of what brings inner health—and not *just* outer wealth—requires seeing past our culture's bias toward perpetual more-ness (which is a petri dish for denial, fantasy, and addiction).

In medieval times, the church developed the idea of striking a balance between what it called the *via positiva* and the *via negativa* (Latin terms for "positive path" and "negative path"). The *via positiva* is a form of addition, referring to what we can positively bring into our lives to get closer to the good. This might mean, variously, committing to the sacrament of marriage; raising a goodly brood; founding an orphanage to help abandoned children; celebrating the great feast days; nourishing oneself through the beauties of music, art, and nature; or, perhaps, supporting an artist as a patron.

The *via negativa*, by contrast, points toward how life can be nurtured by subtraction, or letting go. The graduate-level examples of that are the monastic vows of poverty, chastity, and obedience. On a more moderate level, this *via negativa* can be expressed through fasting, letting go of a bad habit, or giving away some segment of our money or goods. The insight here is that we need to recognize those times or circumstances when certain things no longer serve us because they claim too much attention, or are distractions, or threaten our health, or have simply outlived their time of usefulness.

The value of letting go was brought home to me in my early adulthood from the time I used to smoke cigarettes. I know well how enslaving that habit can be. (Mark Twain once said, "It's easy to quit smoking. I've done it hundreds of times." And I know whereof he speaks.)

When I decided I wanted to stop smoking, my attempts to do so were painful. But after several tries, and eventual success, I came to view such stopping, which first seemed like a small death, as a large enhancement of my life. What *felt* like a subtraction at first, became an unambiguous addition over time. I added better breathing, improved health, and psychological confidence. I eventually grew into a new part of me that now says, "How could I have ever actually *wanted* that in the first place?"

Letting go of an addiction like that is an example of the *via negativa*. It offers a tangible, practical example that letting such things go (or letting them "fall" away, as happens in autumn) can help us to restructure our lives in ways that offer a better future.

In one of his most direct teachings about resurrection, Jesus says, "Unless a seed falls and dies it stays alone; but if it does die, it bears much fruit." He then explains further, "Those who cling to their life as it is will lose it; but those willing to let it go will truly gain it" (John 12:24–25).

That is a reminder from one of history's greatest and most advanced souls that the spiritual life, in its essence, is a developmental process. In the wisdom of its own rhythms, life leads us through cycles, the fluctuations of which include accepting necessary losses. Those subtractions can be, paradoxically, vehicles for adding in—and for gaining—whatever next higher stages of life may await us when they are ready to present themselves. And when we are ready to let go of what came before.

BELOVED AND
UNBELOVED GHOSTS

⌖

WHEN MY fourteen-year-old daughter and I talked about possible movies to go to last weekend, *Beloved* was the one option I didn't much want to see. Its focus on racism and misogyny, though of course important, sounded too grim for some weekend entertainment with my kid. But I had told Emma she could decide. And wouldn't you know—the one I didn't want was the one she picked. So off we went.

I was right about the grimness. But although I would critique this movie on some technical grounds (too long, hard to follow), its power can't be denied. As befits Halloween coming this week, *Beloved* is a ghost story of sorts. But the "ghosts" in the movie are far removed from the playthings of sci-fi or trick-or-treating. It would be hard to see this film and deny that the ghosts of our culture's racial past—about which we continue to be in great denial—can haunt us as much as any supposedly real ghouls.

The story line in *Beloved* starts by showing us former slaves in the post–Civil War South. They are living in a large rundown house that is being terrorized by an unnamed, fiendish force. Dishes fly, mirrors break, a dog's eye pops out.

The house, we learn, has been haunted by the daughter of the main character, Sethe (played by Oprah Winfrey). The girl died horribly years before. But now her somewhat grown-up spirit (played brilliantly by Thandie Newton) starts to re-appear, haunting and troubling the house. We soon learn that this girl's death took place in a way that was not only tragic, but laced with agonizing moral ambiguity.

Behind all this, always, lies the specter of slavery and its horrors. The real ghost is not just that of this one child, but of all those brutalized by American slavery. Beyond reminding us of the evil of enslaving human beings, this film's power derives from giving us a taste of what being enslaved *felt* like: not just the fear of being brutalized, but of dreading that our children could be taken from us, and even raped or brutalized themselves. It helps us enter a psychological world so despairing that we could even comprehend killing our own children as—yes—acts of love and protection.

In interviews about bringing this novel to film, Oprah Winfrey described her preparation for eliciting "a sense of what slavery actually felt like." As a part of that process she arranged to be blindfolded and dumped in an unfamiliar forest. As described in *Time*, this was "part of an effort to regress back to the slavery years" and give a sense of what it felt like to be not Oprah, but "Rebecca, a freed slave who had been recaptured."

Initially, Winfrey thought of this as just a thespian exercise. But after hours of sitting alone and then hearing horses gallop up, with threatening men harassing her, calling her "nigger," and uttering sexual threats, she eventually lost control. "I became hysterical," she said. "It was raw, raw pain. I went to the darkest place. I thought: *So this is where I'm from.*" But because of her courageous openness to experience such feelings, and her subsequent work to create this movie for us to see, we too have the chance to face—and work through—at least some of our own pained emotions that live on in us so tenaciously, given our collective history of slavery, racism, and brutalization.

Through its archetypal metaphor of the "haunted house," this film unmasks the unhealed haunting of our *national* house. It points to how much we Americans have kept ourselves in a state of sustained denial about the ongoing effects of slavery, and the resulting racial fault lines that are still greatly with us.

We have done so—and continue to do so—by failing to fully face not just the historical knowledge, but also the *emotional* awareness of the ghosts of our own national legacy of racial oppression. The time for all of us to acknowledge, address, and move beyond such denial is long, long overdue.

"THANK U" FOR EVERYTHING

◁▷

NOVEMBER 1998

THANKSGIVING is a favorite time for many of us, given its simple pleasures of enjoying good food with loved people. It's a holiday of scale, unsullied by the over-buying of Christmas (or the over-drinking of New Year's). And though it is based on a spiritual principle, it is also nonreligious in format. Why spiritual? Because gratitude points us toward a larger, divine Source of our lives and blessings prior to any human doing. Why nonreligious? Because gratitude is not unique to any given faith but is common to them all, transcending any specific religion.

As I sat at table last Thursday with my family, our host for the day suggested we each take time to say what we're thankful for. Among the several things that occurred to me, the one that has stayed in my mind the most is my appreciation for the gift of music. This has been highlighted by a song that has been buoying my spirits recently: Alanis Morissette's new hit, "Thank U." I've been listening to it again and again.

Though only twenty-four, this young Canadian has a spiritual sense beyond her years. After her first US album sold a breathtaking twenty-eight million copies, and after a long and lucrative tour to promote it, she took an extended break to study meditation in

India. During this hiatus, she gave serious thought to quitting her music career. She decided against that. And that's lucky for us.

One result of her spiritual quest is this current hit. In various parts of "Thank U" she sings, "Thank you, India . . . thank you, terror/providence . . . thank you, disillusionment/clarity . . . thank you, silence . . . "

Beyond the song's musical beauty, what strikes me here is the sense of gratitude not just for the easy times, but also for hard ones. Morissette sings of thanks for the providence *and* the fear, for the clarity *and* the disillusionment. She sings, "Thank you, consequence . . . "—even the kind that comes from unwise choices.

This is a contemporary version of the ancient spiritual concept of the inherent goodness and divinity within all things. (At another point in the song the lyrics ask, "How about remembering your Divinity? How about not equating death with stopping?")

What is being prescribed here is a radical openness to each moment or event, regardless of whether our immediate experience of it feels positive or negative. With such attitudinal openness, we are enabled to see new forms of value, not only in our blessings but in the banes too.

An obvious instance of this is the process of physical birth. That can be painful and terrifying not just to a mother, but also to the baby when they are both in its throes. To be sure, saying "Thank you" with a polite smile right then might be a bit much! At various times later, though, both mom and child can come to see that earlier painful event as the precious gift it is. They do so because they come into a larger frame of consciousness. They see that even the intense pain they went through together was part of a larger life-process.

Just as the seed dies *as* a seed but becomes a plant; just as the caterpillar dies *as* a caterpillar but becomes a butterfly; so also, even death can reappear as another face of birth. Some births are hard; some relatively easy. But all are, or can be, opportunities for yet another day of saying—or singing—"Thank U."

RELIGION AS RESOURCE
NOT AUTHORITY

<>

DECEMBER 1998

S EVERAL WEEKS AGO, I attended a seminar in Chicago led
by the medical clairvoyant and spiritual writer Caroline
Myss (pronounced "Mace"). Thirteen hundred people came.
What drew so many?

As I talked with my fellow attendees, I heard a recurrent theme.
They were looking for spiritual experiences that go deeper than
what they have found as being available in institutional religion.
I couldn't help but wonder if the act of gathering with other spiritual seekers in this kind of workshop/seminar format might in
itself be, or become, a new, emerging form of "church" idiomatic
to our time. This differentiation of religion from spirituality is a
growing trend. Let's consider what distinguishes these two terms.

Religion, first, is something that is external to, and has an
independent existence from, the people who may (or may not)
believe in, or belong to it. More specifically, a religion is a specific,
identifiable social organization, created by human societies. It is a
grouping that is characterized by preformulated beliefs and practices which, in turn, are structured around texts and leaders that
have come to be considered as authorities. Adherents of a specific
religion are generally expected to adopt and correspond themselves to some real degree to these external authorities, with the

dual aim of pointing people in the direction of the Ultimate, while also regulating their behaviors in the service of social cohesion.

Spirituality, by contrast, is not mainly about external adherence, but about internal experience. It involves, and to some degree depends on, a dynamic unity between mind and spirit, and emotion and body, within the practitioner. Spirituality points toward an actual, felt sense of vitality, depth, wholeness, hope, connectedness, spirit—and of the Godhead itself. And it involves the internal choice to proactively seek in order to reliably find. And although a "practice" of spiritual awareness necessarily includes individual initiative and self-development, in its healthiest forms it equally honors the human need for connectedness and community. Like religion, there is a dual aim here. On the one hand, an active spirituality helps us attain a direct and clear consciousness of the Ultimate, while also developing our own behavioral skills in service of a greater ability to love. And that, in turn, is a skill that strengthens the well-being of human communities, both spiritual and secular.

In short, where religion emphasizes externally given beliefs and behaviors, spirituality emphasizes internally sensed experience and awareness (as the necessary basis for bringing more love and connectedness into the world). When Jung was asked near the end of his life if he believed God exists, he said, "No, I don't believe it. I know it." That's one expression of the kind of confidence and faith that a spirituality based on inner experience can lead us toward.

Although spirituality and religion are often in tension, they each have their place and role. I think of them as having existed in a necessary symbiosis through the many centuries of human history, like the two snakes of Aesculapius's staff, or the helix strings of DNA. Religion and spirituality can exist apart for a time. But for each to fulfill its function—to move people not only toward an experience of the Ultimate, but also toward individual and societal well-being—they are at their best when they work as mutually supportive partners.

One way to describe that partnership is to say that although religion is indeed greatly valuable, it is not in itself primary, and no specific form of it is superior or required. We humans *do* need at least some form of structured religious-spiritual community for our optimal spiritual development. But in the final analysis, spirituality is both prior to, and holds a priority over, religion. It is "prior to" because the great religions themselves initially sprang from direct spiritual experiences. The revelatory perceptions that came to Christ and the Buddha, for example, provided the original raw material from which the religions named after them first arose, grew, and developed.

Spirituality, however, holds "priority over" religion because a core purpose of religion itself, after all, is to foster spiritual awareness. By contrast, the purpose of spirituality is most certainly not to foster allegiance to or belief in the doctrinal system of any particular religion. The key to remember is this: a religion should never be an object of faith. It is never the main event. A religion is always and only a midwife to faith. A religion works best as a servant, but not as a master.

Those of us who are clergy would do well to remember that the religious entities we serve are never final authorities. But they are—when at their best—invaluable resources to the necessary structuring of a humane society. Religion and spirituality can and must work hand in hand to embody and serve the qualities of love and wisdom that the divine Spirit stands ready to bestow on us, if and as we are ready to receive and embody such grand gifts.

BEYOND GOD THE JUDGE

⌁

JANUARY 1999

T HIS WEEK I saw the new movie *Prince of Egypt*. I was curious about how it treats one of our culture's core stories: the Hebrew exodus from Egyptian slavery, as depicted in the Bible. The film itself is great entertainment, with rapturous animation. The producers, to their credit, consulted with leaders of the three Western faiths that revere this narrative. Several Muslims have lauded DreamWorks for avoiding demeaning stereotypes about their religion in the making of this movie.

But what strikes me most in this film is its harsh depiction of the nature of God (a portrayal, I might add, that is true to several parts of the Bible). This story that depicts the Supreme Being as showing compassion by freeing the Hebrew slaves also depicts that same God as inflicting horrific plagues on the Egyptians, slaughtering their firstborn as payback for Pharaoh's earlier killing of Hebrew children.

That dichotomy between divine mercy and cruelty found in Exodus appears often in the Bible. On the "loving" side we hear the Hebrew prophet, Hosea, have God say, "I will not inflict fierce anger; nor will I destroy . . . for I am God and not a mere mortal human . . . and thus will not come in wrath" (Hosea 11:9). And Saint John likewise, in the New Testament, affirms that "God is love," and that "there is no fear in love, for fear arises in the face of punishment" (1 John 4:16–18).

But in stark contrast, this same Bible has Leviticus say that God's law condemns adulterers and gays (along with other kinds of offenders), and that they must be stoned to death as punishment. In a similar vein, we hear the Book of Deuteronomy depict God as commanding those entering the Promised Land to "utterly destroy all the people" already living there. (These days we call that genocide.)

What are we to make of these conflicting—and mutually incompatible—portrayals of God? First, we need to be clear that any belief that the Bible is either literally true, or fully authoritative, is untenable. The biblical text *does* include a remarkable collection of rich insights and instructive stories. But some parts of it are more valuable than others. And some parts of the Bible, if taken at face value as science or history—or ethics—are fully wrong.

In light of this, making the fullest and best possible use of the Bible requires a well-developed and carefully thought-through methodology for sifting its materials. In order to benefit from the parts of the Bible that are lastingly wise, we need to sift out and leave behind many other biblical sections that were culturally conditioned when originally written, but are now anachronistic. There are many prejudices and mores found in various scriptures (both Christian and non-Christian) that were once culturally normative, but aren't anymore—and now need to be let go.

How might this methodology of sifting apply to these divergent views of the Deity? Does God judge, act with cruelty, or even send some people to an everlasting hell, as some parts of the Bible describe it? I would say, emphatically, "No." The core quality of the Divine is the quality of love. And love alone. Hosea and Saint John were right to say that love and judgment are fundamentally incompatible. And from them we hear this freeing "good news" that neither condemnation nor punishment of any kind exists in or from the Divine. The realm of the Ultimate is a judgment-free zone. This is an affirmation that is especially needed, to my eye, in today's so-called Abrahamic Western religions, some versions of which continue to hold a misplaced biblical literalism that perpetuates concepts of a wrathful, condemning Deity.

Having said all that, though, there is a subtlety to this subject that we would do well to notice and integrate into our thinking. Spiritual understanding includes the awareness that even though the Divine does not, in fact, judge or condemn, there is nonetheless a principle that *does* exist within the structure of the universe that can easily be misperceived as divine judgment or harshness.

I am referring here to what is sometimes called the "law of consequences." Consider two other statements, also from the Bible. We hear Jesus say, "The measure you give is the measure you get" (Mark 4:23). There is also this from Saint Paul: "Whatever you sow, that shall you also reap" (Galatians 6:7). These statements from within Western religion correspond to what we find in several Eastern thought systems, often referred to as "the law of karma."

The popularized idea of karma is that doing bad things in one lifetime may lead to "paying for it" in another. More accurately, though, karma is an Eastern version of the same spiritual principle that Jesus and Paul referred to, as cited above: causes have effects; actions have consequences. This is a principle in the field of ethics analogous to what Isaac Newton outlined in the field of physics, that "for every action there is an equal and opposite reaction."

Looking again at biblical portrayals of God, I would speculate that the writers of texts portraying God as a judge (or sending sinners to an eternal hell) were people who, although working in an era of relatively primitive consciousness, nonetheless had an inkling, an incipient insight, into the law of consequences, which, as I am suggesting, is a real dynamic within things. But they then proceeded, as we all do to some degree, to intermix that relatively *advanced* insight with other relatively less developed beliefs current in their day. In this case that meant that those early biblical writers were including a projection of the merely human qualities of judgment, condemnation, and retribution into their conception of God.

This happened in three important ways. First, they used language that was highly anthropomorphic, depicting the Divine as if it had human qualities, especially some version of human-like personhood. Second, they projected onto God the same kind of *emotional* reactions that commonly appear in human personhood, especially anger, disapproval, self-justification, and judgment. And, third, they legitimized the collective beliefs in the value of punishment and vengeance, killing and destruction that were normative in the societies of that era (and are still very much with us).

The people who wrote or compiled early biblical texts, then, were *partly* right in sensing that, in the larger scheme of things, life includes this phenomenon of cause and effect (and consequences for choices) that is evident in the fabric of the material world. But the thinking behind these biblical writings was also partly— and importantly—*wrong* in describing such naturally occurring consequences in an anthropomorphic way, by interpreting them as punishment or judgment coming from God. Cause and effect, action and reaction, consequences for choices—those things all actually happen in the actual universe (prior to and independent of human beings). But attitudes of judgment, and actions of punishment, are undertaken by human personal agents—*only*. They do not exist in, or proceed from, the Godhead, which is neither human, nor a person, nor a person-like agent.

These are subtle distinctions. But they are important ones that Western theology would do well to integrate more fully into its thinking. They are hard to grasp, even now, let alone for our theological forebears of three thousand (or so) years ago, whom we ourselves should not judge too harshly for not yet having fully parsed them within these Bible texts we're talking about.

The deeper issue here is not so much whether we believe in a punishing, judging God, but whether we believe in punishment and judgment at all. We need to see that those are beliefs, attitudes, and practices that human beings have created (approaches that humans have tried out, we might say). And we also need to see that our experiments with punishing and judging have not worked very well, and that the time has come to let our belief in them go, first within our own psyches, and then in the practices of our societies. The more we can see that, the less we'll be prone to projecting our own negativities onto a supposedly wrathful and punitive Deity.

Hosea was right: the real Divinity does not judge. And Saint John was right, too: the real Godhead is a life-giving and life-enhancing Force, whose name is Love itself. And the time has come to embrace these kernels of theological wisdom as the "keepers," and leave the judging God—the one we've made in our own image—well behind.

OF LOVE AND COMPASSION

JANUARY 1999

A S THE IMPEACHMENT PROCESS against President Clinton grinds on, there is a battle going on behind the scenes for the soul of the Republican Party.

Last week the Conservative Political Action Committee met in Washington. Heavily dominated by fundamentalist Christians, CPAC sees itself as the conscience of the nation (if not the world). At that gathering, Dan Quayle, Lamar Alexander, and Steve Forbes (would-be presidents all) were featured. They tried to outdo each other in criticizing the concept of "compassionate conservatism" put forward by another Republican candidate, Governor George W. Bush of Texas. One speaker suggested that even the Texas governor's father, former president George H. W. Bush, had "betrayed" the conservative movement with his "kinder, gentler" approach.

Far-right columnists, including George Will in *Newsweek*, and Don Feder in the *Boston Herald*, have recently taken up this trope, arguing that those calling for government policies based on compassion are "weak."

What is remarkable here is that this same conservative movement that is negating the role of love and compassion in public policy is heavily dominated by devout adherents to Jesus Christ, in whose teachings compassion is, unambiguously, the central ethic!

Curiously, these same devout Christians, who argue so strenuously that this ethical heart of their own religion should *not* apply to public policy, have brought the business of American government to a near standstill by impeaching the president because—you guessed it—they want to apply religious values to, well, public policy.

So here is a question. How can conservative Christians argue that the values of their Judeo-Christian faith should be *divorced* from American governance when it comes to meeting human needs among the people, but should be put at the *forefront* of American governance when it comes to personal behavior by a government leader?

This contradiction derives from several conceptual flaws. One is the notion that morality applies mainly to behavior by individuals, but not to actions undertaken by collective entities. My conservative colleagues would do well to read the American theologian Reinhold Niebuhr. Shortly before World War II, he wrote *Moral Man and Immoral Society*, which argued that the world's most dangerous evils almost always spring from collective entities: nation-states, political movements, armies, ethnic groups, religions, corporations, and economic classes.

The conservative movement is right when it says that we need a return to values in American life. But it is wrong when it asserts that those values apply mainly to individual acts (especially those of a sexual nature), but not to those of institutions and corporate entities (especially those of an *economic* nature).

But the morality of choices made by collective entities is at least as important as the moral choices and behaviors of individuals. Here are some examples of situations where those collective choices become crucial: whether the world's kids are fed and educated; whether the world's rainforests survive; whether the gap between rich and poor is shrunk rather than grown; whether women can attain full equality and physical safety in the face of misogyny, discrimination, and abuse; whether slavery (yes, it still happens) is ended in today's world; and whether torture (which, very much, still happens) is finally abolished. The collective choices that determine how these issues play out are much more important, and will have far greater effects, than whether a powerful but strangely lonely man in the White House engages in sex-play with a young woman and later tries to hide it.

That list of issues contains the clear priorities our public officials should be focusing on if they are interested in making our world a better place (we might even venture to say, a more "Christian" place) for all of humankind to inhabit.

A TALE OF TWO LEADERS

✑

I DON'T CRY OFTEN OR EASILY, but I did on Sunday after hearing that King Hussein of Jordan died. Why such tears?

The answer, for me, has to do with greatness. I'm thinking today of President Lincoln, whose birthday we observe this weekend. Elton Trueblood, a Lincoln scholar, wrote about the nourishment he drew from spending eight years in that man's company. "The next best thing to being great," he wrote, "is walking with the great." As I reflect on my palpable sorrow at Hussein's death, I can sense my own, similar hunger for real leadership in today's world, given its current short supply. When greatness leaves the stage, we lose something inherently needed by the human spirit. Of the myriad rulers that come and go, many are malignant and most mediocre, but few are to be revered. Hussein of Jordan, like Lincoln, was one of those jewel-like few.

This was so, first, because of his ability to resist being fully programmed by his surroundings, most especially by the chronic negativity draping the Middle East. In one of his later interviews he said, "Rulers cannot depend on others to guide them; they must make their own decisions and go their own way." With his peers fixated on the notion that leadership lies in toughness and confrontation, Hussein was the rare soul able to break free of this hostility-imprisonment, and see the greater potentials of conciliation and creative solutions.

What is remarkable here is that he did not start out that way. Educated at a British military school, his early actions were standard tough-guy fare. He supported the war on Israel in 1948. He called out troops in martial law against his own people in 1956. He joined in attacking Israel again in 1967, and ordered a bloody crack-down against Palestinian dissidents in 1970. If his career had ended there, he would be barely remembered as an average petty despot.

But his legacy became different because he allowed himself to change. When a third chance to try to destroy Israel arose in 1973, he abstained. When the Arab–Israeli peace process began to bud in 1979, he joined in.

There are parallels here to Lincoln. Few who watched his pre-presidential life predicted greatness. The Lincoln of the 1850s was a somewhat average pol, veering this way and that to suit the crowd of the day. Even his language was often bloated and hackneyed. But when faced with the severity of office and crisis, Lincoln evolved. So did Hussein. Both men were notable in their capacity for growth.

As time advanced, though, these two leaders found their highest selves in their ability to forgive. King Hussein survived several plots for coups or assassination. When an army officer who had failed at one of them was awaiting death in jail, word came of a pardon from the king. To the officer's astonishment, Hussein himself soon arrived to drive him home personally with an admonishment not to stray again. Beyond forgiving that one man, he could also lay aside his enmity for, and seek reconciliation with, his nation's larger, much more powerful foe, the nation of Israel.

We hear echoes there again of Lincoln, just hours from death, saying in his final cabinet meeting, "There will be no persecution (of the South) after the war . . . no hanging or killing those men, even the worst of them. Enough lives have been (lost)."

Many leaders speak of high goals with grand words. Hussein, like Lincoln, found ways to actually live them out and make them real. We need more like him. And we need to *be* more like him in our attitudes and actions.

THE WORK OF WINTER

⋖⋗

MARCH 1999

As I sit at my screen for this electronic chat with you, I'm aware how long this winter is starting to feel. And I'm remembering my post-Christmas fantasy, with little snow or ice yet in sight, that this winter might be an easy run. But the higher powers (i.e., the editors of the *Farmer's Almanac*) had other plans.

Winter is always hard for me. In summer, the nourishments of nature are right at hand. The smells of the plants and grasses, even the farm animals in their barns, seem like sweet perfume to me. Walking barefoot on moist grass, or soft sand, brings a molecular reminder of our kinship with earth. And what a balm when the breeze is a warm kiss to be nuzzled, not a cold assault to be braved.

Theologians have long argued about how many sacraments there are. (Catholics say seven, Protestants two.) I've never seen summer placed on one of those lists of church sacraments. But to me, that summer season of warmth and green could easily be included, and right near the top at that.

Despite this, though, I find that as the years advance, I'm negotiating more of a peace with winter. Whereas I might think of summer as a longtime friend, I'm coming to think of winter as something of a high-demand coach.

My now fourteen-year-old daughter told me this week about some of her times on team sports over the years. It was interesting to hear how the coaches she liked best were the ones who demanded the most.

I had a parallel experience as a child with my piano teacher, Charlotte Rogers (in Bridgehampton, NY). She expected a lot, often critiquing my practice habits and performance. But I learned how to play. As I told a friend the other week, "I could go five years without playing a piano, but then sit down and play certain pieces without hardly thinking." That wouldn't have been true if I hadn't had a teacher who made me work, pushing me past my comfort points, and making me practice my repertoire again and again. The long-term effect of those unenjoyable moments has been, paradoxically, lifelong musical *enjoyment*.

What does all this have to do with winter? Winter makes demands on us. It makes us work. In summertime, the livin' may be easy, but in winter, we have to become more proactive in sustaining our aliveness and well-being. Winter makes us vigilant about what keeps us vital.

In the summer, I can skip my fruits and vegetables; I can eat or drink almost anything and stay well. But if I do that in the winter, I'm setting myself up for sick days. In the summer, our nourishment is right there on the bush, with berries ripe for the picking. But in the winter, my physical and psychic diet needs to be tended much more mindfully.

If summer, then, highlights accepting grace, winter calls for embracing choice. And each needs the other. As I develop my relationship with this teacher-coach of a season, I'm learning to work through the rigors of its longer-term rhythms. And I'm able to see its cold fields and leafless trees less as absence, and more as a kind of pregnant emptiness.

But all that doesn't mean I can't still look forward to spring, does it?

RISEN INDEED

↭

APRIL 1999

ONCE UPON A NIGHT, two fleshy cells did meet and merge. What resulted was quickly larger and stronger than those first two cells combined. It fast became a being in its own right, with an amazing bent toward constant morphing into something new, while still remaining itself.

Before long, this fast-growing cluster of cells became a place where something wondrous came to the forefront: awareness. It was hard to pinpoint just what this was, but it included a noticing of rhythms and repetitive motions, and a sensing of subtle pulses and shifts. As time went on, this new growing thing had something like an "aha": it could set itself in motion. It could decide to make its appendages move this way or that. And when it did so, the world around seemed to respond, setting off new sensations in return.

Some of the most delightful new awarenesses were of sounds. One in particular, high-pitched and song-like, became a constant. Its intonations had endless variations, some quite matter-of-fact, some more energetic, some melodic. The sounds that flowed from it produced a buzz of good feelings for the cell-cluster, and during the times that it rang out, it was as if the whole world arose in song. New sounds and sensations, the one more wondrous than the next, just kept coming, day by day.

One day, however, something major changed. The cluster, by now a veritable cell-civilization, was suddenly wrenched by a completely unexpected development. Its whole world seemed to be cramping in on it. And soon its whole orientation was getting reversed, with the upper part of itself being turned increasingly downward. And soon there was an unaccustomed and unwelcome pressure on its top—which was now, dizzyingly, on the bottom, and being pressed down.

Although at first this had seemed just one more new sensation, that downward pressure quickly shifted from neutral to painful, and brought a sickening new feeling: fear. But soon, after the fear feeling arose, another, happier event took place. It was the sensing of a different feeling, as if a still, small voice within were saying, "Not to worry; all is well." And the fear faded.

That fear, though, soon came back, and this birthing being thought to itself, *Everything was a blessing till now, but this is a curse.* But then it noticed that still voice again saying, "Your despair is fully understandable; but this will all lead to a new 'wonderful,' too. All will be well again. I know." When the sense of being pushed down was inexorable, and the pain became intense, the growing cluster, if it could have, might have screamed out, "What I've been is ending! All is lost—I'm dying!" But this was followed by the voice of that comforter, saying one more time: "Yes, but it is also a new beginning, a way of coming to be, yet again."

The pain then became so intense, and lasted so long, that this new being went into a kind of shock, or sleep—a time of losing even its awareness of being aware. And that seemed to be a kind of end.

But that too, eventually, gave way to the awareness being renewed yet again, but now in very different ways. This time it came in the form of frigid cold and intense shaking, of being jerked this way and that. *I'm doomed,* the new being sometimes felt—*done for and lost.* But then there returned that still, small voice of calm that said, "But you could also say, *I felt all was lost, but will soon feel found.*" Soon, mercifully, things again went dark and blank. The pain ceased, as did the wondering and sometimes warring voices. Had it fallen asleep? Or was everything simply finished?

But then something unexpected happened. The noticing part of the cell-civilization became aware: *I'm noticing again.* It felt some of the same feelings of well-being it had known prior to that hard passage down and out of its original world. Soon, though, there was again that wonderful higher-pitched sound it had enjoyed before, but now much louder and clearer—a heartening *voice*, direct and unmuffled. There was also now the addition of a new, delicious, deep-toned voice, and there were several sets of sure and loving hands, offering aid and help, caressing touch and food. There were many new and different things to feel, like pulling in, and then letting out a cool, mysterious presence through the openings on its face; or being nuzzled in, and drinking from, an astounding magic fountain.

This is not so bad after all, thought the new being. *This is at least as good as what I had before—and maybe better. Perhaps that still, small voice was right when it led me to think that the bad dream of going down was not completely bad. For this life of mine seemed lost, but now is found. I had thought I was dead but now am very much alive.*

And the silent, inner voice of comfort returned again to say, "Yes, you are alive indeed, and your life will go on. And then on again." And the two voices kept on sharing knowings back and forth, teaching and learning of many more things in heaven and on earth than they ever could have dreamed on.

In a world without end. Amen.

THE LESSONS OF LITTLETON

᪈

MAY 1999

On April 20, 1999, Dylan Klebold and Eric Harris entered the Columbine High School they attended near Littleton, Colorado, and gunned down thirty-two of their fellow students and one teacher, twelve of whom died of their wounds. The gunmen themselves died by suicide after exchanging fire with the police. The massacre animated ongoing debates about gun control, school safety, and the "culture of violence" in American society.[12]*

A S THE LITTLETON school shootings come into clearer focus, what stays most in my mind—beyond the tears and caskets—are the human vignettes emerging from its rubble. Two in particular stand out.

In one, a reporter said to a Columbine girl, "What a terrible thing, to have your innocence taken away like this." The girl said, "Yeah, but maybe not totally, because this has forced us to grow up." If that is true for her, these agonizing losses could help *all* Americans "grow up" into a much fuller consciousness of what is happening to the world of our kids, and of how we might better raise and protect them.

12* Editor's note.

A second vignette comes from the Christian-right Republican presidential candidate Gary Bauer, who said, "The lesson of Littleton is not more gun control but more . . . spiritual life." That is a comment that I would classify as obscene, if not virtually pornographic. The mindset behind those words will lead directly to the murder of many, many more children and citizens in the decades to come. Bauer's concept of an either/or choice between spiritual truth and practical safety is utterly fallacious. Real wisdom clearly calls for both. This is so obvious it shouldn't even have to be said.

But what makes Bauer's comment even more galling is that this is a blatant instance of a "Christian" politician taking an anti-gun-control position in no small part to ensure that the NRA demographic in American politics will continue to be a reliable voting bloc for the conservative constituency of the Republican Party. That may be clever politics. But given the large number of future killings that such an approach all but guarantees, it is light years divorced from anything remotely resembling Christian values. Gary Bauer and his ilk should be deeply ashamed of such self-prostitution.

The starting point of any lessons from the Littleton tragedy must be only this: recommitting ourselves to raising our children in the most loving way possible, including doing all in our power to ensure their basic physical safety. How can we do that? Two things stand out. One is that we need to slap ourselves into sanity, and acknowledge that letting our kids have easy, physical access to guns is profoundly, radically, and inexcusably unloving, unacceptable, and irresponsible. There is no possible rationale that Gary Bauer, Charlton Heston,[13] or anyone else can make to the contrary.

If a parent or child-care worker routinely allowed toddlers to play with matches near curtains or dry hay, that action would be criminal. But we Americans routinely allow their older siblings

---

[13] American movie actor (1923–2008), famed for his roles in biblical epics such as *The Ten Commandments* (1956) and *Ben-Hur* (1959). A fierce defender of gun rights, he served as president of the National Rifle Association from 1998 to 2003.

access to instruments of far greater danger. And will we then pretend that the supposed abridgement of a constitutional "right" is a greater threat than the potential firing of actual bullets?

Consider how we deal with cars. Every car in this country must be registered and traceable. It can be driven only by licensed persons who must legally demonstrate competence to drive. Police are empowered to stop unlicensed, and thus illegal, drivers. Can any sane person deny that the same principle must apply to guns? The line that "Guns don't kill people, people do" is an obscene fiction. Those twelve people in Colorado were all killed by bullets fired from guns. No rhetoric can euphemize that away.

Comparing the record of other countries to our own is instructive. In England, where guns are carefully controlled, there is only one annual gun death per 100,000 population, compared to 46 per 100,000 in America. In Japan, on a per capita basis, there is one death-by-gun for every 176 in America. The correlation is plain as day: less access to guns, fewer deaths.

The lessons of Littleton? There are many. The most important is learning to love our children enough to protect them not only from troubled peers like Klebold and Harris, but also, and equally, from the gun lobby and the radical right. Such policies, if handled rightly, have nothing to do with abridging constitutional rights. But they have everything to do with a much more fundamental responsibility: to keep our children physically alive, and our population safe.

ME AS THE MANTRA
OF ALL THINGS

✑

JUNE 1999

B ROWN UNIVERSITY has made unusual news for an Ivy League school in its recent announcement of a new academic requirement. Undergraduates in all majors will soon have to take at least one course in "values" in order to receive diplomas.

That might not seem earthshaking, but this program has received quick criticism. Opponents claim that, unlike a church-related school, a secular university should be value-free. Those who make this argument for separating morality from inquiry appear to be presenting an academic analogue to the value of separating church and state in society at large.

Although these concerns may seem reasonable at first glance, I think they are, in the end, untenable. History does clearly show the dangers of religious orthodoxy interfering with the free pursuit of truth, as the legal proceedings against Giordano Bruno, Galileo, Scopes, and many others attest. But upon deeper reflection, I don't think that those fears are relevant to the Brown experiment for two reasons.

First, Brown's program will be denominationally nonspecific, and will examine and draw from a wide range of perspectives. And although these might *include* viewpoints from world religions, none of those would be considered privileged or normative. And such studies would, presumably, also examine ideas from science and psychology, as well as those of various philosophical, political, and economic approaches.

Second, although taking a seemingly value-free stance sounds like it provides the neutrality needed for free inquiry, a closer look shows something different. It is easy to overlook that fact that no institution can ever be completely value-free. When a university, for example, has a medical or law school, it is making an implicit value judgment that law and medicine are good things. If a medical school teaches prospective doctors to "first do no harm," or a law school teaches its students not to advocate for lying under oath, those are also judgments of value. And the values in question are not based on any religious or sectarian dogma, but on a common cultural consensus that the overall societal benefits of health and law, harm-avoidance and truth-telling, are, in Jefferson's phrase, self-evident.

I see Brown's program as a creative and worthwhile attempt to counter the erosion of consensual values that is a real, current threat to our culture's well-being. And I believe that addressing and reversing that erosion is as crucial to securing a strong future as any potential developments in technology and science, or in governmental programs.

The cultural convulsions of the sixties and since may have freed us of many psychological inhibitions and outmoded churchly dogmas. But alongside that is the recent emergence of a culture-wide value system in which, as we might describe it, "*me* is the mantra of all things." But if the ethic of "doing what's right for *me*" submerges the equally necessary values of self-transcendence, and of serving the common good, our culture as a whole becomes not only shallow, but wounded.

I'll share two vignettes that encapsulate this imbalance. One is a comment I saw on TV recently made by a seventeen-year-old girl whose grandparents had just celebrated their fiftieth wedding anniversary. When asked if she thought she might ever be married that long, she said, "I doubt it. But maybe as long as I still feel love for him."

The second is an ancient Middle Eastern tale of two brothers who inherited a field and a mill. They decided to share it, and split the meal from it equally. One brother lived alone, the other had a large family. One day, the unmarried one thought, *It isn't fair that I take half, for I am only one; but my brother must feed many.* So each night he secretly took grain to his brother's barn to ensure that his family wasn't lacking.

Meanwhile the married brother thought, *It isn't fair that I take half, because I have children to tend me when I get old; but how will my brother be cared for?* So he too delivered grain to his brother's barn at night. But one night they bumped into each other on the path, and when each came to know the other's deed, they embraced in a river of tears.

These stories describe two fundamental value-choices that are available for our culture. The first, in which relational choices are based on personal feelings alone, is a prescription for cultural decay. The second, in which such choices include empathy and a capacity for selflessness, offers the best available road to social progress.

Which religion or philosophy does that second option come from? Virtually all of them. It's called the Golden Rule. It's a key component of any real hope for a good future. And it's one that should be included—as at Brown—in the education of our students at all ages.

ON PARADES AND THE FOURTH

❦

JULY 1999

LIKE MOST OF US, I love a good parade. Despite my wariness of all things militaristic, I don't seem to have much trouble finding my way down to some parade route each Fourth of July. It makes me smile to see the bands march by, playing great Sousa tunes, in flashy red threads, amidst fluttering flags.

For an almost-pacifist, it turns out my patriotic juices can get surprisingly stoked sometimes. As we approach this year's Fourth, two memories are surfacing in me. The first is from over a decade ago when I was minister of the Congregational Church in Newfane, Vermont. One of my parishioners, the late Gene Godt, was our representative in the Vermont Legislature. While standing next to Gene one day at a July Fourth event, I looked over and saw tears streaming down his face as the national anthem ended. I leaned over and whispered, "Yeah, I can get choked up like that too sometimes." But Gene waved me off and said, "Oh, don't mind me. I can get crying even at supermarket openings."

The second memory comes from a time I was reading a bedtime story to my then five-year-old daughter. It was the book *When the Stars Come Out*, which describes an older woman reading her grandchild a story based on her own mother's emigration to America decades earlier. Near the end of the book there is a grand image of the Statue of Liberty appearing in New York Harbor as the immigrants' boat enters American waters. I remember reading this book to Emma for the first time (for both of us). When I turned the page and saw that picture of the statue, I burst into tears. It was completely unexpected, for me as much as her. As my tears came, she looked puzzled and said, "Daddy, why are you crying?"

I wasn't sure what to say. I did my best to put into words that the statue meant something important to me; that it had to do with freedom; that freedom is sacred; that countless people in the world don't have it, often suffering greatly because they don't; and that we are among the luckiest people alive to have some real freedom.

I don't know how much of this registered with her at the time, but what I was trying to tell her was that the liberty that statue stands for has a hold on my heart, not just my head. She may not have understood it much then, but I hope she's starting to now. And I hope that as her life unfolds, she and I and all of us will keep doing the hard work of keeping that freedom alive.

I also hope I'll find a good parade to watch sometime this weekend with some good bands and marching. And some snappy red threads.

FINDING GOD IN NATURE

◆

AUGUST 1999

A s a kid, I loved science experiments in school. One that especially intrigued me involved holding a magnet under a piece of paper that had iron filings placed on top of it. When the magnet moved, the filings followed. As I see the increased traffic on our Vermont roads this delicious week of mid-August, I'm aware of how the natural splendor around us is also a kind of magnet. It pulls people with an elemental power, like those filings, to the breathtaking beauties of this verdant landscape.

Beyond the health benefits of spending time in nature, taking a break from our usual busyness to bask in natural beauty can feed our spiritual lives also. I think of the first two chapters of the Bible, which speak metaphorically of God taking Sabbath-rest after the first six days of creating. The idea is that if God weaves rest into the rhythms of the divine work, so should we. We see Jesus follow a similar rhythm. When his students finish their days of labor out on the road, he calls them to "Come away by yourselves to a place in the wilderness, and rest for a while" (Mark 6:31).

Time for rest in nature, then, is an opportunity for more than just enjoying recreation as we usually think of it. Being out in the wild is also a way to return to the divine Source of things. In the Bible, again, we hear that "Ever since the world came to be, God's invisible nature . . . has been clearly seen in created things." (Romans 1:20). Our divine Source, in other words, is first and foremost the creative Force manifesting itself, playing itself out, in and as the universe itself, in and as the world of nature.

Consider that word *recreation*, and its original meaning as "*re*-creation": being created *again*. In that core sense, recreation involves allowing the generative powers of the universe to re-energize us, to re-charge, or even re-structure, both our bodies and our inner selves. In line with this, I would suggest that the most authentic forms of recreation come from making proactive choices to re-establish contact with the original spiritual Power that has splayed out the world we live in. And since that Power inhabits and radically pervades the universe, life-enhancing recreation includes taking time apart to connect with the blessings our physical world bestows.

When we do make such contacts with nature, the spiritual nourishment from those experiences can stay alive in us far beyond the actual time frames they occurred in. I'm remembering today a trip I made to Florida in the winter of 1981, during which I visited the Corkscrew Audubon Preserve near Naples. After hiking the two miles of its central trail, I came upon an unexpected vista: a glistening sunset over some majestic marshlands. The breathtaking beauty of that scene unloosed a sudden flood of ecstasy inside me. And the energies of that delight were flowing out from a visceral, sensual certainty of life's invincibility—and of my own vitality as an integral thread and member of a cosmic fabric.

As that awareness grew, I started to weep, soon to the point of long, joyful sobbing. Through a happy confluence of natural beauty, divine grace, and my own readiness, that one corner of creation gifted me, in that short but endless-seeming moment, with a tangible, sacramental taste of the Totality. And although eighteen years have come and gone, the splendor of that experience is, on certain days, so vivid in my mind that it can feel like it is still unfolding in present time.

That occasion was more than just a nice vacation memory. Beyond that, it helped strengthen in me a deeply rooted knowing that the Divine is real, as surely as I know that this keyboard and screen are real. And what I am most aware of today is that I was able to carry that epiphany with me. Something of the power, grace, and grandeur I felt in those moments on vacation in Florida feeds me even now, all these years later.

These green glories we are enjoying now in Vermont will soon wind down. But even as we savor them today, we can also store them away in the food banks of our memories—like squirrels with their acorns. Such memories of divine aliveness can come in quite handy later on. They can bless us after the fact as a form of spiritual sustenance during the leaner, hungrier days of winter that will cycle back this way soon enough.

THE UNIVERSAL MIND

✧

AUGUST 1999

E ARLIER THIS SUMMER, when I was looking for a preacher
to fill in for me this next Sunday, the clergy on our usual
"supply" list were all unavailable. But when I spoke with
our head deacon on the phone, she did have one new name to
add: the Reverend Dr. James Carpenter, who summers here in
Greensboro (where I live and work in northern Vermont). Jim is
an Episcopal priest and a theology professor at General Seminary
in New York. I had never heard of Jim, but I took his number so
I could call him.

But then something interesting happened. Just as I was putting
down the phone after talking with my deacon, I heard the church
door open. A man soon walked into my office to introduce
himself. It was Jim Carpenter, the selfsame person we'd just
been discussing! When he and I talked, I asked if my deacon had
suggested that he meet me. He said no, he was driving by and it
just popped into his mind to drop in since I was new in town, and
he wanted to say hello. (And, yes, he'll be filling in for me this
coming Sunday.) That was quite a "coincidence," wasn't it? What
underlying dynamic might be at work when such synchronicities
happen?

I'd start with this: there are forms of consciousness at work in things that transcend what takes place in any individual human psyche. Our culture's prevailing scientific worldview would, of course, disagree. That worldview would more likely depict consciousness as a phenomenon that is, fundamentally, a function of individuals—or, more precisely, of the biological brains that exist within individual people. But on examining the natural world, we see something notably different. In nature, there are clear instances of consciousness operating not only within, but also *between* organisms and entities. In such instances, an important attribute of consciousness comes to the fore: it is not always limited to, or confined within, mere individual functioning.

Yesterday, for example, as I paused during my morning walk beside Caspian Lake near my home, I saw a school of small fish darting this way and that in the water. What struck me was how coherently those fish moved as a *group*; how they changed their direction repeatedly with a near-simultaneous choreography; and how they gracefully sustained their structure as a "school."

What enables those fish to swim like that with such unity? Why don't they dart off individually and disperse? What, in other words, leads them to swim as a collective—as a *community*—rather than as single separate fish? And while I'm at it: how can Anthony Acheson hear the name Jim Carpenter for the first time, and be about to phone him, only to see that same man "just happen" to walk in minutes later?

To answer that, we need to move past the assumption, culturally prevalent but misleading, that each human mind is, in its most essential nature, a separate entity. For many of us, letting go of that assumption calls for a revised model of how reality is structured. It calls specifically for a more expansive model of what consciousness is, and how it works.

As an analogy, consider a wave in the ocean. It has an aspect that includes *some* measure of distinct existence. But if someone spoke about such a wave as if it were a freestanding, individual entity, or asserted that an ocean wave was a distinct being that

was inherently separate from the ocean, most of us would immediately see the flaw in that depiction. Whatever distinctness that
wave may have, it exists, much more essentially, in a continuum
with the whole ocean. The wave's existence is much more fundamentally a manifestation of connection than of separation. The
nature of its being is that of a fluctuation within a field, rather
than that of a stand-alone, individual entity that exists within a
collection of separate entities.

I would argue that the same principle applies to the nature
of a human mind (and of human persons more generally). The
continuum-aspect of reality, which is so self-evident in the ocean
wave, is also to be seen behind and between *all* entities and phenomena in the universe, including the human mind, and human
consciousness, and human beings more generally. Just as it would
be inaccurate to think of an ocean wave as an inherently separate
entity, so also we are on the wrong track if we conceptualize any
human mind, or body, or person as a fully separate, or completely
independent, entity. But most of us are caught in precisely that
kind of misperception. Why? Because that is how our culture
heavily programs each of us to think about and define ourselves:
as individual, *separate* beings.

When it comes to human consciousness, though, what is much
closer to the case is its existence in an organic interrelatedness
with and within a larger divine Field of Consciousness. We could
think of this larger Field as the universal Mind. (I am using that
term here as a name, or synonym, for what is more traditionally called God.) We could also refer to it as a universal divine
Intelligence, one that generates, pervades, and *runs* all things.

Just as our school of fish is organized and animated by a field
of vital intelligence that is more extensive than the mind found
in any single fish, so too our individual human minds are subtly
connected to, and within, fields of consciousness that are larger
than any single mind. I see this as what the Bible hints at when it
cites the "unknown God" in which "we live and move and have
our being" (Acts 17: 23, 28).

We would do well, then, to ask: What was happening when my deacon suggested I make that call to Jim Carpenter, and when Jim Carpenter had a near-simultaneous thought "pop into his mind" to come and visit me? To my way of thinking, that suggests the workings of a larger field of consciousness, one that permeates Being itself, just as your and my consciousness permeates our local bodies—a consciousness that Jim, and my deacon and I, were all participating in and receiving information from.

Recognizing how our particular minds participate in this larger Consciousness Field can be both empowering and awe-inspiring. The same radically powerful divine Intelligence that generates and organizes the stunning miracles of biological life is also available to generate new and better ways of ordering and living our lives, both individually and collectively.

As we increasingly grasp this continuum aspect of reality, we can learn more about how to access the animating Field of Consciousness that operates within the world, and within human-kind, through that continuum. And in the process we human beings could learn some things about living and moving together harmoniously, just as that school of fish was doing, as it swam with such coherence and beauty in Caspian Lake during my walk yesterday morning.

IN PRAISE OF FASTING

∾

SEPTEMBER 1999

TODAY I'M ON the second and final day of a brief fast. I don't fast often, and when I do, it's hard to stay with. The first day is especially tough, considering how so much of the eating I do is more for emotional comfort than physical need. And indeed, one of the benefits of fasting is the way it reminds me how strong a hold that psychological pattern has on me.

Undertaking this fast is also a way to help clear and focus my mind in preparation for a workshop I'll be co-leading in a few days. The topic is "Religion and Spirituality: Do They Need Each Other?" This is a charged topic for ministers these days, given the difficulties for our religious communities in fostering vital spiritual experience among their people.

Fasting is a spiritual tool commended by every major religion. On first glance, not eating may seem primarily negative. Many people associate it with a life-denying asceticism, or with seemingly rote rituals such as giving things up for Lent, or abstaining from meat on Fridays.

Fasting may be "negative" in the immediate sense that it does say "no" to food for a brief period. And in some cases, fasting could be unhelpful, or even dangerous if it is undertaken for too long, or if it is embraced as part of an overall life-denying attitude.

But the real goal of healthy fasting does not have to do with negating food, appetite, or the body. In fasting, the temporary "no" to food is really part of a larger "yes."

As an analogy, if an educator says "no" to one child hitting another, that is part of a larger "yes" she is saying to safety, mutual respect, and relational skill. Or if a legislator votes "no" to allowing large donations to political campaigns, he is promoting a broader "yes" to expanded democratic power for all citizens, regardless of wealth. It's the same when we fast. The temporary "no" to the food is also part of a complex and multi-faceted "yes" to cleansing and well-being for body, mind, and spirit.

One helpful way to wrap our minds around the function of fasting is to see it as a form of meditation. When we meditate, we abstain, for periods of time, from our usual thoughts and patterns of thinking. Meditators don't do that because thinking is bad, or because the mind needs to be negated. Rather, we do so to give our cognitive mind a bit of a break—a vacation, we might say, a time for Sabbath and for rest.

The same principle holds in fasting. Whereas in meditation we let go of thinking for a period of time, in fasting we do the same with food. (And, as an important bonus, during those food-free times, we can also let go of some of our habitual thinking—as happens in meditation—*about* food and eating, including our illusory beliefs that we need to eat as much as we often do.) Beyond that, meditative fasting, by saying a temporary "no" to our customary eating patterns, helps to remind us of the enjoyment that can come from feeling the spiritual Presence directly.

Our ordinary, cognitive mind tends to think that the good things in life are to be found in food but not fasting. It also thinks it sees the same in wealth but not simplicity; companionship but not aloneness; activity but not stillness; sound but not quiet; sense but not nonsense; visibility but not the unseen; youth but not age; life but not death. The good that life offers is indeed present in the food, the wealth, the companionship, etc. But it is equally present in the seemingly empty places.

Meditative fasting, then, is a tool for reinstituting balance. By helping us let go of too great a tilt toward what we can taste and touch with our senses, it can correspondingly help us commune with the parts of life that are beyond sensory awareness.

Fasting, in short, is a major tool, a major spiritual practice, for accessing the subtler spiritual substratum of reality which, at the deepest levels of things, is the real living Source of all we are and all we have in every instant.

MEETING JESUS AGAIN
FOR THE FIRST TIME

OCTOBER 1999

THIS FALL I'm leading a study group (at my church here in Greensboro, VT) on Marcus Borg's book *Meeting Jesus Again for the First Time*. In our first session, the talk turned quickly to the question of "demythologizing" Jesus (a major talking-point for theologians in the last century). This starts with learning how the early church turned quickly toward depicting Christ by means of concepts drawn from Greco-Roman mythology.

One clear case of using such Greco-Roman ideas is the story (later a doctrine) that Christ had one human and one divine parent. Jesus himself, of course, never claimed any such thing. His references to God as his "father" were clearly metaphorical rather than literal. And, importantly, he spoke of God as the father of all human beings, not just himself.

But in the mythological mindset of that era, one common part of the definition of who might even be *considered* a hero lay in asserting that such a figure had at least one divine parent. In one mythic story, for example, the Greeks described Dionysus as a son of their supreme god, Zeus, but claimed for him a human mother, Semele. (Hercules, Achilles, and Odysseus are other Greek figures who were deemed to have both a human parent *and* a divine parent.)

Such claims of divinity were initially applied to gods, but later were seen to be useful by high-profile political figures as well. The Egyptian pharaohs, for example, when at the height of their powers, were routinely seen as divine incarnations. And when Alexander the Great conquered Egypt centuries later, he arranged for some Egyptian priests to declare him the official "son" of the chief god, Amun-Ra. That was a common form of legitimization then. Only a full "son of God" could claim supreme respect.

Or again, consider how in 42 BCE, the Roman Senate declared the recently assassinated Julius Caesar as divine, designating him to be *Divi Filius*—"Son of God." (They did this posthumously, just as the early Christians did for Jesus.) And, to cite one more example, when Octavian became the undisputed emperor of Rome a few years later, he too had himself declared "the Son of God" (along with another new title: *Caesar Augustus*—"the Ruler who expands the realm").

All of this can help us see that when first-century Christians turned to depicting Jesus as "the Son of God," they were following a long-standing practice of claiming divine parentage for their own principal figure. And when they claimed that "the One True God" was Jesus's father (along with his virginal mother), this was their way of adding the Nazarene to the group of those already called "Son of God." They were saying: "Our Jesus is also 'the real thing' along with other world-historical figures." (The early Christians, of course, went on to assert that this same Jesus was now to take precedence over all the supposed "sons of God" who had come before him.)

But the important thing to notice is this: that before this version of Jesus (increasingly called "Christ" by the church)[14] had any chance of superseding Dionysus as a god, Hercules as a hero, or

14 The term *Christ* comes from the Greek *khristos*, meaning "anointed one." That, in turn, translates the Hebrew *messiach*, meaning "one anointed to be a liberating king."

one of the Caesars as a ruler, he first had to be located on the same main stage that those other greats already played on. The church's elevation of Jesus into the cultural conversation by depicting him as divine proved effective indeed, as the remarkable spread of historic Christianity makes clear.

I understand fully how some people might hear this analysis as disrespectful of Christ and/or demeaning to Christianity. But I don't mean it that way at all. The skillful use of mythological imagery by those early Christians made full sense in that mythological era. Every meaning-system has to express itself, at least to some degree, in the language of its time. The early church did precisely that, and did so quite effectively.

But the issue for today is not what the early Christians thought then, but how you and I frame our thinking now. Although believing literally in mythological concepts made a certain kind of sense in *their* mythologically-based era, the same is no longer the case in ours.[15†] And this leads back to the work of demythologizing, which our church's study-group is addressing this fall. Given that the prevailing worldviews of our own time have evolved beyond being structured around mythological concepts (such as were predominant in the first century), our religious traditions have a major need now to let go of those anachronistic mythological images as objects of literal belief, or as required doctrines.

Just as the church of the first century interpreted Christ in the language and thought-categories of *their* time, so can—and must—current spiritual seekers (both Christian and non-Christian) do the work of interpreting Jesus in ways that are viable in *our* time. This means that we need to go beyond the merely *negative*

15† The nature and meaning of both myth and demythologizing is complex, and, in the context of a short article such as this, does not lend itself to the full treatment it deserves. My comments here about demythologizing point to the value—I would say the necessity—of moving past formal religious belief in mythically framed concepts as literally factual. But such a process should also avoid the frequent mistake of disparaging the value of myth altogether. The gist of my view is this: myth is not to be believed in literally. But it can nonetheless be utilized consciously and psychologically as one valuable tool, among others, by which to access truths and insights that are not amenable to direct verbal formulation.

work of deconstructing (or "de-literalizing") obsolete, mythological ways of thinking. We also need to do the correspondingly *positive* work of articulating new ways of thinking about Christ, and do so by utilizing contemporary thought-categories, where appropriate, in ways that *do* work for today's people.

This might include, among other possibilities, learning to see Christ as a sage and wisdom-source; a mentor of spiritual discipline and practice; a teacher who prioritized spirituality over formal religion; and an advocate for, and builder of, an intimate and inclusive community. And such an emerging new view must also include an understanding of Jesus as a prophet and activist; an advocate for the poor and oppressed; a healthy male; and a supporter of female equality. The texts that depict Jesus all contain ample evidence for each of these available interpretive categories.

Although the Palestinian Jesus of old did not, we may assume, have a biologically virginal mother, or literal heavenly Father, and although he certainly does not need to be seen as "the Son of God," "the *only* Son of God," or "God incarnate," there *was* a real, rabbinic Jesus who continues to be radically significant and worth listening to. That real Jesus was one of history's most significant voices, offering teachings and modeling that are still profoundly relevant for the spiritual and cultural needs of today.

What Jesus taught and modeled is needed as much now as ever: engaging in committed spiritual seeking and finding; cultivating conscious awareness; asking questions and questioning pre-packaged answers; loving and serving; including rather than excluding; forgiving and reconciling; staying free of fear; committing ourselves to the health of both body and mind; and protecting life on this planet—even while simultaneously accepting and embracing death with faith and courage.

The legitimate work of demythologizing the Roman-era version of Jesus is not at all a process of diminishing him. Nor does it involve minimizing what Christianity as a whole has to offer. Rather, such work has the exact opposite goal. Such work is an invaluable tool by which to reintroduce the voice of Christ to our culture as the profoundly important spiritual master that he is, and to do so in terms and concepts that our culture can hear and understand.

In this critical period of mind-numbing and anxiety-producing change, we of today need all the life-affirming wisdom and spiritual guidance we can find.

THE DEEP MANTRA
OF THE AMERICAN MIND

⊷

NOVEMBER 1999

I N THE CLASSIC MOVIE *Shenandoah*, Jimmy Stewart, playing a prosperous Civil War–era farmer, sits to dinner with his kids and offers grace. He prays: "Lord, we cleared this land. We plowed it, sowed it, and harvested it. We cooked the harvest. It wouldn't be here, we wouldn't be eatin' it, if we hadn't done it all ourselves. We worked dog bone hard for every crumb and morsel, but we thank you just the same anyway, Lord, for this food we're about to eat. Amen."

Beyond whatever humor may be triggered by that crusty old Jimmy Stewart character, the underlying belief that shows up in his prayer—the idea of having "done it all ourselves"—expresses what might well be described as a deep mantra of the American mind. We Americans are the can-do kids, aren't we? "I'm rich and I deserve it," we think. "I built this ranch/house/family/business/ career/life with my own two hands and my own hard work." As Paul Anka wrote (and Sinatra and Elvis sang) we Americans love to believe that "I did it *my* way." When politicians promise to cut taxes, they often say, "That's *your* money that you made." But they rarely say, "These are *our* resources that you've been graced to be given some of."

In contrast to this American "My Way" creed, consider the question the rabbi Jesus frequently asks, "What is it like under the reign of the Divine?" (This is my paraphrased translation of what is rendered, more traditionally, in the King James Version as "Whereunto shall we liken the kingdom of God?") One of the answers Jesus gives to his own question is this: "Where God reigns, (again, my paraphrased translation of "In the kingdom of God") it is like a farmer scattering seed upon the ground. He goes to sleep and rises night and day. The seeds sprout and grow, but the farmer knows not how, for the earth keeps producing on its own and from within itself" (Mark 4:26–30).

That's a bit different from Jimmy Stewart's "We did it all," isn't it? Yes, of course, each of us must do our part. When it comes to growing food, we *do* have to pick up the hoe and the plow, first learning their ways, then putting them to use. Without that—and many other steps of choice and effort—there would be no lasting harvest. But we don't do it *all.* Because even when we do what we can and must, there is nevertheless a power much greater than us that actually grows the grain (and, yes, the turkeys, potatoes, cranberries, etc., that most of us will enjoy at our Thanksgiving tables later this week).

This is where gratitude comes in. This is not just a matter of being polite and saying, "Thank you," gracious as that may be in daily life. Gratitude goes an important step further in its acknowledgment that there is a larger generative Life-Process we are blessed to benefit from; and that no matter how hard you and I work to plow the ground, gather the grain, or trim and baste the turkey, we cannot *grow* either grain or turkeys. I chuckle inwardly sometimes when I hear people say, "I grow corn." Really? You may tend it, but you don't grow it. Gratitude is the acknowledgment of the higher, larger Power that actually *grows* the corn and the turkeys.

In the end, then, being thankful is not so much a moral imperative as a mode of perception; not so much a code of conduct as an attunement of consciousness; not so much an obligation we owe as a noticing of the divine grace that buoys us.

Most specifically, thankfulness helps remind us that the ultimate Process that grows our corn and turkeys is continually working *in us* to keep us growing also. And despite our frequent, all-too-human fears to the contrary, that divine Process is a Force that will never leave us or forsake us.

ALWAYS AND FOR EVERYTHING

✧

NOVEMBER 1999

MY PREVIOUS ESSAY discussed gratitude as a practice that helps grow our spiritual perception. I suggested that being thankful includes recognizing that even our successes are gifts to be grateful for. Most of our achievements, after all, are greatly helped along by favorable social and economic circumstances that we ourselves did nothing to put in place.

My additional thoughts about gratitude today have been prompted by a verse in the Bible that urges people to practice thankfulness "always and for everything" (Ephesians 5:20). The first reaction many of us might have to that verse is to dismiss it as a pious but unrealistic ideal. Are we really to give thanks always and for everything in a world that includes injustice and cruelty, not to mention death, disease, suffering, and grief? From the point of view of ordinary awareness, giving thanks in such situations would seem a clear nonstarter.

But here is another possibility: that whoever wrote those words was *not* writing from the point of view of ordinary awareness but had grown into a more expansive perception about how life happens, and was encouraging his or her readers to do the same. Growing into more awareness—i.e., looking with a wider view, and thus perceiving and understanding more of what actually is the case—can make things appear quite different.

Over the centuries, mystics and visionaries who have gained glimpses of larger perspectives have reported back on what they've seen: that the universe is beneficent to its core; that life, in its essence, is an expression of Love; that all events can be or become meaningful; that even our hard experiences are, from the perspective of the Ultimate, opportunities; and that whatever happens can be a conduit to a larger process that is fundamentally life-enhancing and creative.

This week a friend and I got talking about our daughters. I became tearful when reminded of the preciousness my daughter, Emma, holds for me. As we talked, I started remembering an event in my life in the late seventies. I lived in Hamilton, Ohio, then, and was one year into my first ministry at a church there. It was a great job. In addition to being the assistant minister, I was also the organist and choir director. I loved it.

After that first year, the senior minister left, and I was put in charge of the church as the interim pastor. Before long I was enjoying my new role greatly. As a result, I decided to apply for the senior position. I was doing good work and the people liked me. I wanted the job and started to believe I would get it. But in the end, it went to someone else.

That decision to hire someone with more experience made a lot of sense from the church's point of view. But for me it was a big disappointment. At the time, I thought those people had made a big mistake and a *bad* decision. And on an emotional level, I felt that something bad had happened to me.

But from my perspective of this week, as I talked with my friend about how precious my daughter is to me, and as I looked back on that "bad" experience of not getting the job in Ohio, I can only say now: Thank God I didn't get it! If I had, I never would have met her mom back East, and my gem of a daughter would have never come to be. What *seemed* bad in my perspective of 1978 has turned out to be unambiguously good in my perspective of 1999.

The Muslim poet Rumi once wrote, "Your old grandmother says, 'Maybe you shouldn't go to school. You look a little pale.' Run when you hear that. A father's stern slaps are better . . . Pray for a tough instructor to hear and act and stay within you. We have been busy accumulating solace. Make us afraid of how we were."

One gift of the spiritual life is learning that what we may initially, or habitually, view as bad can also be seen as bearing hidden benefits that don't become apparent till we learn to look from a larger view. And in light of this, maybe it isn't such nonsense after all when that ancient text urges us to give thanks "always." (And maybe even, to a very advanced spiritual eye, "for everything.")

GAYNESS, PORK, AND PERIODS

FEBRUARY 2000

MARRIAGE EQUALITY for gays has been much in the news of late. But even here in (relatively) liberal Vermont, this is still a hard sell for many people. Momentum does seem to be shifting, though, toward legalizing civil unions in the state. And that would be at least a step forward on this emotional issue.

Last week, a Vermont newspaper ran an opinion piece that opposed gay marriage and cited "four places in the Bible" declaring homosexuality to be wrong. After reading that, I couldn't help but think that the real news there is how low this number is. In a text as long as the Bible, the fact that it offers so *little* commentary about homosexuality offers scant support for the idea of a coherent, "biblical" viewpoint on that subject. (There are, in fact, a few more than the four cited in the opinion piece, but not many. And several passages utilized to bolster an anti-gay stance are quite ambiguous in their meaning.)

Of those cited anti-gay Bible verses, the most explicit are in the book of Leviticus (Leviticus 18:22 and 20:13). But here is a curious and significant fact: that same book of the Bible also prohibits eating pork (Leviticus 11:27). And—O yes—it declares as well that women are "impure" while having their periods; and that they must sequester themselves during those times, during which men must have no contact with them (Leviticus 15:19–33). We might also add that this same biblical book requires that those caught in adultery must be put to death (Leviticus 20:10).

In regard to these varying prohibitions it is noteworthy that those who advocate the "no" to homosexuality, as found in Leviticus, don't preach a corresponding "no" to eating pork or bacon. Nor do they insist that individuals, or society generally, enforce those other commands regarding menstruation or capital punishment for adultery. I would challenge my conservative Christian friends to re-examine their belief that some of those Levitical laws about gayness should be given such intense attention and allegiance, while they themselves leave those other Levitical laws unmentioned and un-obeyed. The conservative stance that gayness must be seen as wrong because "the Bible tells me so" doesn't hold up, because they *don't* espouse those other teachings in the very same text.

Just exactly why is it, then, that those same conservatives who assert the authoritativeness of that Levitical "no" to gay sex do, in fact, fail to accept those corresponding laws about pork, adultery, and menstruation? To me, it seems clear that the real reason for this contradiction stems from psychological factors rather than from a thoughtful and cogent approach to biblical interpretation. The obvious selectivity here concerning which prohibitions are or are not binding today springs from an attitudinal dynamic which needs to be named and examined.

What should be clear is that conservative Christians are clearly using the Bible here to buttress what is most essentially a *psychological* aversion to homosexuality within their own mental attitudes, and that this aversion derives from how they've been socialized by their families, churches, or social communities to think of same-gender sex as reprehensible. Among those influenced by such psychological influences (especially if from early childhood), there is a strong tendency to latch onto the idea—or, more precisely, to latch onto an inner emotional *feeling*—that biblical anti-gay verses "make sense" (and, thus, must be authoritative). But because those same people have not been inculcated with a corresponding aversion, say, to pork or bacon, etc., they do not have a corresponding belief or feeling that these other strictures that I've cited from Leviticus are also binding and authoritative.

All of this leads to a key question: What is the real nature of legitimate authority? That word—*authority*—has a fascinating background. It derives from the Latin verb *augere*, which means "to grow, increase, or create," and which gives us our English word *augment*. It is also behind the name of our eighth month of *August*, so labeled because late summer is the time when crops have grown and increased to their fullest extent. (Likewise, when the Caesar at the time of Christ chose to have himself called *Augustus*, that term was chosen to highlight his role in increasing the Roman Empire to its greatest level of growth.) All of these words, as well as *authority, author,* and *authentic,* come from that same linguistic root, implying some form of creating, increasing, or growing.

In light of this root sense of growth and increase standing behind the core idea of authority, we would do well to re-examine our current concepts *about* authority in religion and society. This is sorely needed because the original sense of what constitutes authority, as I've been describing it here, has been corrupted, if not fully reversed, in current usage. Over time, the meaning of authority has become co-opted to refer to those who have been *authorized* (i.e., empowered) to exercise control or domination in the enforcement of whatever social norms predominate at a particular time. And in the process, those things seen as authoritative are often used as instruments of suppression. And they are often wielded in ways that manipulate people through fear of, and obedience to, those in positions of authority.

That way of thinking often carries with it the idea that such "authorities" have legitimate power to injure, kill, and even torture people in the service of such enforcement. Authority has been reframed in this way so as to become an agent of restriction, if not outright destruction. That is a full reversal of the original sense. Over time, the natural beneficence of the fully grown cereals of *August* has been beaten down to justify the horrors of mass crucifixion under Caesar *Augustus* and his many heirs (who wield their supremacy through domination and enforcement, threat and violence).

With these thoughts about the nature of authority in mind, let's return to the question of homosexuality and the scriptures. The Bible's real authority here doesn't lie in cherry-picking isolated verses to use as hammers against groups of "others," including gays. That approach reflects the later, co-opted concept of authority as a tool for control and enforcement.

By contrast, the real nature of biblical authority and wisdom can only be found by doing the hard work of mining Bible texts for their core treasures about what is life-*enhancing*, not life-denying. We need to be focusing on those sections of the Bible that offer liberation, not domination—the ones that point in the direction of growth and increase in the well-being of both individuals and society.

And here is a remarkable and important fact: that same biblical book of Leviticus that says that homosexuality, pork, and menstruating women are to be avoided *also* says, "Love your neighbor as yourself" (Leviticus 19:18). With the significant help of that love-of-neighbor precept from within the Judeo-Christian tradition, our culture has come to recognize, over time, that those ancient instances of saying "no" to menstruation and "yes" to capital punishment for adultery are cultural relics that needed to be outgrown—and, thankfully, *have* been outgrown, at least within much of Western culture. And just as we have seen such successful growth beyond *those* approaches, should we not also grow beyond the discrimination and cruelty that homophobia inflicts on so many of our people? And should we not also grow into the biblical wisdom of loving *all* our neighbors as ourselves—including those who have sexual orientations that may be different from our own?

This is what real authority points us toward: whatever helps increase our commitment to the lovingkindness that supports and includes *all* our fellow human beings. The important thing is not that the Bible is always authoritative in each and every statement, but that we make the choice for love to be authoritative in each and every situation. Real authority lies in the aspect of love that manifests as a refusal to exclude any pre-defined groups, classes, or categories of people, regardless of whatever surrounding religious and cultural influences may tempt us to stigmatize those groups and the people in them.

Social attitudes about such things as gayness, pork, and periods come and go. But the one thing that does not come and go is the ongoing value of loving all our neighbors around us, regardless of whether they're gay or straight. And regardless of whether they do or don't eat bacon. (At whatever time of the month.)

RECLAIMING CHRIST
FROM CHRISTIANITY

⤶

MARCH 2000

A S A MINISTER, I cringe when I hear the negative attitudes about sex and the body that are present in some streams of Christian thinking (though, thankfully, not all). This negativity is evident in the opposition to homosexual behavior that is so prevalent in conservative Protestant churches. And we see it too in the Catholic bans on priestly marriage, women's ordination, and abortion. All those views, to my eye, are fueled by an attitudinal dynamic of distrust in the energies of physical life, especially those related to sex and gender.

Such positions are unfortunate not just because they are hurtful to flesh-and-blood human beings, but also because they promote forms of Christianity that are at odds with the actual teachings of Christ himself. As a minister, I believe that one of the most important things to know about Jesus is his deeply organic, nature-based cast of mind. The sage of Nazareth, in fact, consistently teaches *from* nature, not against it.

In his parables, for example, Jesus often points to seeds and plants for analogies. He says, "Unless a grain of wheat falls and dies, it remains alone; but when it does die, that is when it bears much fruit" (John 12:24). He talks of mustard seeds becoming large trees (Luke 13:19), and of seeds being sown on soils that are less or more receptive (Mark 4:3–20). We hear of helpful and unhelpful seeds growing together to produce wheat or weeds (Matthew 13:24–30,36–43). And in the Sermon on the Mount we are counseled to have the same kind of faith possessed by "the lilies of the field," which trustingly await what they need to grow and flourish (Matthew 6:28–29).

Jesus also frequently cites animals as teaching tools. He draws our attention to "the birds of the air who sow not, nor gather into barns; yet (God) fully feeds them" (Matthew 6:29). He talks of each sparrow being precious in the eyes of Heaven (Matthew 10:29) and speaks of sheep trusting in the guidance of a "good shepherd" (John 10:11).

What is noteworthy about these examples is their clear implication that spiritual truths are fully present *within* the natural order, within biological life itself. Christ is telling us that if we want to contact our divine Source, we don't have to look far, because it is present in the very tissue of pulsing flesh and living things. The life of God, in other words, far from being antagonistic to physical life, is radically present in the processes of our own bodies and beings. The Nazarene is telling us, unmistakably and repeatedly, that deepened spirituality requires *returning* to the organic and embodying it, not recoiling from it.

In addition to these nature-based metaphors, Jesus's actions and choices point in the same direction. For example, when he is about to start his public life, he first goes on a retreat into nature (his forty days and nights in the desert). That time in natural wildness demonstrates a version of what Native Americans call a "vision quest."

Consider also that when Jesus returns from the wilderness and begins his public life, we see him again and again utilizing organic things as teaching tools. One of his first public acts is to bathe ritually in water (Mark 1:9). He then uses a cornfield as an occasion to teach about the meaning of Sabbath (Mark 2:23–28). The message is clear when our eyes are ready to see it: there is spiritual power to be found in the natural world's sights and smells, blessings and snares, rhythms and stasis.

I think also of the wonderful story in which Jesus takes a blind man by the hand, spits on the ground, and makes clay of the spittle with which he then anoints the man's eyes as part of the process of healing him (John 9:6). Or again, we see him not only dine with lepers, but physically touch them, contrary to cultural taboo (Luke 5:12–13). In another instance, we see him bend down and write with his finger in the dirt, just before he models forgiveness for a woman caught in adultery (John 8:6–8).

And then there is the exquisite story in which, prior to Jesus's torture and execution, a woman comes with an alabaster flask of expensive ointment, and pours it on his head. When his disciples object that the ointment might better be sold to raise money for the poor, he says, "Why do you trouble this woman? She has done a beautiful thing" (Matthew 26:10).

Jesus, then, was a man highly at ease with flesh and touch, with the earthy and the organic. And those who look to him as a spiritual guide will do well to follow his lead of finding the spiritual *by means of* organic, fleshy things—not in opposition to them.

NOT BY BREAD ALONE

✌

APRIL 2000

THIS WEEK'S NEWS has brought us a spate of painful stories: yet another shooting of an unarmed black man in New York City; more resistance to gun control in Congress; a new breakdown of Arab–Israeli talks over a veritable postage stamp of disputed land. And then there was the killing of several hundred cultists in Uganda. What first seemed a group suicide now appears to have been a mass murder by the cult's leader. (His flock had the temerity to ask for their money back when his repeated predictions of the world's end kept being wrong.)

In the face of so many stories like this, I find myself wondering how much time I want to spend absorbing such grimness by watching the "news." (The stories there seem less and less new these days.) I certainly intend to keep myself informed. And for my work as a minister and writer, staying abreast of world events is a must.

But I am noticing more and more the degree to which too much exposure to negative events in the world triggers a subtle but unmistakable stress in my mind. Last week I gave a talk in which I cited the biblical admonition: "Whatsoever is true (or) honorable . . . if there is anything excellent, or worthy of praise, think on these things; and you will know the peace of heaven"

(Philippians 4:8). Those are wise words. But how do I balance my desire to keep my mind focused on things that are positive and good with my need to stay aware of the world scene, including all the tragic things that happen?

One thing I've found helpful is seeking less news from TV (and electronic screens generally), while getting more from print. Although I used to be a TV news junkie, my screen-based news-watching is now minimal. For me, TV news reports tend to be more intrusive upon the mind. Those electronic images with all their motion and sound tend to be hypnotic, drawing us into themselves, riveting us to them in a way that makes it hard for the psyche to be alertly selective about what to let in, and what to filter out. Such formats, I think, reduce our freedom to manage how the world's negativities will influence us.

By contrast, when I focus more on news articles in printed form, if there's been another school shooting or atrocity, I can get the gist of what's happened, but be selective about the details. And I can more easily look to, or away from, these stories at times of my own choosing. Staying informed is important, but I also want to make sure my psyche doesn't get over-influenced by the world's chronic fear-patterns, and by our culture's repetitive focus on negativity and bad behavior. And for me, at least, the video-based and multi-sensory formats of TV newscasts feel like a kind of assault on my consciousness. And I find myself, more and more, wanting to minimize that.

In addition, we would all do well to focus less on problems per se, and more on hopeful, potential *solutions* to our problems. And to that end we will do well to take some time each day to feed our minds not just from the world's same-old, same-old version of the news, but from larger and more nourishing helpings of positive, constructive information.

The ancient Hebrews knew something about this in their saying that we should not "live by bread alone, but by every word that proceeds from the mouth of the Divine" (Deuteronomy 8:3). That is a good reminder about where our truest and best "news" can be sought and found.

THE PRODIGAL BROTHERS

～◇～

APRIL 2000

IN THE BIBLICAL STORY of the prodigal son, the younger of two sons asks the father for his share of the inheritance. When the father complies, the son travels off, but soon squanders what he's been given. The elder son stays home, faithful and hard-working. But when the wayward one returns, and the father extends forgiving welcome, the elder bitterly resents his father's generosity to the younger.

When I was growing up, this parable was presented to me as a teaching tale mainly about the foolishness of the younger son, with a nod toward the forbearance of the father. That is all to the good. But as I look at it again now, I see it as having further layers than that, especially with respect to the two sons. Each has not only weaknesses but corresponding strengths, which archetypally represent qualities that exist and need to be accounted for in all of us. Let's take a look at these two sons and brothers.

The younger one is often cast as a stick figure representing self-indulgence to be avoided. But in addition to that, he also embodies another quality that is positive, and deeply necessary to human progress: the willingness to take risks and to explore what is yet unmapped and unfamiliar. We might think of the younger son as the "liberal" in the family, representing change, flexibility, spontaneity, fascination, experimentation, innovation, intuition, and self-discovery. He represents, it seems to me, an archetype of society's inventors, modernists, and voyagers—those who look at the stars and translate their wonder to conscious (and eventually practical) use. He stands for those who walk daringly into the deep, dark forest farther than yesterday's scouts—even if told not to. The younger son stands for Jesus's truth that "new wine belongs in new skins" (Luke 5:38).

The older son is also often cast in a stereotype of being rigid and hard-hearted. But as the one who might be considered the "conservative" in the tale, he too stands for essential and necessary values. He is sensible and hard-working, and represents those who do the work of safeguarding and transmitting already-established learnings and practices so that they can benefit succeeding generations. People on the progressive side of things—like me—sometimes minimize the importance of such legitimate conservative/conserving functions. But where would we all be without that older brother's values of order, duty, discipline, practicality, planning, work ethic, responsibility, and common sense? In his tending of the family farm, he represents those who make sure that the farm keeps producing enough food to last through winter. The older son embodies another truth spoken by Jesus when he said, "The old is good" (Luke 5:39).

These two brothers, then, one standing for the needed known, the other for the equally needed new, are humanity's two legs—the one moving forward, the other holding a connection to the ground already reached.

If we read this tale archetypally, each brother embodies not only weaknesses to be avoided, but necessary strengths to be honored. We would do well to avoid denigrating or demonizing the strengths of either brother—whether in this ancient story or in current society. We have equally much to learn from those who seek to liberate us to embrace new ways and those who wish to conserve established ways that help maintain social cohesion and continuity.

LIVING IN PRESENT TIME

⤸

APRIL 2000

WHILE BROWSING on the internet recently, I read about a survey in which some grade-school kids were asked, "Would you rather live now, in the past, or in the future?"

Among those who chose the future, one said, "Well, nowadays if you want to wash clothes, you just have a regular old washing machine. But in the future, you'll probably be able to push a button and as the machine washes the clothes, some computer will be able to play lots of neat music and give weather reports, too." (Who would doubt any of that?)

Would you rather live in the future? If our minds focus on the potential benefits of new technology, the world of a century from now might seem bright indeed. But if we think about how our entrenched social problems could unfold—the degradation of the environment, untrammeled population growth, and economic inequality—living in 2100 might well be a nightmare.

Although most of us may not spend much time pondering a century ahead, virtually all of us *do* spend a great deal of time in *some* form of living in the future. If you doubt that, try an experiment. Take a few moments to become still and quiet. Then choose to let your mind come to complete rest. Do your best to be free of all thoughts, and notice what happens. In almost all cases—usually within a few seconds—our minds are busy at work imagining some future scenario we need to deal with, or something on our to-do list to attend to.

What I just described represents a core dynamic of what happens in meditation. Anyone who meditates learns fast that it's a hard thing to keep the mind at rest and in immediate, present experience. Our mental chatter pulls us "back to the future" quickly and addictively. Our minds are incessantly rehearsing what we're going to do or experience in some future situation, or how we might address some portion of tomorrow's problems. One of the most essential elements of becoming a genuinely conscious person starts here: learning to notice and experience how much of our life-energy is pulled (mostly unconsciously) into the future-oriented scenarios of our minds.

The same dynamic is at work in what our minds do with the past. A substantial majority of those grade-schoolers I mentioned said that they would, in fact, rather live in the past. One girl said, "In the past, all that people had to worry about was dinosaurs and stuff. When the first cavemen fought, they only used clubs. Now we use bullets, even in our schools. It's harder to dodge a bullet than get out of the way of a club. I'd rather live in the past. It was a lot safer then." That response is a young person's version of how we can all easily romanticize the "good old days" as preferable to the present.

But whether we point our minds forward or back in time, there is a key common element either way: a loss of present-time focus and awareness. Being aware of that is crucial because everything we do in our lives—without exception—springs from our consciousness, from some aspect of our psyches and our mental functioning. Every choice and action we take has a thought, or some form of thought-process, or some activity in our consciousness lying behind it. Because of that, the thoughts we think, and the places we put our mental focus, have a major impact on everything that goes on within us, most especially our reactions and responses to events that happen *to* us from the outside in.

That's why meditation is so valuable. It is a tool by which we can learn how to make choices about what happens in our minds (and also, to a considerable extent, our bodies). It is only when we can calm our inner beings, and learn to still our thoughts, that we can start to learn how to *choose* our thoughts, and thereby experience what the New Testament describes as being "transformed by the renewal of our minds" (Romans 12:2).

The more we can choose what happens in our consciousness, the more you and I can become free to choose how to be, and to become, our best and most capable potential selves.

THE CROSS REVISITED

⤸

JULY 2000

THE TV SHOW *60 Minutes* recently aired a segment about John Shelby Spong, the Episcopal bishop and author. His challenges to orthodox Christian dogma have offered hope and inspiration to progressive Christians. But they have also angered traditionalists. One doctrinal lightning rod has been this bishop's notable rejection of the idea that Jesus "died on the cross for our sins." He considers any view of God as a being that punishes all sins to be "grotesque" and outmoded.

To represent the orthodox disagreement with Bishop Spong, the CBS reporter Lesley Stahl interviewed Diane Knippers, of the Institute on Religion and Democracy. I was struck by the ferocity of her opposition to the bishop's concept of the crucifixion. She calls it a denial of "the very heart of our faith." And she describes him personally as "very dangerous," and as "pushing a deadly product." She adds that "having the cross denigrated and discounted," as she believes he does, "is like someone trashing your mother."

As a minister, I know that such words are not confined to a few overheated people. Diane Knippers' comments represent a deeply held belief, not only in the idea that Christ *did* die for our sins, but that this, somehow, is at the very heart of what Christianity is about.

To my eye, however, Bishop Spong is offering us a major service by exposing the outmoded, if not fully faulty, nature of this doctrine of the crucifixion. The traditional view is based on four core assumptions that have roots in primitive thought systems and no longer make sense to the modern mind.

First, there is the idea that God is a judging, punishing being. Second is the corresponding thought that human misbehavior calls for and must necessarily be dealt with by punishment and judgment. The third idea is the belief that God chose to inflict terrible punishment onto "his own Son" instead of onto the rest of us humans, who were the ones who in fact deserved it (this being, somehow, a demonstration of God's "mercy")! And finally, there is the idea that Jesus willingly obeyed God's decree to take onto himself that "necessary and just" punishment that we humans deserve.

The more I have become aware of what I see as being the wrongness of all four of those concepts, the more I have come to agree with Bishop Spong's critique. That orthodox view is wrong, most essentially, because it misperceives God as punitive. No power or being that is essentially punitive in nature, and that could submit its own child to torture and death, would be a fit object to be believed in—let alone worshipped.

Put simply, the harsh God-concept in that doctrine does not correspond to the much more central Christian vision of a God of Love. The God that I sense experientially is a power and presence that is deeply loving in its nature. The divine Presence that I have come to know, through my spiritual practice and life experience, is a force for forgiveness and healing, self-betterment and growth—not one of guilt, threat, or punishment. And given the grip which that "dying for our sins" doctrine has come to hold on the thinking of orthodox Christianity, Bishop Spong's work to dismantle it is theologically necessary, not to mention personally courageous.

It is important to note that Bishop Spong does not disparage, or urge us to discard, the symbolism of the cross altogether. Rather, he urges us to re-vision the cross, to think it through carefully and in a new way, so we can interpret it more intelligently. His critique can free us to newly see this iconic image for what, in my view, it more accurately is: one of religious history's most powerful symbols of our need for courage in the face of fear, pain, and mortality.

From this perspective, the crucifixion story can be seen as a high-level teaching tool about what I would call *necessary suffering*. No matter how responsibly we live, and no matter how much self-mastery we achieve, some degree of suffering is inescapable. The law of impermanence inevitably causes all our possessions, achievements, and human connections to fade and dissolve. And in the face of such loss, one of the core tasks of being human is to cultivate the psycho-spiritual skills that can deal with that hard and all-too-difficult side of life, and to do so without bitterness or blame, without shutting down our willingness to feel, and without numbing our hearts and our hope. The cross, seen in this light, shows Christ as one of humanity's highest spiritual masters. It shows him demonstrating what spiritual maturity and courage look like, and how they can be practiced when pain, loss, and death knock at the door.

The cross, then, in its core meaning, is not about guilt as a result of sin. Much more, it is about courage in the face of suffering. The story of Christ's Passion can be a guidepost for helping us find our way courageously and consciously through the minefield of mortality and loss. "Accepting" the cross is not a requirement for avoiding hell after death, but a window into how we can best navigate the aspects of *this* life (which can sometimes seem hellish) *before* death.

In my next article, I'll say more about how we can utilize this great spiritual symbol in a useful and healthy way.

NECESSARY SUFFERING

‹›

Y PREVIOUS ARTICLE discussed the cross in Christian thought, and described why more and more Christians, including myself, have come to reject the traditional idea that Christ "died on the cross for our sins"; i.e., the idea that God meted out punishment onto "his own son," Jesus, for sins that were committed by the rest of us more generally.

Despite my rejection of that older view, I continue to see the Christian cross as a powerful spiritual symbol, the deeper meaning of which revolves around the inescapability of impermanence and loss, suffering and death. The cross is a tangible and conceptual resource for learning how to live with and through necessary suffering. In my view, one helpful way to think about the symbolism of the cross is to see it as a Christian concept that corresponds to, and parallels, the core teaching of Buddhism known as the Four Noble Truths.

The first of these Noble Truths is the Buddha's assertion that "All life is pervaded by suffering." The Second declares that suffering is generated by attachment; while the Third, in turn, says that freedom from suffering comes from letting go of attachment, i.e., letting go of grasping, or holding onto, things as they are—or as we want them to be. The Fourth Noble Truth then asserts that letting go of such attachments can be learned with the help of following various moral and behavioral precepts (as outlined in the Buddha's "Eight-Fold Path").

The Buddha's starting point, that "all life is pervaded by suffering" (which I am here calling "necessary suffering"), might seem obvious. But the real meaning of that First Noble Truth lies not just in *stating* an objective reality—that suffering happens a lot. Rather, it consists in confronting the *subjective* reality of how our minds tend to maintain various forms of denial about the inevitability of our pains and losses. Our ordinary thinking (sometimes referred to as the ego-mind) tries to seduce us into believing that pain and discomfort either can or should always be avoided—and that pleasure and convenience should always be sought.

In service to that goal of denial, our minds urge us to grasp tightly to things we already have that give us comfort (as a way to forestall suffering). And they also urge us to acquire—and then attach ourselves firmly to—things we don't currently have that might *bring* us comfort (again, as a way to forestall suffering).

But this is where things get tricky, because enjoying what we have and gaining new things are not bad or unworthy goals *per se*. Nor is it wrong to steer clear of immediate, physical pain. Those are all natural, normal activities in and of themselves. (And it should be noted that both the Buddha and Christ counsel engagement in, and enjoyment of, the normal activities of everyday life.)

But here is a key point: although acquiring and enjoying are natural and normal, impermanence and loss are also natural and normal. We often want to skip over the second part of that equation. What we need to reckon with is that although the human mind strongly pursues the acquiring/enjoying side of what is natural, it has a corresponding resistance toward the impermanence side of "natural": i.e., the psyche strongly resists the pain/loss that comes with the impermanence that is inherent to nature itself, and thus to the "natural" world.

This is a point where Christ and the Buddha offer an important common teaching. Although their modes of expression are different, their core message is much the same. It says: Yes, enjoy the good things that life gives you in the normal course of things; but also be prepared to relinquish them freely and without resistance when their time is up, and when life takes them away.

That is the main sense, I think, of the part of the Noble Truths that counsels non-attachment. That teaching needs to be taken in conjunction with the Buddha's parallel idea of the "Middle Way," which recommends moderate, normal enjoyment of natural life (free of the extremes of both indulgence and asceticism).

As a parallel to that, I would suggest that the cross in Christianity is, in its essence, saying much the same. Think about Jesus's advice to his students that they "take up their cross and follow my way. For those who cling to their life as it is will lose it; but those ready to let go of their life will find it. For what profit is there to gain even the whole world, but forfeit one's larger field of life?" (Matthew 16:24–26).

Just as the Buddha's Noble Truths need to be seen in conjunction with his concept of the Middle Way, so this call to "take up the cross" needs to be taken in conjunction with the biblical portrait of how Jesus freely ate and drank, enjoyed the company of women and children, celebrated marriage, and engaged in playful conversation with a wide range of colorful and vitally alive people. When compared to the Buddha's Middle Way and Noble Truths, the way of Christ, including the way of the cross, tells us something quite similar: Enjoy the natural gifts of life as they are given, but when pain and loss come, claim the courage to practice surrender and letting go, doing your best to walk through those struggles with faith and hope, and keeping your heart open to love and new life, despite whatever you may also suffer in the process.

Any approach to life that is worth following must include ways of moving beyond denial of the inevitability of loss and pain. And that includes moving beyond the parallel denial that loss and pain are essentially bad, or always to be avoided. The principle I am describing here is present not just in Christianity and Buddhism, but throughout most of humanity's wisdom-streams. We hear it in the words of the Greek playwright Aeschylus that "In suffering is our learning." We hear it in Islam, when Rumi declares that "your pain is your medicine." We see it lived out in history's saints and martyrs.

Jesus himself puts the paradoxical nature of all this as well as anyone, in the gnostic text known as the *Apocryphon of John*, when he says, "If you learn how to suffer, only then will you learn to acquire the power to move beyond suffering."

RELIGION AND POLITICS

❧

SEPTEMBER 2000

A FUNNY THING happened this week on the way to the election. Last Sunday, the Democrats' vice-presidential candidate, Joe Lieberman, gave a speech (or was it a sermon?) at a predominantly African American church in Detroit, in which he called on Americans "to renew our dedication to God and God's purposes."

Such talk is not unusual in our politics, but this didn't come from one of the "usual suspects" (conservative Christian Republicans), but from an observant Jew, who is a (somewhat) liberal Democrat. I liked the implication in Lieberman's message that neither the religious right nor Christianity itself has a lock on the landscape of spiritually based values.

Lieberman's talk brought quick criticism from several parties (including the Anti-Defamation League) that don't want the line between church and state blurred. I share that concern generally, but I don't think it fits this case. The Connecticut senator was careful to emphasize that "the Constitution wisely separates church from state." In Lieberman's case, that is not mere rhetoric, as evidenced by his consistent opposition to allowing prayer in public schools, or to unduly shifting social services from government to religious groups.

The relationship between religion and politics has vexed Americans for a long time. One complicating factor is semantic, given that the words *politics* and *religion* have different meanings when used by different people in differing contexts. Sometimes, for example, when people talk of religion and politics they are referring to the relationship between church and state—i.e., the relationship of specific religious groups to specific government bodies. (One example is when a Christian pastor leads the Lord's Prayer at a public school event.) But at other times, when people speak of "religion and politics" they are referencing a substantially different subject: the relationship of *values* to public policy. Unfortunately, though, we often fail to take note of the fact that church/state issues are not at all the same as values/public policy issues. Clarifying that distinction is important and necessary.

American law has long required that religion and government (i.e., church and state) be kept separate. That is as it should be. But when America has been at its best, it has also insisted—with equal rightness—on the inseparability of our core values from public policy. This, I think, is what Senator Lieberman was trying to get at last Sunday in Detroit. What is the relationship of religion and politics? The operative principle is this: although church and state must *always* be kept separate, values and public policy must *never* be kept separate.

That distinction is simple to state, but hard to achieve in the real world. In my next article, I'll give some examples about how these principles have been successfully brought to bear at key points in America's past.

RELIGION AND POLITICS
REVISITED

☙

SEPTEMBER 2000

L AST WEEK I wrote about Senator (and Democratic vice-
presidential candidate) Joseph Lieberman's introduction
of spiritual themes into this year's presidential campaign.
Addressing concerns about mixing politics and religion, I argued
for semantic clarity in remembering that "church" does not
refer to the same thing as "values," nor are "state" and "public
policy" the same. I said that although church (religion) and state
(government) must always be kept separate, values and public
policy must always be linked.

No specific religion, in other words, should ever be embraced
or favored by the state, or by a specific government. But consensual, humane values must, equally importantly, never be set
aside in our societal decisions. Here are some examples from our
shared history that demonstrate this distinction.

Consider, first, the American Quakers of the seventeenth century. They proclaimed the then-radical idea that *all* people should
be treated equally, not just in theory, but tangibly. They said that
blacks must be treated as respectfully as whites, that the poor
were of equal value as the rich. And they affirmed, long before it
was popular, that women should hold equal status to men. Some

of them were treated harshly—some even hanged by the government of Massachusetts—for espousing such views.

Those Quakers never tried to make Quakerism the official American religion. They knew better than to mix church and state. But they also knew to insist on a basic moral *value* based on spiritual truth: that the equality and respectful treatment of all persons must become public policy. That view was right, then and now. Where would America be today if not for those courageous Quakers of the seventeenth century?

And where would America be if not for the social gospel movement in the nineteenth and early twentieth centuries? The advocates of that social gospel insisted that slavery was wrong, that women should have the vote, and that workers had not just the human right, but a divine right to organize and to share economic power with management. They never tried to make their brand of faith the official religion of America. They too knew not to mix church and state. But they also knew to promote the moral imperative—as well as an effective political program—to work for equal access to social power for all. That view was also right, then and now. Where would America be today if not for those practitioners of the social gospel?

And where would America be if not for that brave, Black Baptist preacher who carried the message of Moses across the centuries to many of us still living when he said, "Let my people go"? Martin Luther King Jr. had the courage to insist that America live up to her best self, and to guarantee her people the sharing of her good.

He then had the courage to call the Vietnam War wrong—militarily, economically, and morally. Dr. King never tried to make Washington an arm of the Baptist faith. He knew better than to mix church and state. But he also knew to insist that human rights be more than just another element of public policy. They must be its *main basis*. That view was right, then and now. Where would America be today without the spiritual vision of Martin Luther King?

As we move into an unpredictable future bedeviled by complexities that will determine the lives of millions, no one religion, and no single spiritual approach, whether liberal or conservative, traditional or progressive, Western, Eastern, or indigenous, can or will have all the answers. But just as the past problems of slavery and social injustice could only be addressed by invoking values grounded in spiritual and moral insights, so too will the problems of tomorrow require a continual search for similar, life-enhancing values.

Embracing such values is the most important resource we have for moving forward as a society in a healthy and harmonious way.

A MORE HUMBLE CHURCH

✥

SEPTEMBER 2000

THE VATICAN published an official declaration last month on the relationship of Catholicism to other religious approaches. It is not encouraging.

The document, called *Dominus Iesus* (*Lord Jesus*), was put forward by Rome's Congregation for the Doctrine of the Faith. This is, essentially, an orthodoxy commission led by the theological reactionary Cardinal Joseph Ratzinger, whose main claim to fame has been making life miserable for some of the best Catholic thinkers—German theologian Hans Küng, for one, as well as the American monk and author Matthew Fox. Under Ratzinger's screws, Rev. Fox was forced out of Catholicism entirely and is now an Episcopal priest.

What makes *Dominus Iesus* so newsworthy—and unsettling— is its assertion that Catholicism is superior not just over other religions, but even over other branches of Christianity itself. The document says that other denominations are "not (true) churches in the proper sense." Only Roman Catholicism, in other words, is the real deal.

The ideas in *Dominus Iesus* are not new. They have been "on the books" for centuries. What is troubling here is the way Rome is stirring up old wounds arising from its own well-documented history of exclusivity and intolerance. Catholicism does, to be sure, have many riches to offer, as does Christianity as a whole. There is a deep vein of spirituality within the Catholic tradition that, frankly, dwarfs much of what my own Protestant tradition offers.

I have no problem with advocating for the legitimate strengths and insights of one's own tradition. But there is a big difference between saying "Our way is a good way," versus saying "Our way is the best way." The fact that there is much that is wonderful in Catholicism, as in Christianity generally, does not make either Catholicism or Christianity superior to other approaches, given the great value to be found in other spiritual paths as well.

One of the repeated self-inflicted wounds throughout the history of Christianity has been the profound misconception that divine revelation is *exclusive to* the church, or that it is found only, or mainly, in Christ himself. The greater truth is that important clues about the divine Mystery have, yes indeed, been revealed in Christ and the church. But the same can be said with equal validity about multiple faiths and philosophies throughout our long human journey.

The church has long taught that humility is a cardinal virtue. The Holy Father and his staff in Rome would do well to remind themselves that such humility must be practiced not only by individual believers—but also by the church itself.

IT'S BEYOND BELIEF

৵

September 2000

L AST WEEK in this space I critiqued the Vatican's recent document *Dominus Iesus* (*Lord Jesus*) because of its dubious assertion of the superior status of Catholic beliefs over those of other faiths.

This week I want to also point out that when a religion exalts its own beliefs (Catholicism is far from being the sole example), that approach is also flawed for reasons that go beyond institutional arrogance. I say that because whenever any religion (or other movement) makes the mistake of ultimizing its own beliefs, it is making the even deeper mistake of implicitly asserting the centrality of *belief itself.* The widespread disaffection with organized religion these days is, in no small part, a reaction against some religious bodies having oversold the role of belief in the spiritual life more generally.

In my own Christian tradition, for example, consider how much focus has been placed over the years on disputing beliefs about the nature of Jesus, the various definitions of God, and the authority of the Bible and/or the church. But when we look at the teachings of Jesus himself, we see him taking a quite different approach.

In the Gospels, Jesus never tells people (in effect): You must have this belief or adopt that doctrine. Rather, the gist of what he does have to say, much more often, is found in the kinds of questions he poses, which tend to ask, by implication: What is the state of your attitude? Are you cultivating openness of heart and mind? Are you willing to examine your actions to see if they reflect good-heartedness, love, and courage? Again and again, Jesus says to people: You need an attitude that is merciful and gentle, tender and forgiving. And you need to cultivate an attitude of trust toward, and confidence in, the Ultimate Realm.

In the worldview of Christ, the wheel of spiritual living clearly revolves around the state of our hearts and of our psycho-spiritual *attitudes*, not the correctness of our thinking about doctrinal *beliefs*. That distinction between attitude and belief is very important. For Jesus himself, a legitimate spiritual life does not revolve around affiliation, allegiance, or adherence to any specific institution or religious approach, or to any speculative belief system, to which people so often look for a sense of identity.

Does this mean that ideas or worldviews are unimportant generally? Not at all. Good paradigms, including well-thought-out beliefs, have some legitimate role in the scheme of things. Clear thinking and proper uses of the mind are important parts of being human. And in light of that, we humans have a need to keep on developing intellectually viable views of how things are and how they work. When this happens in a healthy, clear way, it can lead to real insight. So, yes, beliefs and paradigms have their own value and importance. But they are never what is *most* important.

What is in fact much more important is the *attitudinal* commitment to love and openness of heart, to spiritual experience and discovery, and to the search for truth more generally, in all its forms. This is a journey centered around finding greater acceptance and empathy; living with greater courage; becoming more conscious of how reality itself unfolds and operates; and surrendering our lives more and more to the Divine. This is a journey of embodying greater trust and confidence, and of having more wonder, amazement, and delight in our life's adventures.

On the spiritual path, beliefs and paradigms are like maps that can help us navigate. Maps have an important role. But all our maps—whether geographical or conceptual—are always incomplete, and thus in need of ongoing revision. They need to be updated by what we learn during the journey itself. In the end, having attitudes characterized by trust, courage, curiosity, and openness as we move into the unknown are much more import-ant than any doctrinal mapping of what has already become par-tially known.

When we get this balance right, we learn that the experiential riches we can gain on the spiritual path are—quite literally—beyond belief.

SHIFT HAPPENS

❧

OCTOBER 2000

THIS PAST WEEK had a "good news / bad news" element for me. First, the bad news. When my daughter came down with a cold, I gave her some vitamins along with my usual "take-care-of-yourself" sermon. So far, so good. (She says she has even been *taking* the vitamins.)

The problem, though, was that instead of just giving her the pills, I added a spiel about my own increasing vitamin use, and about how much better I'm feeling as a result. I even said (and this is where things started going south), "Do you remember how I used to get a lot of colds? And have you noticed how few I've had recently? Well," I went on, "a lot of that is from these vitamins I'm taking."

By now, my brilliant readers (do I have any other kind?), you've likely guessed the rest. Within a few days I came down with, yes, a really bad cold, vitamins notwithstanding. But even worse than the cold itself is my nagging thought that if I'd just kept my mouth shut about those pills keeping me cold-free, I might have, in fact, *stayed* cold-free. Not this time, though. Hubris strikes again.

But there was also some good news. Even though being sick was no fun, it also taught me some things about my own tendency to self-isolate when I get into a down place. When I get sick, or get the "blues" in some form, I often regress into a self-sufficiency mentality, a core attitude that says, "I can handle this myself." This is my inner American male speaking—the dutiful son of Mark and Cecilia Acheson, the long-suffering clergyman who must always look good and project a happy, hopeful face.

But as I grappled with all that this week, a shift took place in me. When I was in the midst of my low time, I did something uncharacteristic: I reached out. I called several friends, including some members of the church I serve. I asked a couple of people to visit and spend time with me when I was in bed. In the past, I would have just toughed it out. Reaching out is unfamiliar to me. It's a new behavior. But after I did so, I felt noticeably better. And I now think that this reaching out, and the increased human connection it fostered, may have helped me recover faster. (Perhaps my revised sermon for my daughter should be titled: "Connection Is the New Vitamin.")

There's a bumper sticker I like that says, "Shift Happens." I write and speak often of our human need for attitudinal shifts. For me, the shift this week was toward being willing to ask for more help, and toward a willingness to be more vulnerable and humble. It was a shift away from going-it-alone, and it was a welcome change.

Next time, maybe I can find a way to keep growing in that same direction—without getting sick in the process.

SIFTING THE TRADITION

&

November 2000

W HEN JESUS was once asked which commandment was the greatest, he replied, "Love God (fully) . . . and love your neighbor as yourself" (Mark 12:29–31). That covers a lot of ground in a minimum of words.

This "summation of the law," as it's often called, was not in itself original to the Nazarene. He was quoting it from the Hebrew Scriptures (Deuteronomy 6:5 and Leviticus 19:18), and was offering what he saw as the core of his own Jewish birth tradition. His use of these quotations makes clear the priority he gave to studying his own religious and cultural background carefully. And by so doing he made their core meanings his own.

But beyond acquiring that textual knowledge and, in this case, quoting it, he did something else of enormous significance. He didn't simply restate the parts of his native Judaism that he embraced. In addition, he did the much harder work of "sifting the tradition" he had grown up in—of evaluating and culling its various elements.

Such sifting has two sides. The positive side has to do with reaffirming what has enduring value in a tradition. In the summation of the law noted above, Jesus put his finger on the living essence of his Jewish faith, and beyond that, of all life-affirming religion: the principle of love. This starts with loving the Divine, and further manifests through loving other people, loving our own selves, loving all living beings, loving life itself, loving wisdom and truth.

But sifting our traditions has another critical function, which is equally important. This has to do with, first, identifying, and, second, letting go of those parts of a tradition that have become outdated or outlived their usefulness (or, in some cases, were not valid or worth embracing in the first place). The work of sifting a tradition, then, includes two parallel tasks: saying "yes" to some parts of it that need to be retained, while saying "no" to other parts that need to be released.

Here is an example. We've seen how Jesus elevates that one verse in Leviticus 19:18 ("Love your neighbor as yourself") as representing the second half of the great law. But alongside that, Jesus also strongly *rejects* several other teachings in that same Book of Leviticus.

In the Sermon on the Mount, for instance (in Matthew 5), Jesus proclaims, "You have heard it said, 'An eye for an eye and a tooth for a tooth' [Leviticus 24:19–20]; but I say unto you, do not resist an evildoer. For if anyone strikes you on the right cheek, turn the other also." This is an important example of how Jesus doesn't simply *restate* Leviticus. He *sifts and culls* it. He elevates and emphasizes one part of it (love your neighbor). But he also rejects and lets go of another part (an eye for an eye).

Jesus's significance as a teacher, then, lies not just in the specific teachings he presented, important as those are, but also in the process by which he *arrived* at those teachings. Learning from the Nazarene involves not just hearing or obeying his sayings. It also involves engaging in the harder, subtler work of discerning not only what he said "yes" to, but also what he said "no" to. And then—most importantly—it also involves discerning *how and why* he went about sifting the parts of scripture and tradition that needed to be affirmed from those that needed to be negated.

And here is a key point. When it comes to our current spiritual-religious scene, we have the same task set before us. As many of us engage in the complex work of helping bring our faith traditions forward into a new century, and present them in ways that can "work" and speak effectively to new generations, an essential part of our job is to engage in the same kind of discernment process that Jesus engaged in. Our job is not just to restate and transmit our traditions, but also to *sift out* their outmoded and anachronistic elements—and to cull for posterity those truths that need to be sustained and strengthened.

This is a difficult dance: learning how to both preserve *and* transcend our religious traditions, and how to do both simultaneously. But it's a dance that we greatly need to be dancing.

MY SAME NEW FACE

֍

DECEMBER 2000

THE CHRISTMAS SEASON is a hard time for many people, including me. The various cultural pressures to smile and be joyful on cue have never sat well with me. I can fake it. And usually make it. But I don't like it.

Recently I read an account about the Swiss sculptor and painter, Alberto Giacometti (1901–1966). His work often depicts people with thin, stick-like figures, which several critics have seen as symbols of cultural alienation, or psychological malnutrition.

In his personal life, though, Giacometti understood a key part of one possible solution to such alienation. Throughout his career, Giacometti used only a small group of models. He favored a select few he had long known: his wife, his sister, and both his brothers. When asked why he didn't use a greater range of models, he said, "The joy for me is to look at the same face each day, but to see something new there."

For many of us, I think, our default tendency is quite different. When we look at a face repeatedly (including our own in the mirror), we may think, "Oh, it's the same old face" (or "the same old face getting older"). But this man saw value in familiarity, and he trained himself to discern the yet unnoticed in the already seen. He had the wisdom to seek out new ways to delight in those accustomed images by continually scanning their expressions for what they might newly embody and express. The ability to see in that way is itself an art, potentially as great as any skill with a brush or chisel. Since I came across that information about Giacometti, it has become fodder for me to think about seeing these "same-old" holidays with friendlier, more possibility-oriented eyes.

And—here is one more thing. After writing the previous paragraphs a few hours ago, I was stumped for a while about how to end this article. But then a serendipity happened not many minutes ago, and it was sweet indeed.

When I got up to turn down the thermostat in my office, I saw something just beneath the sleeve of my minister's robe. It's a large yellow Post-It that an anonymous angel left for me as a gift. The words on it say: "Dear Tony, I know you miss me, but I'm going to start heading back your way soon—around Dec. 21st, in fact. Love, The Sun."

As I reached to pull off the Post-It, I saw that it had been placed on the full-length mirror that hangs behind my robe. As I removed the note, I could see the reflection of my own face in that mirror—my own same-old, same-new face. And it was smiling. Someone (I think I know who you are!) cared enough about me to leave that gift. And because of that small confection of unmerited grace, there were suddenly no frowns on my face about the burdens of the holidays.

I'm going to cherish that Post-It for a long time. For all my grousing, maybe there's something to this holiday-spirit thing after all.

RELIGION AS SURRENDER
TO LOVE

↭

DECEMBER 2000

THE SURGE OF INTEREST in spirituality these days is evident all around us. Most bookstores now have large sections devoted to spiritual topics. The New Age movement is booming, in no small part because of the wide appeal of its eclectic approach. Spiritual seekers can take a little of this, and some of that, from an array of spiritual offerings. Even in corporate America, a growing number of companies—Xerox and Boeing among them—have hired "spirituality workers" to offer ecumenical, in-house options, including prayer and meditation groups, yoga, and studies of the Bible and the Quran.

Despite this growing interest in spiritual matters, the trends are more mixed when it comes to religion in its traditional forms. Some religious groups are growing, especially among evangelicals. Some have been holding roughly even, as with Catholics. But for quite a few years, mainline, non-evangelical Protestant churches have been losing significant ground in attendance, contributions, etc.

The eclectic, nonsectarian ethos of today's spiritual climate has some clear advantages. It has served us well, I think, in challenging and replacing the dogmatism and exclusivity we see in some religious groups. But it has disadvantages too. Disengaging from specific religious groups can deprive us of the benefits of solid relational and community structures that can help us develop positive patterns in how we live.

In the zeal that many of us have for prioritizing spiritual experience over religious doctrine, we would be wise not to overlook the evident benefits that organized religion has also provided historically. Specifically, the various disciplines fostered by many religious groups have a rich record of mobilizing their members to humane service, and to working for social repair and justice. Such collective works of service constitute a major part of an authentic spiritual life. And that is an element that is often lacking in some of the self-fulfillment orientation found in many New Age approaches.

Years ago, I heard someone ask Ram Dass at a lecture if he thought it mattered which religion people believed in. His answer: Pick a lineage (i.e., a specific religious-spiritual approach) to be based in. It may be your birth religion, or a path you are drawn to later in your life. But pick one. And stick with it as your spiritual home base.

That advice has stayed with me over the years. I'd even go so far as to say that hearing that one statement on that one night has played a significant role in my choosing to become an ordained minister in the Christian tradition, and then staying with that choice despite having more than my share of disagreement and discomfort with formal Christianity.

In the process, one thing I've learned clearly is that having a defined religious framework as your starting point does not require elevating it to a privileged status. To expand the metaphor, we might think of one's choice of tradition as representing a kind of spiritual marriage. When we fall in love, or when we feel an ongoing sense of devotion to our beloved, we might say or feel that our actual, human spouse is "the best in the world." But that doesn't mean we believe that to be true in an actual, or literal way.

I see an analogy there to how we can frame our relationship to our religion of choice (for those of us who have one). When we do choose—or recommit ourselves to—a religious or spiritual "lineage," we certainly need to feel a resonance with its essential core (as is needed for a healthy marriage or relationship). But that doesn't mean we can't also disagree with some of its specific beliefs or practices within the religious tradition we have committed ourselves to. Nor does it mean we can't supplement the offerings of our principal tradition with insights or practices from other traditions.

All those forms of flexibility are integral to marriage, as to any committed relationship. We may have deep love for our beloved, and we may experience her or him as a life-giving presence. But that doesn't mean we have to hold to a belief that they are perfect, or be blind to their human faults, or have a crisis of faith in the viability of the relationship if we are sometimes infuriated by those faults. And it also doesn't mean we can't feel love for, or learn new things from, people other than our spouse. In religion, as in marriage, there is a primary focal commitment that exists *despite* the fact that the object of that commitment is humanly imperfect. And in both cases that commitment can be honored alongside connections with, and learnings from, sources outside or beyond that focal commitment.

When it comes to religion, then, it is essential to be able to see and affirm its value *and* its faults simultaneously. But the fact that it has real faults doesn't necessarily mean we need to leave it. We can also share in the work of helping it grow and better itself.

As a personal example, within my own religious commitment there are several doctrines within Christianity that church authorities have long considered essential to it, but that I no longer believe in. I no longer think, for example, that God exists literally as three persons in a Trinity—or that God is even a person (or person-like being) at all. I no longer believe that Christ is God uniquely incarnated into a single person, or that he "died for our sins" on the cross. Nor do I believe that God judges or punishes at all.

But despite those shifts of belief (and I understand fully that for many they would be deal-breakers), there is a core to my

Christian-ness that is different from (and deeper than) those relinquished beliefs. To my mind that core of cores lies in a different set of views: that Christ was and is one of history's greatest spiritual voices and wisdom teachers; that the quality of love Jesus taught about is an expression in human form of the nature of the Divine itself; that the ancient Judeo-Christian admonition to love neighbor, self, and the Divine is a tried-and-true guide for living life; and that our core purpose in this life is to become conscious of the spiritual Presence that permeates all things, as Jesus also taught in his many parables about the "Reign of Heaven" (traditionally translated as "the Kingdom of Heaven"). But despite the earlier *versions* of Christianity that I have moved through and left behind, there is still a living core of vital spirituality that continues to resonate for me at the heart of the Christian tradition, and that I hear calling me to stay on a significantly Christ-focused path.

For someone else, the call may be to embark upon, or stay with, a different path. But whatever group or tradition we are in, the core of cores stays the same: becoming more conscious of the ways of the heart and of the Spirit, and then, by means of that, surrendering more and more to the resources and powers of the divine Presence.

AN EPIPHANY OF RADICAL
SIGNIFICANCE

ᕲ

JANUARY 2001

OR CHRISTIANS, the season of Epiphany has just begun. While everyone in our culture is fully aware of Christmas, many people have no awareness at all of Epiphany. But it wasn't always so. During much of the church's history (including quite a few centuries in which Christianity was the dominant force in Western culture), Epiphany was given substantially more emphasis than Christmas.

This word *epiphany* refers to some form of revealing or appearing. Webster's dictionary describes it as a "usually sudden perception of the nature or meaning of something." In traditional Christian thought, there is a natural progression from Christmas to Epiphany. Whereas Christmas points to a potential but yet un-actualized boon (in the form of a prophesied baby), Epiphany points to the time when that potential becomes *actualized* in a fully functional adult. At Christmas we gaze at Jesus, the newborn, with a living hope for the benefits to come. At Epiphany we celebrate those benefits as we meet the adult Christ, who has now fully grown into his role as a master and sage we can learn from, emulate, and draw life from in the context of spiritual community.

Over the years countless ways of interpreting Jesus have been put forward. I no longer believe that there is any single formulation about Christ that is "correct," or that requires assent in order for a person to be a valid Christian or a legitimate spiritual seeker. I myself have long since ceased to believe that Christ is "the Son of God," or a savior or redeemer, or that it is necessary to "accept Christ" in order to be "right with God," let alone "get to heaven."

But having said all that, I continue to believe strongly—and increasingly—that this Nazarene rabbi was a radically significant wisdom-source that the human race can deeply benefit from listening to. According to this perspective, Christ was in fact, and continues to be, a priceless window into the nature of the Divine. And he was and is an ongoing fountain of invaluable teaching and guidance from within Western culture that can help us humans live well and thrive both individually and collectively.

Accepting this affirmation of the radical significance of Jesus does not mean denying that the Buddha, for example (along with Krishna, Socrates, Rumi, etc.), was *also* radically significant. And—importantly—acknowledging that radical significance of Christ does not mean, and is not necessarily synonymous with, "becoming a Christian." Gandhi is an important example of someone who accepted the radical significance of what Jesus offered. Christ was, in fact, one of Gandhi's main spiritual lights. But this never led him to convert and "become a Christian." Nor is there any reason it should have.

Gandhi's continued religious identity as a Hindu, then, did not lessen his ability to learn from Christ. Nor did it make him less an instrument of the Nazarene's teachings about love-based, nonviolent resistance. And indeed, it would appear that Jesus had much more actual influence on this committed *non-Christian* (Gandhi) than can be seen in the lives of many self-proclaimed *Christians*. That influence did not manifest itself by Gandhi affiliating with official, institutional Christianity. But it did manifest through him studying the actual teachings of Christ, and making a choice to take them seriously. Put simply, being a student (the original meaning of the word *disciple*) of Christ is not at all synonymous with "being a Christian."

The key here is attitude, not affiliation. What is important is not how finely we frame, or fervently proclaim, any beliefs or doctrines *about* Jesus. What counts, much more, is the degree to which any of us are actively seeking to *emulate* Jesus. Such emulation means embracing his call to seek and find, to be curious and experimental, to be conscious and compassionate, to be fear-free and peaceful, to be trusting and confident, to be welcoming and inclusive. Those are the essential teachings of the Christ. And they can be embraced by anyone, Christian and non-Christian alike.

That view about what it means to be a mature and healthy adult is a significantly different perspective from what traditional Christianity presents. And seeing it that way can be, well . . . quite an epiphany.

NO TO NORTON

⚘

I N THIS WEEK's confirmation hearings in Washington, George
W. Bush's[16*] choice of John Ashcroft for attorney general has
been getting much of the attention. But on Thursday, hearings
will start for another lower-profile nomination: Gale Norton for
secretary of the interior (the department that oversees our public
lands). To my eye, her appointment deserves much more scru-
tiny—and opposition—than it's been getting.

For an environmental post as sensitive as that one, it seems odd
that this nominee's defense of property rights (as well as states'
rights) seems much more impassioned than her concern about
environmental degradation itself. She is on record saying that a
property owner has a "right to pollute" as one legitimate element
to be factored into public policy. And she has been unapologetic
about her tilt toward business development of public lands at the
expense of preserving, let alone enlarging, lands that are currently
protected.

When Norton was attorney general of Colorado, she publicly
opposed the Americans with Disabilities Act. (At one point she

---

16' That is, the forty-third president of the United States (served 2001–2009), not
to be confused with his father, George H. W. Bush, the forty-first president (served
1989–1993).

expressed her disdain for "this really ugly addition"—a wheel-chair ramp—that the state had been required to affix to its capitol building.) Since leaving that office in 1998, Gale Norton the lawyer has represented NL Industries, a lead producer that has been the subject of more than a dozen lawsuits for possible lead poisoning of children.

Another troubling fact about Gale Norton is her vocal opposition to the Endangered Species Act, which she sees as unconstitutional. Also concerning is her minimization of the threat of an increase in the cancers arising from ozone depletion, as well as mercury in fish. And then there is Ms. Norton's blithe denial of the advance of global warming. Its sobering potential for coastal flooding, drought, forest fires, and increasingly severe storms is a growing threat to our future safety and well-being. But Gail Norton's record of raising the alarm on this issue is nonexistent.[17†]

Given that the interior secretary is one of the two main officers of government (along with the EPA head) charged with *protecting* the environment, it is bizarre indeed that the person nominated to this post would be someone so *hostile* to environmental protection. This appointment, if approved, can only signal four years of hard struggle in the work of protecting our air, water, and lands.

[17†] In the summer of 1988, NASA climate scientist James Hansen drew wide attention with his statement that "global warming has reached a level such that we can ascribe with a high degree of confidence a cause-and-effect relationship between the greenhouse effect and the observed warming." He further testified that human activity, especially the burning of fossil fuels, was the main driver of what he called "global warming," of which the possible long-term results could be: increasingly severe storms, rising sea levels, droughts, disruption of agriculture, and widespread extinctions. Although Hansen's views reflected an already widespread consensus among scientists, they sparked a fierce backlash among those who deny that human-caused warming is taking place. By "warming," of course, Hansen meant rising *average* annual temperatures on a worldwide scale. But detractors deride the idea of "global warming" every time there is a cold snap or a chilly spring. Realizing the political consequences of their terminology, scientists have come to refer more frequently to "global climate change." But the phrase "global warming" has remained lodged in the public's consciousness, especially among those who deny its reality. [Editor's note.]

All of us who are concerned about tending the environment should join to oppose this foolish and shortsighted choice. One way to do that is to e-mail (or phone) our Vermont senators. Equally helpful would be to take the time to e-mail your friends to ask them to do the same. The full roster of senators' e-mail addresses can be found at www.senate.gov.

Doing those things will be time well spent indeed.

THE REAL PRESENT DANGER

⤴

JANUARY 2001

IN LAST WEEK'S ARTICLE, I advocated for rejecting Gale Norton's nomination as interior secretary. I highlighted her lack of commitment to protecting the environment (a key responsibility in that post). Today I'll focus on her views about states' rights in relation to those same Interior Department duties.

In 1996, Norton described an "epiphany" she had in a Civil War graveyard. It was triggered by a headstone with the inscription: "In Memory of Virginians Who Died Defending the Sovereignty of Their State." She said then that although slavery was wrong, nevertheless, in the defeat of the South, "we lost too much. We lost the idea that the states were to stand against the federal government having too much power over our lives."

This is flawed thinking, to put it mildly. Norton assumes that our main societal danger is too much power in *national* government. Yes, of course, if a Stalin, Hitler, or Pol Pot is in charge, centralized government power would be the big threat. But serious dangers are often located somewhere other than in the concentrated powers of a central government.

Consider the lynching era in America. The core threat then was to be found in horrific mob violence and the racist social attitudes that produced it. It is essential to remember that when lynchings were taking place, one of the main problems was precisely the *weakness* of the federal government, as shown through its inability to stop those murders. And that danger of weak federal power went hand in hand with the equally great danger of strong Southern *state* governments, most of which actively condoned such crimes.

The core danger then was definitely *not* too much federal power (or too little power for state governments). The real danger was that federal power was too weak, and thus unable to counteract the racist social attitudes that allowed the violence of the segregationist South to continue. The truth is that the overwhelmingly real function of the states' rights philosophy in the segregation/ lynching era was precisely its usefulness to let Southern whites continue to murder blacks, prevent them from voting, and keep them in the state of permanent servitude.

But here we have Gail Norton saying that the Civil War made states' rights too weak! What universe is she living in? There are two possibilities. She is either fully deluded about the real role of states' rights (to continue racial oppression), or she actively maintains a racist worldview herself. And how could any sane person think a person who is mentally deluded or actively racist should hold high office?

What today's conservatives don't see is that the real danger for society is not in national government *per se*, but in *any* power center that has become too strong and is consequently liable to being misused in ways that result in large-scale harm. In one time or place that misuse of power *might* stem from a national government. But in another time and place, the main threat might come from somewhere else entirely. It might come from within an economic system or a religion, or from militarism or an entrenched social prejudice. To say "always limit national government" because national government is always the main danger is to make a major oversimplification. It is remarkable to me that educated people can talk themselves into such nonsense.

The real, deeper need in any given era is to discern which power centers in society have too much sway in *that* era and context. In the days of lynching and segregation, the main threat came from too *much* power residing in the very states' rights that Gail Norton thinks were too weak after the Civil War. This should be self-evident from the fact that those supposed "rights" were being used to actively promote the widespread murder of blacks by whites. Norton, therefore, has it exactly wrong. The aftermath of the Civil War left the power of the national government too *weak*, not too *great*.

And if that was true then it is certainly still true now. One important instance of this is, precisely, in our environmental crisis, which is an issue Gail Norton would have to address as interior secretary. The danger facing us from the degradation of our atmosphere, soil, and waters is far greater than any possible threat from federal bureaucracy. The danger of global warming, especially, is a far greater worry than any potential power grab that might take place by the Interior Department or the Environmental Protection Agency.

Since our most serious environmental woes are being fed by the discharge of greenhouse gasses by large corporate entities, today's most threatening "centralized power" is not at all our federal government, but the *corporations* that are generating and emitting those gases. I would argue that the broader corporate system creating and allowing such pollution is the real main power center that exists in our society. It is the power of that *system* that most pressingly needs to be curbed. And that can only be done through strong regulatory power in Washington (and in other governments globally).

The real "present danger" today, in other words, is not government doing too *much*, but doing far too *little* to rein in those corporate power-centers, which pose a far greater threat than can be found anywhere in our central government.

Today's conservative call for states' rights is a regressive, backward-looking view. A more forward-facing approach lies in opening our thinking toward a larger global consciousness, not a smaller, more parochial worldview. Doing so is analogous to the mind-shift that citizens of the thirteen colonies once underwent when they looked beyond self-identification with their individual "states" and grew into a larger, more inclusive identification with the new American nation.

Our task now is similar. But instead of transferring our self-identification from a state to the nation, as the colonists did, our present need is to transfer our self-identification from the American-based corporate system to fulfilling our role in the global human community. Our emerging sense of identity—and responsibility—must focus on the needs and interests of the entire human race more than any particular nation or economic system.

SACRAMENTAL CHOCOLATE

⊸

MARCH 2001

THE AWARDS SHOW on Sunday was a lot of fun. Steve Martin's hosting was hilarious. And I loved hearing Bob Dylan sing his entry for best new song, "Things Have Changed," which appears in the film *Wonder Boys*. When he won, it was great to see his happy smile, a different look from the studied aloofness we've so often seen from him.

As for the movies themselves, I saw all five Best Picture nominees. To me, it is hard to see how people could consider *Crouching Tiger, Hidden Dragon* one of the top five. *Gladiator*, which won, wouldn't have been my choice either, though I thought it was quite good. *Traffic* and *Erin Brockovich* are also outstanding. *Brockovich* makes a powerful statement about the evil that is so often perpetrated by corporate power that is underregulated by the federal government. And *Traffic* sears into the brain the futility of trying to physically dam up the flow of drugs across borders. It implies (I think rightly) that the only real way forward is to help people heal their addictions.

If it were up to me, though, I would have given Best Picture to *Chocolat*. It's about a nomadic single mother called Vianne (played by Juliette Binoche), who not only makes delectable

203

chocolate, but infuses her confections with medicinal herbs, and then prescribes just the right batch for each person based on her reading of their needs and condition.

The constant counterpoint to her work comes from the local Catholic church. Many of its folk, especially the ever-righteous mayor, oppose her harshly. Beyond her nonattendance at church, she commits the sin of offering candy during Lent. The subtext of the movie lies in the contrast between her power to heal through lovingly made chocolates and the inability of the church to do the same through its less-than-lovingly delivered sacraments.

A central offering of the church, especially in Catholicism, lies in just those sacraments, intended to be visible signs of heaven's grace. The first among them is communion, its bread and wine being potential medicine for both soul and flesh. But in this movie, the sacramental food that has real healing force is the chocolate. And why does that chocolate work? There is, of course, the ancient plant-knowledge that Vianne has garnered. But the greater factor is that all the treats are made with loving affection.

There is an important sense in which all physical life can be, and is, sacramental, if we let it be so. Whether the shrines we enter elevate bread and wine or medicinal chocolates (or peyote, or something else entirely) on their central altars is relatively unimportant.

What is more important—and what is real, recurring good news—is that nearly anything, when offered from the heart, can carry sacramental force; and as such, nearly anything can be, at least potentially, an effectual tool for bringing the healing grace of heaven into the needs of flesh and form.

COMPASSIONLESS CONSERVATISM

~❧~

APRIL 2001

P RESIDENT BUSH's recent speech at the Gridiron Club in Washington included quite a bit of self-deprecating humor. He was playing the tired old political game of disarming critics by making the same kind of jokes about himself that others make about him.

The psychology of this approach says, in effect, "Since I can laugh at myself and my own foibles, they probably aren't all that serious, right?" If a president gets irritated or defensive about criticism, the public is likely to think the critics are on to something. But his own chuckling about those same qualities is a way to manipulate people to think, "He sounds like a guy comfortable in his own skin, so maybe the problem isn't in *him*. Maybe those critiques are mostly politically motivated, or if they *are* real foibles, they're probably not big a deal."

In this vein, Mr. Bush mused about how great it would be to clone a second Dick Cheney, because then he "wouldn't have to do any work at all." He laughed about his recent statement that "more and more of our imports come from overseas." And from the leader of the free world, another self-quotation: "When I was coming up, it was a dangerous world, and we knew exactly who the 'they' were. It was 'us' vs. 'them.'. . . . Today, we're not so sure who the 'they' are, but we know they're there." The audience ate it up. The idea was to get people thinking, "Yes, he may seem confrontational at times, but thank God he can laugh about it. That probably shows he understands what's at stake, and if he can joke about having a simplistic view, he probably *isn't* actually simplistic, right?"

In the most telling joke Bush told on himself, he said, "As you know, we're studying safe levels for arsenic in drinking water [laughter]. To base our decision on sound science, the scientists told us we needed to test the water glasses of about 3,000 people [laughter]. Thank you for participating [more laughter]." Only days earlier, of course, the new Bush EPA had reversed a Clinton order tightening standards for arsenic levels in the country's drinking water.

Behind the president's jokes, though, the real message is, well, laced with arsenic. The psychology, again, is: "If I (the president) can laugh about potentially high arsenic in drinking water, and most importantly, if I can get *you* to laugh about that, then the arsenic in question is probably not that bad a problem."

That may be good psychology for manipulating people politically, but where does truth fit into this picture? The truth is that toxins and poisons in our drinking water *are* a serious problem, and they are *not* a problem that can be made to go away through comedy—or denial. A president who tries to deal with serious matters this way is not a real leader, but a follower. In this case, he is a mere bag-carrier for the self-interest of businesses and wealthy contributors who value corporate profits more than the health of the people.

The deeper tragedy is that this foolish action on arsenic is not simply one unfortunate slip. It as part of a clear trend favoring profit over protection. In its still-young life, this Bush Administration has canceled recent government rules to prevent repetitive-stress injuries; given initial approval to an industry-backed measure to allow higher levels of salmonella in public-school lunches (later withdrawn because of public furor); declared that carbon dioxide (CO_2—a major cause of global warming) is not a pollutant; withdrawn from the Kyoto climate agreement; proposed weakened enforcement of the Endangered Species Act; and reversed candidate Bush's pledge to budget $100 million to support the exchange of debt-relief for the protection of tropical rain forests.

George Bush says he's a compassionate conservative. His first weeks in the White House have been plenty conservative. But the compassion—and wisdom—is nowhere in sight.

A GOD WITH SOME SKIN

⌁

MAY 2001

MOTHER'S DAY this year is especially poignant for me. In April, I took my sixteen-year-old daughter to see my ninety-year-old mother in Illinois. At one point, the three of us were looking at a photo from my niece's wedding three years prior. My mom stands alert and beaming there with her just-wed grandchild. Since then, though, the "silent artillery of time," in Lincoln's telling phrase, has taken its toll. The other night on the phone she spoke of her now clearly shortened time. "You should be preparing yourself," she said. And I am.

Mother's Day is a good time to remind ourselves how mother-love can be a conduit to life's best blessings. To borrow from the Catholic catechism, the mother–child connection is sacramental: an "outward and visible sign" of the Life-Force itself. The energies of that Power, of course, come to us in myriad ways. But with all due respect to the "Mother Church," for most of us it is our physical, tangible mothers who are our first and primary mediators to the Divine.

In Christianity, and Western religion generally, we often speak of God as Father (or with other male imagery). But even amid the mainly male metaphors of the Bible, the feminine, nurturing side of divine love manages to nudge its way onto the stage with persistent regularity.

In the Hebrew Scriptures, for example, we hear the heavenly Voice say, "As a mother comforts her child, so will I comfort you" (Isaiah 66:13). And in Proverbs, as well as the Song of Songs, one of the main names for God is "Wisdom," which is referred to with female pronouns.

Likewise, in the New Testament, Jesus says, "O Jerusalem, Jerusalem, how often have I wished to gather your young as a hen gathers chicks under her wings" (Luke 13:34). Here again, divine shelter and protection is presented in female, maternal terms.

It is important to remind ourselves that these images—"mother" or "father," "hen" or "chicks"—are all metaphors, and as such are neither literal nor definitive ways to depict God. But when we do use metaphorical language (as we must if we want to use any words at all to describe the Divine), more and more of us are moving beyond using exclusively masculine metaphors to refer to God. To the degree that we use personalistic and/or gendered metaphors at all, we would do well to think more in terms such as "Mother-Father" God. This can remind us that the divine Love is here for us in a broader range of guises than given by male-only imagery. In light of that, Mother's Day is a good chance to expand our menu of images for depicting the Divine.

There is a lovely parable that's been told about the power of the mother–child bond. It's about an eight-year-old girl, Marie, who had a great fear of the dark and, especially, thunderstorms. Whenever Marie became anxious her lower lip would quiver. And when her mother saw that, she would hug her and say, "Marie, Marie, there's nothing to fear. You are safe right here because God loves you, and so do I."

One night, Marie was awakened by a violent thunderstorm. In a panic, she looked for her usually reliable nightlight. But this time, it wasn't on. In the raging turbulence of that moment, confronted by her two worst fears, darkness and thunderstorms, she was terrified. She cried out for her mother, who quickly rushed into the blacked-out room and found Marie curled in a ball under the bed. She coaxed her out, wrapped her in a hug, and said, "Marie, Marie, you are safe. God loves you and so do I."

Normally, that was enough to calm her down. But not quite this time. Little Marie snuggled closer and said, "Mommy, I know that God is stronger than this storm, but please, don't leave me alone. Right now, I need a God with some skin."

To all our mothers who have been, sacramentally, just that, we give our heartfelt thanks.

BLAME AS ANESTHESIA

WHILE WRITING a Memorial Day sermon last week, my thoughts turned to the news stories about former Nebraska Senator Bob Kerrey's tour of duty in Vietnam. One night in 1969, his squad killed about twenty unarmed Vietnamese civilians. Kerrey claims the shootings were accidental and at a distance. A fellow soldier (Gerhard Klann) says Kerrey ordered it intentionally and at close range. As with similar Vietnam tales over the years, most of the media have buzzed around the potential culpability of Bob Kerrey as an *individual.*

Are lethal actions by Bob Kerrey from a 1969 war zone newsworthy now? To some extent, of course, they are, especially since this former senator is a once and could-be candidate for president. Individuals *are* responsible for their acts in war, especially if their actions fall egregiously outside the rules. (Whether this is so for Senator Kerrey, I can't know.)

What is most important in our ongoing talk about Vietnam, though, lies not so much in what specific individuals may have done (though that does have its own importance). What is much more relevant, in my mind, is coming to terms with the institutional and collective factors by which the country as a whole entered and waged that war.

What were the rules and practices under which Kerrey, Klann, and millions of other soldiers waged war in Vietnam? What collective assumptions lay behind America being there at all? What forms of killing were deemed acceptable in the context of that military culture? Were there rules of engagement that were not approved on paper, but *were* approved, man to man, for "doing what it takes" in order to "get the job done"? And what were the attitudes in the American public at large that allowed our military to concoct massive "body-counts" and report them with blithe banality as if they were just routine news?

I would argue that answering such collective questions is much more important than detailing whatever Bob Kerrey or Gerhard Klann did or did not do on the night of February 25, 1969. We mustn't minimize the heart-wrench of the ensuing deaths. Nor can we overlook individual responsibility. But the devastation of the war in its entirety—including more than two million dead—dwarfs any specific act that occurred in any single engagement.

The knee-jerk blaming that follows incidents such as we're discussing here is often a tool of denial about those larger institutional dynamics. Overfocusing on individual actions (that, yes, might be blameworthy in and of themselves) can be an anesthesia for the pain of confronting the *national* actions that allowed such a war-tragedy to unfold in the first place (and that *might* allow for another such war in the future).

Broadening our vision to include those collective cultural patterns—and our own role in them—is much harder than focusing narrowly on possible individual misbehaviors. It takes time and study to learn what took place, and what produced the war. It requires acknowledging dysfunctions for which we ourselves share some responsibility—if and as we assent to the prevailing culture, as most of us do to some degree. Scapegoating the questionable deeds of one or a few people is a way we often try to let ourselves off the hook by conveniently categorizing our own current versions of "them" as culpable outliers.

Vietnam has been called, in Joseph Conrad's phrase, a "heart of darkness." The darkness there had no single source. But its horror is to be found much more in what America did *as a nation* than in what a handful of Bob Kerreys may (or may not) have done as individuals.

America is a land of numbing denial. Just as we have relentlessly refused to exorcise the ghosts of slavery and racism, so we have come nowhere close to exorcising the ghosts of the violence and death we inflicted on Vietnam.

But there is hope for moving on. It lies in focusing far less on the Bob Kerreys of this world, and greatly more on dealing with the long-term collective patterns in our national psyche that said "yes" to that "crazy Asian war" (as a song of the sixties called it).

If we don't move beyond our customary denial of those underlying national tendencies, we will most likely set ourselves up for similar—and similarly disastrous—American wars in the future.

THE WOUNDS OF THE FATHERS

↤

JUNE 2001

MY DAUGHTER sent me a fun Father's Day card last weekend. The envelope had a big pink crayon-drawn heart on the back. On the front it said, "Dad, you've always been my hero. Could I have your autograph?" Inside? A check for big bucks awaiting my signature! (But what dad doesn't love spending money on his princess?)

Some other things from last weekend, though, didn't tickle my fancy quite so much. On Father's Day itself, I heard an ad for the sitcom *Sex and the City*, which contained a string of put-downs of men (*incompetent, sloppy, boorish*). That same day, *USA Today* had an interview with Patricia Heaton from *Everybody Loves Raymond*. When asked why TV moms are "so often collected, while husbands are bumblers," she said: "Because it's true?" Such denigration of males is common these days.

Here is another example. A friend of mine attends an urban church with a well-educated and mostly liberal membership. On Mother's Day last month, one part of the Sunday service there was set aside to honor mothers. But on Father's Day (which was on the summer solstice), no honoring of fathers was mentioned in the service. There *was*, however, a liturgy for "the Goddess of the Summer Solstice." Think about it. On Mother's Day they honored the female principle. And on Father's Day? They again honored the female principle (but did not include any corresponding honoring of men or male-ness).

Why that imbalance? The psychological subtext in such cases, I think, is an attitude that says, roughly, "Since patriarchy has ruled for so long, and has done such damage, we can now redress the imbalance by giving more attention to femininity and females, and less to masculinity and males." Although the premise there about patriarchal damage is accurate, the attempted remedy for that damage is flawed, for several reasons.

First, it assumes that past suppression of females by the patriarchy has been overwhelmingly advantageous to males. There are, to be sure, some important aspects of our society's life where that is all too true. Men are far less likely to be physically or sexually abused by the opposite sex. We make more money on average, and we get more pay for equivalent work. And we certainly have more institutional power, most especially in business and government (and religion). These are major injustices that need to be brought to conscious awareness and corrected.

But there are other ways—often less obvious—by which the patriarchal system has proven just as disadvantageous to males as to females. Alongside the horrific violence done to women and girls across the centuries (which is still happening), there has been the correspondingly massive violence done to young men through military conscription, and the resulting maiming and slaughter of millions of young male soldiers in our near-endless wars. (Have you visited a VA hospital recently? The patients lying wounded and crippled in those beds are mostly men.) I would argue that the very fact that our culture routinely forces and trains males to be warriors—and in the process programs them to be oppressors—is, in itself, a major form of oppression that is inflicted heavily against males.

Consider also that most prison inmates are male, and virtually all executions are inflicted on men. And indeed (a surprise to most people), a majority of rapes in this country are committed against males. Yes, a *majority!* But since most of those rapes take place in jails, and are violations against convicted criminals, they are rarely reported in our media, aren't generally included in national rape statistics, and spark little public outrage or empathy.

In addition to all this is the fact that alongside all the major crippling of women's access to social power, there is in our culture a corresponding crippling of men's capacity for emotional depth and healthy expression of feeling. (And indeed, many men often have trouble identifying what they *are* feeling at all.)

Males in our culture have been overwhelmingly encultur-ated for thousands of years into playing out psychological roles in which they must substantially suppress forms of emotional expression, especially crying. Males are routinely programmed to stay "in control," to project consistent confidence, and to main-tain the proverbial stiff upper lip. We males are taught to be tough (definitely not "soft"). And we have been programmed for millen-nia to develop *cognitive* intelligence to an exaggerated degree—but at the great cost of stunting growth in *emotional* intelligence.

We need to see such patterns of cultural conditioning for the forms of major oppression—and victimization—that they are. And we need to find ways to change and heal that patterning in boys and men. I would argue that liberating our males from those cultural stereotypes is as greatly needed as ending the parallel oppressions suffered by females. It should be obvious—if we let ourselves see it—that the emotional crippling prevalent in the raising of our boys is, in itself, a major cause of the ongoing cycles of oppressive behaviors that so many men continue to commit against girls and women.

Any male that victimizes a female is, by definition, precisely that: emotionally crippled. Victimizing behaviors are always unacceptable in themselves. But that shouldn't—mustn't—stop us from asking how and why so much of our male population has become so emotionally crippled as to become such frequent vic-timizers. In twelve-step programs there is a saying that "the hurt hurt." Those who have been hurt, in other words, are those most likely to inflict hurt. When it comes to winding down our gender wars, our society would do well to utilize that insight toward the goal of raising our boys, and educating their psyches, in curriculums of emotional intelligence.

In light of this, we need to steer clear of embracing our now-common assumption that yesterday's delegitimization of females is best countered by delegitimizing today's males. Activating new cycles of negativity is hardly the best way to lessen the negativity that already bedevils us. The needed healing of the male psyche may be harder to see than the healing needed by women, but it is no less real.

The only sustained way that gender healing can happen in the years ahead is through building up *both* genders, not through the dead-end practice of enhancing one by denigrating the other.

BEYOND ECO-DENIAL

〜〰〜

JULY 2001

IN THE GOSPELS, Jesus is often quoted as saying, "Those who have ears to hear, let them hear." But today, if there is one thing many of us clearly don't want to hear about, it is the severity of the environmental crisis.

This spring, a group of us from several local faith communities has been meeting to address this issue. In our initial gathering, we focused on how we might engage in "right action" through adjusting our local and personal behaviors: making our houses of worship more environmentally efficient; buying more socially responsible products; supporting the companies that make them; and engaging in political advocacy.

Our group also has talked about the "right consciousness" that goes hand in hand with effective action. Important as practical action-steps are, dealing with our environmental woes calls for more awareness of our own inner attitudes that may contribute to environmental problems. Pollution is not caused solely by a small cadre of high-placed people doing bad things. It is produced, rather, by a systemic lifestyle we *all* take part in through the ways we drive and eat, purchase and consume.

Right consciousness, then, starts with noticing how we participate in our society's consumption systems. But it also includes the psycho-spiritual work of learning *why* our consumption—and consequent waste production—is so excessive.

Much of this can be traced back to the prevalence of fear. Most of us give enormous attention to stuffing down our anxieties, especially our fear of lack, our feelings of disconnection and incompleteness, weakness, and unworthiness. And underlying all that we chronically push our dread of death to the side, safely off the screen of direct awareness. One of the main ways we do so is by filling our lives with constant distractions, material acquisition, and massive consumer usage and waste. Our minds then seek to justify the materialism of this lifestyle by labeling—or should I say mis-labeling it—as some form of "prosperity," or "abundance," or by thinking of it as "living the American Dream."

This is where the spiritual work of right consciousness comes in. It gives us tools for learning to see through, and grow beyond, being captive to the fear, distraction, and denial our culture snares us in. An important starting point is learning to recognize where and how our denial patterns appear and operate.

One place our cultural denial is most visible is in the way our corporations, government and media collude to minimize environmental threats. Consider the recent *New York Times* headline "Nuclear Sites May Be Toxic in Perpetuity." The article cited a study by the US Department of Energy concluding that most of the government sites where nuclear bombs were built will be lethally radioactive for . . . *several hundred thousand years!* The DOE recommends that these now be designated as "national sacrifice sites."

Some of the solutions presented by the DOE are as impractical as they are grim. Here's an example. In the early nineties, the government sold land to be developed as a golf course near the Oak Ridge nuclear facility in Tennessee. The sale came with the stipulation that the ground water (highly toxic with nuclear waste) not be used for drinking. Within a few years, though, a well had indeed been drilled on the course, to irrigate the grass. The justification for the project seems to have been: people won't be *drinking* the radiation; they'll "only" be breathing its vapors and touching it on their fingers when they pick up golf balls, etc.

The *Times* report also described how a "No Fishing" sign had been posted at a creek near this golf course because of the radioactivity in the stream. But high school kids soon stole the signs, and then, of course, fishing *did* take place there. The DOE document goes on to outline how among the country's 144 contaminated nuclear sites, 109 would probably "not be cleaned up for unrestricted use because of insufficient money, technical skill, or political will."

I cite this article partly because the information itself is important to know, but even more so because when the *Times* ran this story, the editors placed it *on page 12!* Can you imagine? Whole pockets of our country have been declared uninhabitable, and this by the government itself. But on the day this news appears in our country's premier newspaper, the story is buried. It appears nowhere close to the front page. Such minimizing of the severity and urgency of ecological damage is one key way our cultural denial-system works.

In the weeks ahead, you might want to do your own personal media-scan of how environmental stories are reported, and of how such coverage corresponds to the actual severity of the damage being described. When we open our "ears to hear" in that way, going back to Jesus's phrase, we soon find that major ecological issues are routinely reported in secondary and relatively less-noticed locations in our newspapers, magazines, and newscasts. This also happens in our personal conversations, and in the messages we send to our politicians about what we consider important (or unimportant) for them to consider.

The attitudinal mindset that is operative here works something like this: if the story appears on page 12, it probably isn't *that* serious—right? And if we adopt that kind of denial through minimization, we create short-term comfort for ourselves. But when it comes to the environment, such supposedly comforting assumptions are often deeply untrue, and the comfort derived is temporary indeed.

We, the public, need to let our news outlets (and government officials) know that we do in fact notice, and disapprove, their treatment of such major issues with scant coverage or other forms of minimizing. We need to take the needs of the environment off page 12 and put them where they belong: on page 1.

Changes of that kind need to happen not just in our newspapers, but more importantly in our own minds, and in the priorities of our political agendas and of how we advocate for them.

SPORTS, SPIRIT, AND PRACTICE

❧

AUGUST 2001

TWO AMERICAN SPORTS held Hall of Fame enshrinements this week. On Saturday, the National Football League welcomed seven greats to its Hall of Fame in Canton, Ohio. These included Lynn Swann, the Pittsburgh Steelers receiver, who caught footballs like a fly-trap and ran with them like a gazelle. Also inducted was Marv Levy, who quit a promising Harvard academic track against parental advice to do what he loved most: coaching football and eventually leading the Buffalo Bills to four consecutive Super Bowl appearances.

On Sunday, it was baseball's turn in Cooperstown, New York. The most memorable moment came when former Pittsburgh Pirates second baseman Bill Mazeroski was so moved by his induction that he started sobbing only seconds into his speech. It was touching to see someone who had been a "real man" tough guy on the field be such a real *person* on that stage.

Turning from sports to my own line of work, I talked recently with a young woman who is contemplating ordination to the ministry and has started working with a spiritual director. In our conversation, she referred several times to her "spiritual practice." Her use of the word "practice" has been lingering in my mind since then. Despite the surface differences between spirituality and sports, they both have an important element in common: the necessity of practice.

Becoming good at *anything* requires practice. The inductees into those halls of fame last weekend did not get there by talent alone. They also had to do years' worth of serious and sustained work to transform their natural talent from carbon to diamond.

Consider the career of Ronnie Lott, the star defensive back with the San Francisco 49ers. When Lott was enshrined in Canton a few years back, one speaker described an incident from Lott's final year of playing. His best days behind him, he was struggling to make use of his remaining skills. After practice one day, three of his teammates were putting in time on exercise bikes. As they looked out over the field, there was Ronnie Lott doing a seemingly endless set of tackling drills even after every other player had gone back inside. It so happened that Lott was already one of the best tacklers in his sport. As his teammates did their time on the bikes in the warmth of the clubhouse, one of them, a veteran, overheard two rookies commenting on Lott's extra practice.

One rookie said to the other, "Look at that Lott. He's a top guy who's been in Pro Bowls. He's a lock for the Hall of Fame. Why does he have to stay out there in the cold doing all those extra drills?" At which point the veteran said, "Don't you guys understand? What you're seeing out there shows why he *will* be in the Hall of Fame. It's because he keeps on going out there doing extra." Beyond his natural talent (of which he had plenty), Ronnie Lott became the great player he was precisely because he never stopped practicing.

Our religious-spiritual communities could learn a lot from high achievers like that. To have a spiritual life that is consistent and growing means knowing what it means to make spirituality a *practice*. Committing to a spiritual practice involves many of the same things as practicing in sports—or art and music, engineering and business.

Just as each of those fields requires ongoing work and learning, so also the spiritual life requires the discipline and hard work of *spiritual* practice. It calls for repetition and regularity. And it demands of us the willingness and mental toughness to engage in such practicing past the point of discomfort. In the context of spirituality, it involves doing our meditating and praying, our studying and serving, on a sustained and daily basis.

Ministers like me have been known to ask, "How is the state of your soul?" But here's another question we might ask more often: How's your spiritual practice these days?

WITH WHAT YOU HAVE LEFT

✎

UP HERE IN VERMONT, summers are short. Even now, in this late August warmth, hints of early fall abound: fading leaves, cooler nights, the need for extra blankets. But summer it still is, and I want to stay present to all of it that's left.

If staying present applies to this shift of seasons, how much more does it speak to our larger transitions from life's summer to its autumn, from youth to becoming a senior. As we age, it takes spiritual and psychological skill to make full use of our remaining time and energy. We need to avoid getting pulled down by regret about what we had but have lost, or about what we still can do that may be getting *harder* to do.

Saturday will be my mother's ninety-first birthday. When she and I talk on the phone these days, I can sense her mounting losses both in mind and body. And then there are all the earlier losses: her parents; her first-born child; her husband; both her siblings. All those disappearances cut hard. Sometimes she speaks of them with equanimity, but mostly with sadness.

As I contemplate calling my mom on Saturday, I can feel my own welling regret about what was lost in my relationship with her. When I was younger, that sense of loss was focused on what I wished she had been for me, but wasn't. Recently, I've become more aware of the steps I myself could have taken to help bridge the gap between us, but didn't. The pain of that regret is magnified by the fact that I know how much she would have welcomed my doing so. But there were times when neither she nor I chose—or knew how—to get closer.

What, then, do I do with these feelings in present time? Emotional honesty is one key. Healing happens best when I let myself acknowledge my pain and regret for those past events, and when I have the courage to feel those emotions.

Alongside that is the value of focusing on the choices I can make now. How can I be the best possible son *today*? How can my mother and I share the most loving moments possible right now, with what is left of her mind, in what is left of our time?

There is a lovely, brief story I came across recently of a great violinist who had one of his violin strings break mid-concert while playing a major concerto. The audience all assumed he would stop to fetch a fresh instrument. But after only a brief pause, he nodded to the conductor to continue. He then proceeded to play the remainder of the piece with remarkable passion and power. The storyteller depicts how people could see him modulating, changing, re-conceptualizing the piece in his head, getting new sounds from the strings in ways he'd never done before.

When he finished, there was first silence, then thunderous applause. The musician smiled, wiped off his sweat, and raised up his bow to quiet the audience. And in a pensive, unboastful tone, he said, "You know, sometimes it is the artist's task to find out how much music you still can make with whatever it is you still have left."

Since I've never played the violin, I have no way of knowing if such a thing could happen in real life. But those words at the end of the story are wise ones indeed. For me, for my mom, for all of us, the same question awaits our response and answer: What will we do with the rest of our lives? What will we do with whatever we have left?

The main artwork, after all, is—always and for all of us—our own ongoing creation of the arc of our own lives.

WITHOUT YOUR CONSENT

⤻

L AST TUESDAY, I drove my seventeen-year-old daughter, Emma, to start her junior year at boarding school (St. Paul's, in Concord, New Hampshire). Although she'll always be my *child*, she seems suddenly, astonishingly, much more young woman than child.

Something intriguing happened when I helped her move into the dorm. Emma's mom had bought her a poster to help decorate the new room. It's a photo of Eleanor Roosevelt, showing her trenchant comment: "No one can make you feel inferior without your consent." When I handed this to Emma, she lit up. Not only did she like it for her wall, but she told me that the quote itself was a favorite of hers. She even said she had been thinking about telling us that if we saw anything with that quote on it, she'd like us to get it for her. But she had never in fact said that to either of us, as her mom later confirmed.

That was an interesting coincidence (getting me wondering about possible telepathy between mother and daughter). And I was quite pleased to hear my offspring express appreciation for such wise words, and the remarkable woman who said them.

That interaction about the poster also triggered a memory in me from Emma's infancy that I remembered writing about in my journal (a practice I have maintained since college). One night, in 1985, after singing baby Emma to sleep, I had a little epiphany. I suddenly saw that this cooing, crying, consuming, diaper-filling, barely differentiated lump of life would one day be a distinct person, a unique individual, an adult woman. I soon set upon some mental meanderings about what kind of person she might become, and what kind of people she might come to admire.

After driving home from Emma's school last Tuesday, and with this memory in mind, I started searching out my old journals. What I found (in my entry for February 9, 1985) included these words: "Who will she become? Will she have positive exemplars that aid her development? What images of woman-ness will she be drawn to as she grows up? And what kind of role models would I *like* her to admire? Susan B. Anthony, Emily Dickinson, Eleanor Roosevelt, Mother Teresa, and Joan Baez are some names that first come to mind.

"But those are *my* names. Who will be *her* heroes? Will they be names known to me or unknown? Will they be people I value more or less? I want to expose her to the best, but I also want to avoid imposing my own values on her too much. Her mother and I can show her a hundred female—and male—exemplars, but she will have to find her own kindred spirits, whether from our lists or from her own. I'll want to lead her, but she'll mainly, eventually have to lead herself. It's just a baby I see in that crib tonight, but someday soon she'll walk and talk. She'll make choices. She'll stand for things. I want life for you, Emma, full rich life. What will you become?"

That question from 1985 is now starting to be answered here in 2001. After that coincidence with the poster in her new dorm room this week, I asked Emma to do a quick free association of some people, women especially, whom she admires. Beyond Eleanor Roosevelt she mentioned Rosa Parks, Joan of Arc, and Princess Diana. Mrs. Roosevelt was the only name on both her list *and* mine. But that's not a bad name to *be* on both lists, is it?

The lists themselves are far from finished—mine as much as hers. But as for who she will become, and what she will evolve into, I'm smiling at what I see so far. I'm delighted that she resonates with those words on the poster. I glad she "gets it" that no one can make her feel—or believe, or choose, or become—anything at all without a unique, personal "yes" from the inner wellspring that waters her own being.

BEYOND THE FREEZE-FRAME

❧

I'M REMEMBERING TODAY a time a few months back when I was driving my daughter back from a softball practice. At one point, the assassination of President Kennedy happened to come up in our conversation. As we talked, I mentioned how shaken I had felt as a sixteen-year-old when the events of that day came down. She said, "Nothing big like that has happened in my lifetime." But this week, for her at seventeen, it suddenly has.

Like so many of us I'm now shaken again, this time by the terrorist attacks this past Tuesday (September 11) on the World Trade Center towers and the Pentagon. After a body blow like this, we wonder how or why such terrible things can happen. And we are reminded of the limited capacity of the rational mind to explain pain and evil in ways that feel satisfactory. And often, understandably enough, we feel there are no answers. But there are at least some clues, I think, that can point us in a helpful direction in the face of such great suffering and loss.

Some of those clues can be seen in the realm of nature. I heard one example of that this week, at a clergy group I attended, when a woman described to me her personal pain of last Tuesday. Her husband's elderly mother had had a bad fall during the night before the attacks. And since he had traveled to help his mom, and since he was still gone throughout the day till after midnight after the attacks, his wife was left to watch the grim news on TV alone during the day.

The rawness of those newscasts was magnified when she heard a cow on an adjoining farm start lowing loudly during the evening. The cow's moans continued into the night, depriving the woman (and soon her husband) of much-needed sleep. But after a while, the husband blurted out, "I think that cow is giving birth; it sounds like a hard one." Sure enough, when they walked over to their neighbor's farm after dawn, they saw the now-quiet cow tending her newborn calf. Even as the darkness had produced morning, so had that cow, though moaning in pain, birthed a new dawn of life.

As most of us now wrestle with how to handle our distress from this horrible event, one place we can look is in the realm of nature, where we find a persistent pattern: out of the seeming finality of pain, and even death, comes a constant re-emergence of new life. We see this in biological birth, as in the arrival of the calf in my friend's story. We see it in the fading glory of flowers, which, even while dying, discharge an abundance of life-giving spores and seeds. And what oak doesn't start as a mere broken acorn?

When it comes to pain and loss, in whatever forms they come, it is important to notice our tendency, when those feelings are most intense, to freeze-frame our focus mainly on the pain of the losses themselves. That tendency is understandable enough. But if we get stuck in that focus for too long, we lose access to a larger perspective through which we can grasp that the pain of birth, the fading of flowers, the death of the acorn are all necessary prequels to a new life-stage coming in.

Holding in mind those larger processes of biology can help provide an analogous glimmer of meaning that is embedded in, and can still be found and felt in, *all* life's losses, including those that are major and those that seem senseless—and even those that result from evil actions. When loss comes, in other words, regardless of the circumstances, we need to avoid the mistake of freeze-framing only on the losses themselves. Difficult as that may be, we need to do our best to allow at least some space in our psyches for an awareness of a larger frame, the one that can also provide a glimpse of the renewed life that follows the various deaths we see in the realm of organic and finite things.

Claiming this kind of perspective does not mean denying the utter devastation of so great a tragedy as happened on Tuesday. And it certainly must not lead to any form of denying the evil nature of murderous acts, or of trying to shut down the feelings of despair that arise in us when terrible things happen. For me, it took a couple of days after those attacks to really "get" how much fear and rage I was feeling from the horror and wickedness of the violence.

I do not mean to suggest that what happened on September 11 can or should be seen in *exactly* the same light as a merely natural event, like the pain of birthing or any other analogy from nature. Nowhere close. I am well aware that the *motivations* behind a terrorist attack and the *processes* of the organic world are in completely different moral categories.

I am fully cognizant, in other words, that these analogies from nature are only partial. But even though they do *not* apply to the moral level pertaining to the perpetrators' intentions, they can apply to the level of our *experience* after the fact of bad things happening. When loss, and the pain of it, come into our lives, the way forward necessarily includes having the courage to live through (and fully feel) the anguish, regardless of what caused that pain, and regardless of what may have motivated the perpetrators if an act of evil was involved.

Even as we live through that anguish, however, we can also claim the spiritual wisdom that comes from learning to see—and keep seeing—a broader range of possibilities that continue to be available as we move forward, ones that we might not be aware of while our initial, emotional reactions are most intense. This brings us into the zone of what religion often calls "having faith," or "sustaining hope," even when things get hard and look dark.

I think of Leonard Cohen's great song "Anthem," which has the lines, "Ring the bells that still can ring / Forget your perfect offering / There is a crack in everything / That's how the light gets in." Those wise words can help remind us that whenever suffering comes, we have the priceless resource of holding firm to the possibility of embracing—and sustaining—a larger, spiritually informed view of what is most real in things. Doing so can help shine some light on the overarching processes of emergence, opportunity, and new life, which, though invisible, are nonetheless still present even when things are breaking apart—and even if that breaking apart seems devastating, total, and permanent.

THE POST-9/11 WORLD

‹⊖›

AS ANOTHER FULL WEEK has gone by since the attacks of September 11, I'm aware of how, when an evil act takes place, it seems to be in our wiring—after first recoiling in horror—to want or need to strike back. To our everyday psyche, this is a way—and many will experience it as *the* way—to numb the pain and fear from such an assault. It's a mechanism by which we try to manage our outrage and sense of powerlessness. I have felt all those things in recent days. And such feelings are more than likely to cycle back within me.

At some point, though, all of us will have to move past being dominated by raw emotion, and face some important questions about how to evaluate what has happened. Those questions are, most especially: Why are there people so deeply enraged at America? And what has led to the series of conflicts with the Arab-Muslim world, which America keeps getting entangled in? Important as these questions are, they are ones that most Americans aren't much asking in these early days after the attack. And, indeed, many among us don't want to even *hear* them asked.

And then there are the parallel questions about how to respond. National leaders, of course, will *always* promise retaliation for attacks, whether "terrorist" or otherwise, and President Bush is no exception. But here again, there are difficult questions: Will retaliation "work" in real life? Will it actually reduce further danger? Do we even care if our retaliations are effective, or will we simply choose to lash out and be content with making ourselves *feel* better as a result?

You and I know—with at least some part of our rational minds—that retaliatory strikes haven't ended terrorism in the past, and that they're not likely to do so now. And since we can see in advance (if we're willing) that escalations of violence don't end violence, but most often increase it—shouldn't we be exploring some different options? Shouldn't we be asking, "What kinds of responses might *really* have the best chance to succeed?" Meeting violence with violence is easy. But in most cases it's not highly effective. And it's often counterproductive.

In my view, the only way to have any real chance of starting to get ourselves free of the terrorism conundrum must begin with seeking answers to just such questions about why terrorism exists at all, and about what tools for defusing it might have an actual chance to bring good results. The truth is that there are specific, historic explanations for why today's terrorism arose, and why it is so fiercely aimed at us. The hard fact is that we Americans have brought a good deal of this on ourselves by the way we have handled our approach to the Middle East, especially since World War II, including the heavy-handed ways we have sought to dominate its politics and economics.

The axle around which our interventionism in that region revolves is the control of its oil. This, for example, was directly behind the folly of America's *coup d'etat* that overthrew the government of Iran in 1953 (with the help of the United Kingdom). The consequences of that act of regime change are still bedeviling us. And the foolishness of our continued interference in Middle Eastern politics has been compounded by our corresponding national refusal to discipline ourselves toward energy independence, even twenty-eight years after the first oil embargo of 1973.

Alongside all that, our country has given active and direct support to Israel (during and after the 1948 war) in its forcible removal of tens of thousands of Palestinian people from the homes in which they lived, the land they owned and worked, and the businesses from which they gained their daily bread. This theft of their lands and homes has been sustained by massive transfers of US dollars and arms to Israel ever since. This is one of the gravest and most consequential acts of wrongdoing in our country's history, the results of which are, again, still bedeviling us.

Until we Americans admit to, and then abandon, such wrongheaded interference in that part of the world (and elsewhere), these attacks will keep coming. Until we cease trying to dominate Middle Eastern oil and politics, and until our policy shifts toward full justice for the Palestinians, terrorism will continue. That's the stark fact.

Let me be clear: the violence committed on Tuesday was unambiguously wrong. It was heartless, cruel, and evil. Its victims were innocent. But the fact that those attacks cannot be *justified* does not mean they cannot be *explained*. This important distinction between justification and explanation is one that our society is slow—if not deeply unwilling—to grasp.

The Jewish rabbi Jesus once asked, "Why do you see the splinter in your brother's eye but do not see (and deal with) the log in your own?" (Luke 6:41). There is a deep wisdom there. We could help ourselves greatly by listening to it, and by taking seriously the best insights of our spiritual traditions more broadly.

As long as we Americans fail to heed the spiritual wisdom that calls us to deal with the "log" of imposing our own oppressive will on the peoples of the Middle East, you and I will continue to feel notably nervous every time we set our feet on board a plane.

A POST-PATRIARCHAL
VIEW OF LOVE

↬

SEPTEMBER 2001

MY LAST TWO ARTICLES in this space have urged that we address our post-9/11 trauma by turning to our spiritual traditions for wisdom about how best to respond, first, to our traumatized emotions and, second, to our need to find effective responses to terrorism going forward. This includes seeking out solutions that are as nonreactive and peaceful as humanly possible. But in the face of the devastating brutality of that day, is there in fact such a spiritual wisdom available that truly "works" in the real world of terrorism, violence, and potential war?

In line with this, it is heartening to hear at least a few voices among us advocating a renunciation of vengeance for those attacks. Though still a minority, more Americans than I expected have called for restraint and conciliation in our responses. And many religious leaders have spoken for turning to forms of love instead of returning violence for violence when evil acts are done.

In my work as a minister, one of my frequent themes over the years has been advocating for social love—i.e., centralizing the principles of love as our main tools and best practices for addressing the problems of society. When properly understood, the range of ways through which social love manifests itself—including policies that focus on strengthening the common good through compassion and social justice—constitutes the best available tool-kit for addressing our major problems, not just for individuals but for society as a whole. I believe strongly that we need to use those tools today in our responses to terrorism.

I am fully aware that such an assertion may seem naïve and highly impractical, if not laughable, to many people. But the reason so many of us might react like that springs from what I see as the narrow and outdated way by which love is commonly conceptualized in our culture. In light of this, we need to do the important work of studying, and clarifying for ourselves, what this word *love* really means. And that clarification must begin by uncovering some of the *faulty* conceptualizations of love that are widespread in our culture, and how those misconceptions can be changed for the better.

There are several forms this misunderstanding of love can take. In this article I'll focus on just one, by pointing out that our most common cultural ideas about love have an often-unnoticed gen-der component. I would suggest that our usual views of love are heavily associated with female qualities—at least, as such qualities are stereotypically and narrowly defined.

In this way of thinking, love is mostly referred to as an emo-tion or feeling, and tends to be thought of as something soft and sentimental, sweet and nice. And, importantly, even when love is taken seriously in its aspect as a moral principle, it is often rele-gated mainly to the realm of individual or interpersonal relation-ships. As a result, love is effectively neutered in its potential power as a large-scale social force by being confined to the small-scale and local levels of romantic or familial relations, or other local, neighborly face-to-face interactions. And all of those, we would do well to take note, have been traditionally seen and defined by our culture as being primarily a domain for women.

By contrast, when it comes to dealing with societal prob-lems, our prevailing cultural paradigm emphasizes a reliance on rationality, and the exercise of power and domination. And those, as we should again take note, are qualities that have—again, stereotypically and narrowly—been associated in our culture with males, who have traditionally been seen as the ones who are best equipped to handle economic, national, and international problems.

In these framings, whereas love is seen as "soft," sentimental, and emotional, our most entrenched social issues are typically described as "hard" problems that call for "hard-headed" solutions in the "real" world. (And heaven forbid that the men charged with solving "hard" social, international, or military challenges should ever let themselves be seen as "soft.")

To think about love in such terms, however, is a profound misconception. It is a viewpoint that, in effect, attempts to manhandle love. It is an approach that tries to take the greatest and most powerful force in the world and domesticate it by corralling it into a small, controlled space. We might draw an analogy to the corrals used in the domestication of livestock. When we humans started putting pigs in pens, we did so as a system of control. The animals there could continue to exist, but only on terms set by their keepers, and only as long as those keepers saw fit.

Using that analogy, I would suggest that the attempt to domesticate, and thus control, these deeply spiritual energies of love is yet one more manifestation of the patriarchal paradigm that still prevails in our cultural attitudes. But in this case, the "corral" into which the patriarchal power-paradigm puts the idea of love-based behaviors is the relatively small designated space of local, individual decision-making and of face-to-face, interpersonal relationships.

The gist of these attitudes that our power elites promote can be expressed, in effect, something like this: "You ordinary folks must, of course, behave lovingly and responsibly to other individuals around you, and thus avoid making trouble on your local level. That way, we can maintain order in your immediate world. But let's not be naïve and imagine that powerful people like us (men) up here on the higher levels, the ones who make the major decisions for society as a whole, are subject to the same rules. We who deal with the big picture," they imply, "aren't required to obey the soft, sweet niceties of acting in a loving, humane way. Doing so would be naïve. Instead, when it comes to major social, economic, and global issues, we will 'do what we have to do,' and 'take care of business' and act in whatever 'tough' ways we deem necessary. We'll meet your daily needs by making sure that you don't starve, and that the police keep things orderly. But when it comes to how we handle the large-scale affairs of state, you ordinary folk at the local level mustn't ask too many questions about morality, or about humane, loving behavior on our part."

According to this line of thinking, ordinary people are supposed to accept the "common sense" approach of our power brokers that, in the realm of societal policies, the wise path is to do whatever it takes in order to "get the job done." If harsh action is required, or if there are reports of major "collateral damage," our population is expected to support whatever our high-level leaders do. Such leaders are, after all, showing the courage to be strong and to do what is needed to keep us safe and maintain our way of life. But when it comes to making such difficult, macro-level decisions, no one should interfere by talking about acting compassionately, or focusing on social love, or quoting Bible verses that call us to "do justice and love kindness" (Micah 6:8).

This brings us, though, to a key point that we mustn't miss. There is a reason that the (male-based) power elites of our major institutions (including religious groups that have strong ties to those power-elites) are eager to promote this domesticated, neutered view of love. That love-limiting, domination-based worldview, and the approaches that it condones, greatly serve their own self-interest. By keeping love confined mainly to the micro level, and by legitimizing power and control, domination, and military violence as tools for handling macro-level social problems, they effectively enhance their ability to maintain their own power and dominance *over* society and its institutions.

In light of all this, I would suggest that one of the main needs of our spiritual-religious traditions today is to unmask the falsity of that patriarchal, domination-oriented approach—and reject it. Our world deeply needs people who are willing to advocate for love as the central standard, not just for individual life, but also for shaping our economic and social policies at home and abroad.

Such advocacy includes saying "yes" to the wisdom espoused by humankind's greatest sages, who have spoken so often on behalf of love as the best and most practically *effective* tool we humans have for solving our most vexing problems—including our largest societal problems. This is very much how Christ and the Hebrew prophets and the Buddha understood their mission: to promote love as a core organizing principle for living life on all its levels, large *and* small, individual *and* societal, spiritual *and* material.

Next week I'll offer some additional thoughts about the nature of this social love we need to utilize in order to address the most pressing problems of our society, including some potential love-based responses to the great challenge of terrorism.

THE POWER OF
INTELLIGENT LOVE

⊸

I N RECENT WEEKS, I've addressed the value of utilizing the resources of our spiritual traditions in addressing social problems, including terrorism. And I've stressed, specifically, the resource of social love. In our current, post-9/11 situation, choosing love-based behaviors includes doing all we can to minimize fear-based emotional reactivity, and its all-too-common results: perpetuating the collective belief in attack and war, and opting for violent policies that pursue vengeance. I've noted also how this discussion must lead us to ask questions about the nature of love generally, and the nature of social love in particular.

Last week, I described the often unnoticed gender component in our society's attitudes about love, and I outlined the extent to which our common cultural thinking (greatly influenced by our patriarchal heritage) tends to consign love to the realm of feeling and emotion, and to over-focus on its local, familial, and interpersonal expressions. But the scope of authentic love extends much more broadly than that.

In this article, I want to take note of a second aspect of love that is also frequently unnoticed among us—namely, that an important part of what constitutes love is to be found in the wise and skillful exercise of *intelligence*. To cite one common example, consider what is involved in being a good parent. Anyone who has had the privilege of raising a child knows that parenting involves surrounding our children with overflowing affection and the kind of unconditional love that is drawn from the well of a loving heart.

But in addition to such loving feelings, raising a child well, especially as he or she grows older, involves thinking through a constant stream of decisions that need to be made carefully and intelligently: What boundaries does this child need? Which of those boundaries need to be firmly enforced today? Which need to be more flexible? When and how often do I say "no"? When and how often do I say "yes"?

Decisions like that must be thought through carefully and repeatedly, rather than being generated through mere habit, emotional reactivity, social patterning, or pre-existing ideological beliefs. (Obeying dogmatic beliefs is, in fact, one of our most habitual modalities by which we often *avoid* exercising real intelligence, by lapsing instead into a kind of decision-making by auto-pilot.) Love, in other words, calls for using the full range, and all forms, of human intelligence. But that phrase, "full range," is important. Because just as love has a much greater range of application than is often acknowledged in our culture, the same must also be said for intelligence.

Consider how, in much of our current cultural thinking, when people talk about human intelligence they are most likely referring to the part of our consciousness that engages in rational, cognitive functions such as deduction and induction, language and logic, controlling physical processes, the use of various technologies, and so forth. That cognitive mode of the mind has enormous advantages, to be sure, when it comes to managing the material world for basic survival—or for convenience, enjoyment, and personal fulfillment.

It is crucial to understand, however, that any view of intelligence that is limited to actualizing such merely cognitive functions is inherently misleading. This is the case not because it is false, but because it is incomplete; i.e., it represents only one part, one aspect, of the full range of what constitutes human intelligence. Beyond the powers of the intellectual part of the mind to manage the *exterior* world, our full intelligence also has enormous potential for managing human *interiors* through helping us develop psychological, emotional, and spiritual skills.

This broader view of intelligence includes the perceptual capabilities that are to be found in what we often call "the heart," as well as "the spirit" or "the soul." And, conversely, for the heart and spirit to come to their fullest fruition requires a partnership with critical thinking and discernment. (And that cluster of capabilities all find specific expression through the physical body, which manifests its own remarkable forms of intelligence.)

Beyond our considerable rational-cognitive intelligence, then, we humans also have a substantial range of inner powers of what we might call *psycho-spiritual* intelligence. This is the part of us that is the source of our ability to develop such interior psychological skills as empathy, compassion, lovingkindness, forgiveness, reconciliation, intuition, resilience, and creativity—as well as our inherent powers of spiritual perception and wisdom.

As we face the looming complexities of the coming century, it is crucial that we humans grasp our need to utilize all those forms of intelligence—both cognitive and psycho-spiritual—if we want to deal successfully with the challenges across the full range of human relationships. And those challenges very much include what comes up not just between individuals, but also between the various groupings of human societies (and also, crucially, between humankind and the Earth's interlocking ecosystems).

The fully developed human being of the future—one who has learned the full range of skills needed to become a mature, responsible person—must be one who has learned how to integrate intellectual skills along with the heart-skills of compassionate empathy and intuition, and along with the resources of humankind's spiritual wisdom-traditions. Put simply, we need to learn what it means to develop an effective working partnership that unites the mind, the heart, and the spirit. And as one important feature of that partnership, the developed, mature human is one who must be committed to learning how to structure his or her life around what we might call "intelligent love."

In recent years, our culture has been learning a good deal about what is increasingly called the "mind–body continuum." That concept is a positive advance in our understanding of human functioning and capability. But that advance, in itself, does not go far enough. We need to see that the structure of a complete and fully alive human being must include developing not just the mind and the body, but also the heart and the spirit. Consequently, a more comprehensive view of the balanced and integrated human self must be seen, more accurately, to be one that includes a healthy *mind–body–heart–spirit* continuum.[18*]

Although all four elements of that continuum are essential, it is important to note that we live in a civilization that has already learned a great deal about skills for mastering the mind and the body. Our great universities and medical complexes bear witness to that. But humankind is still in its infancy when it comes to developing a corresponding curriculum for learning the powers of the heart and the spirit.

Because of that imbalance, we live in a time when special, corrective emphasis needs to be given to the realm of psycho-spiritual intelligence, i.e., to developing those mental, emotional, and spirit-based skills that are inherent potentials in human

---

18* Interestingly, when Jesus offers his "summary of the law" in his Jewish birth-tradition, he makes one change that is noteworthy, though rarely commented on. In the first half of this summation (which counsels people to "love the Lord your God"), Jesus directly quotes Deuteronomy 6:5, in which such a love for God takes three main forms, i.e., to love God with all our heart, soul, and strength. But in Jesus's reference to this, as found at Mark 12:30, he adds a new, fourth mode of expression when he includes the word mind. His expanded version reads, "You shall love the Lord your God with all your heart, soul, mind, and strength." In that simple but significant addition, Jesus does two things. First, he elevates the value of the mind by including it in his list of how we should serve the Divine. But in so doing, he also signals that honoring the Divine requires an equal and balanced partnership among those four parts of the structure of human existence: mind and heart, body and spirit.

consciousness, though they are as yet relatively underdeveloped within humankind. But such capabilities will be crucially needed to meet the great global challenges ahead.

Think about it. Which kind of intelligence does our society now need most? Is it the kind that can build better computers, or produce more consumer products, or deliver military payloads more quickly and efficiently? That is clearly *not* our greatest current need. What we do need much more urgently is the kind of intelligence that can generate healthier human interactions, and a better-functioning social system—and international order. We already have the skills to claim most of the material mastery we need. But we humans are still mere beginners when it comes to relating skillfully with each other and wisely shaping both our individual and societal bonds.

And that is precisely where intelligent love—and social love—comes in. Just as cognitive intelligence needs to be developed (as our schools currently emphasize), so also do we need to "school" each child—each citizen—in the skills of psycho-spiritual intelligence, in the capacities that can empower us to live harmoniously and responsibly with our six billion kin on this planet (and with our increasingly wounded environment).

When we send our kids to school, in other words, we need to do far more than train their intelligence to merely read and write, use computers, learn math and history, engage in the arts—or even learn to think logically and critically. Important as those things are, we also need to train ourselves collectively in the skills of human and social relations: how to resolve problems with social groupings around us in non-conflictual and mutually beneficial ways.

This applies to all forms of relationships, both far and near: how to develop good habits for starting and sustaining intimate relationships; how to be good parents; how to cultivate friendships; how to build strong local communities; how to develop empathy and see the world from the perspective of others; and—crucially—how to be knowledgeable citizens who actively study what is going on in society at large, and who consistently partici-pate in shaping better, more loving societal policies.

Next week I'll offer an example from history of how some of these concepts have manifested themselves in the world of *realpolitik.*

A TALE OF TWO VICTORS

෯

OCTOBER 2001

I N MY LAST FEW ARTICLES, I've advocated ways of responding to the September 11 attacks that involve greater reliance on the wise advice we find in our spiritual traditions to turn away from violence and access the greater powers of love. Specifically, I've been describing some of the elements involved in that mental shift with such terms as "social love," "intelligent love," and "psycho-spiritual intelligence." In the process I've spoken for the idea that a broader understanding of what constitutes intelligence can help lead us to build safer and more sanely structured social systems.

Continuing with these themes, I would suggest that this work of developing both our cognitive *and* psycho-spiritual forms of intelligence involves this key element: committing ourselves to studying and understanding the aspect of human nature that leads us to engage in chronically destructive behaviors. This means coming to grips with what my own Christian tradition has traditionally called "sin" (or what Buddhists call "wrong action," or what depth psychologists call neurotic behavior based on unconscious dynamics).

248

By whatever names we call it, the chronic acting out that humankind *does* engage in so compulsively (as evidenced by war, social oppression, environmental damage, etc.) stems, most essentially, from our ongoing, and largely unconscious, bondage to fear. If we are serious about healing this human tendency toward harmful behavior (and after all, that is one of the major goals of spirituality, religion, and psychology), then our methodology must center on dealing with the phenomenon of fear. And that, in turn, must begin with an increased understanding of how fear works and how it manifests.

This is a large subject indeed. But for our current discussion, I will focus on one crucially important component of how fear shows up in human social systems: it prods us, relentlessly, to think of humankind as being divided into groups of "us" and "them." When fear arises, we easily fall prey to a compulsive wish to strengthen the familiar forms of "us" in which we feel safe, and to counteract—or eliminate—whatever forms of "them" feel dangerous. And this all-too-prevalent tilt toward us–them thinking is one of the most common engines perpetuating the cycles of war and conflict that continue to bedevil human history.

Holding this in mind can point us to one of the most hopeful resources that can be gained by greater psycho-spiritual intelligence: developing ways of thinking that focus more on human commonalities than differences; more on what unites us than what separates us; and more on what can build up trust among us, rather than what generates suspicion or demonization.

Shifting in the direction of those more affirmative attitudes starts with becoming aware of, and transcending, our bondage to fear-based thought patterns. If and as we embrace such attitudinal change, we can progressively replace those fear-patterns with more love-based and life-enhancing modes of thinking, ones that foster connection more than disconnection, creating more than destroying, and pursuing the long-term common good rather than settling for immediate advantage, whether for our individual selves or for the social groupings with which we identify.

Learning to activate those forms of love-as-intelligence can only happen when we activate and access our best selves—our God-given wisdom-minds (which, importantly, include heart-skills as well as brain-skills). In their best versions, the skills of psycho-spiritual intelligence are tools we need to take full advantage of in order to counteract the powerful *dis*connecting tendencies of our more ordinary fear-based thinking (of which the crimes of September 11 are a stark example, and of which emphasizing retaliatory, vengeful responses to terrorism would also be an example).

This way of thinking about intelligence, then, involves a partnership between our cognitive intelligence, as traditionally understood, and the psycho-spiritual capabilities within us conceptualized more broadly—i.e., the fully functioning continuum of mind, heart, body, and spirit. That more inclusive concept of intelligence—which includes the range of skills needed to deal with our social and relational problems *as well as* our technical and material ones—is what our spiritual traditions often refer to as the capacity for wisdom. (This also includes the zone of what some secular psychologists have recently been calling "emotional intelligence.")

What, then, might such intelligent love look like when it comes to dealing with some of the major global challenges facing humankind—including terrorism? Within the limits of this space, let me cite just one example from history that can help flesh out an answer.

Consider how the United States and its allies dealt with Germany after each of the world wars of the last century. The way Germany was treated following World War I was profoundly *unintelligent*. Why? Because it was heavily *punitive* in its approach. But the bad result that ensued could have been easily foreseen—and avoided—had the war's winners been willing to think through the implications of their policy intelligently.

The victors of 1918 had convinced themselves that Germany was culpable for the war (even though the victors themselves were, in truth, also greatly at fault). Consequently, in the postwar Versailles Treaty (signed in 1919), they imposed heavy economic penalties (i.e., punishment) on Germany. This approach enabled the victors to feel powerful through acting out their collective faith in the value of vengeance. And it enabled them to feel righteous in the afterglow of their victory.

But the long-term results were disastrous. Economic recovery for Germany was impossible, and the 1920s saw high unemployment, social unrest, and political conflict there. Most historians agree that such social turmoil was one major cause of the rise of Hitler and Nazism. I would argue that the approach taken by the winners of World War I was impractical and ineffective precisely *because* it was unloving, and that it was unloving in no small part because it was so profoundly *unintelligent*.

All the main elements of the victors' approach—being punitive; inflicting hurt on already-hurting people; being unwilling to forgive; thinking and acting self-righteously; and refusing to acknowledge their own share of responsibility—all these are common aspects of how we humans *refuse* to love. And these are approaches that are also inherently unintelligent because they fail to take into consideration the likely long-term consequences of acting in a harsh and unloving way. This is a clear example from history of an approach that was unloving because in its very essence it was profoundly unintelligent (as evidenced by the enormous human suffering it led to, in the next two and a half decades, in the form of Nazism, genocide, and World War II).

But consider also, by contrast, the approach of the victors after World War II. Their policy was historically unusual—in no small part because of its inherent intelligence. Based, at least partly, on seeing the failure of the harshly punitive Versailles Treaty a generation earlier, the winners in 1945 had learned to let that past experience shape a future action. This time, America and its allies pursued a socially *loving* approach to the ravaged German population, displaying some real measure of compassion. They were, in effect, utilizing the power of social love, insofar as they were focusing on restoration rather than retribution.

In those years after World War II, the war's winners put their main energies into fostering political autonomy rather than national punishment. During the hard winters of 1946 and 1947, they sent food, supplies, and money, and followed that up with the longer-term assistance of the Marshall Plan. This was a policy based on an intelligent analysis of what had the best chance to produce a positive result. And a major part of why that approach *was* intelligent is that it was *compassionate and loving*. (And a major reason we can rightly describe it as *loving* is that it was based on an intelligent analysis of what was needed, rather than on a merely emotional desire to inflict vengeance or punishment.) This is one of history's great examples of the inherent linkage between love and intelligence, broadly understood.

I would argue that this post–World War II policy has become a potential model for us today, a template for applying a wise (i.e., intelligently compassionate) approach to the severe societal and international problems that face us. It is largely because postwar Germany was treated with such wisdom, compassion, and intelligence that Germany and Europe as a whole were able to dig out from under the war's rubble and rebuild so quickly. And, pointedly for Americans, that approach is one of the main reasons that Europe is *not* a threat to us today.

The same principle must guide us again as we prepare to frame post-9/11 policy responses. Our main question must not be: How will we retaliate or punish? Instead, the main questions we ask ourselves must include: What can we learn from history? Why did terrorism arise? What might it mean to take responsibility for our own historic actions? And how can we co-create a future based on conciliation, compassionate action, and creative problem-solving, using only the barest minimum of necessary force?

As I well understand, that is a tall order because it is so different from our usual way of thinking. But if you and I—and many, many of us—will choose, and advocate for, greater reliance on such intelligently loving attitudes and actions, we can, together and over time, make them the new usual.

Doing exactly that is one of our greatest needs, not just for our personal lives, but for society as a whole—and for a more hopeful human future.

LOOKING IN THE MIRROR

⟜

OCTOBER 2001

HERE ARE two stories.

In the first, four monks go on a ten-day silent retreat. After settling in, they start their first session of meditation and prayer. As the first hour passes, they begin to unwind, and then enter a meditative state. After about an hour and a half, though, the eyes of one monk suddenly open wide with a start, and he blurts out, "Oh my God, I think I may have left the stove on."

The monk beside him quickly says, "Brother Robert, look what you've done. This was supposed to be a silent retreat and now you have broken the silence." The third monk then turns and rebukes the second one, saying, "But how about you, brother Eldred; haven't you done exactly the same thing by dressing down Brother Robert?" The three monks look at each other sheepishly, soon acknowledging each has made the same mistake, and try to settle back into their silence.

After a few moments have passed, the fourth monk, with a satisfied smirk on his face, opens his mouth and says, "Hey! Did you guys notice? I'm the only one who didn't talk."

That's a fun story. But consider now another one. This one is actually true. It is far less fun.

After a tour of the post-9/11 rubble in New York with Mayor Giuliani, a Saudi prince, Alwaleed Alsaud, donated $10 million to the fund for families of first responders who had died there. The prince's letter said: "I condemn all forms of terrorism and reiterate Saudi Arabia's strong stance against these horrendous acts." But the mayor soon learned of another statement made by the same prince. This one said: "At times like this we must (also) address some of the issues that led to such a criminal attack. I believe the government of the United States should re-examine its policies in the Middle East [including adopting] a more balanced stance toward the Palestinian cause."

To my ears, each of those statements seems measured, responsible, and defensible. The mayor of New York, however, does not agree. He has responded by saying, "I entirely reject that (second) statement. There is no moral equivalent for this attack. The people who did it lost any right to ask for justification when they slaughtered five or six thousand innocent people. Not only are those statements wrong, they're part of the problem." The mayor then angrily rejected the prince's gift. It was politically advantageous theater, propping up Rudy Giuliani's tough-guy image in the service, no doubt, of future political campaigns. But it also, selfishly, deprived families that suffered grievously on 9/11 of the considerable help those $10 million could have provided.

What do these two stories have in common? They both highlight some of the ways we deal with the flaws, real or perceived, that exist in others—and in our own selves. In the joke about the monks, we are reminded of the all-too-human fact that our attempts to deal with imperfection in others frequently involve some display of—and/or denial of—corresponding imperfection in ourselves. The joke's humor comes precisely from the way that the fourth monk has no trouble at all seeing the mistakes of the first three but can't see his own version of the same mistake in making his critique.

255

Mayor Giuliani (and the whole country) could learn a lot from this simple joke. The fact that the terrorists behind last month's attacks are unambiguously wrong in what they did does *not* mean that we Americans are completely right in how we have related to the peoples of the Middle East in past decades. The fact that those who attacked us were fully guilty of mass murder does not mean that the United States is completely innocent of other, earlier (or ongoing) injustices. The fact that there is no excuse for what those killers did does not mean that we ourselves have no need to understand why terrorism has arisen, and how our own policies might have contributed to that rise.

What the mayor misses is that the hard work of learning why terrorism has come to be, including our own role in that process, is not in any way synonymous with *justifying* terrorist acts. By taking the stance he did, the mayor became a mouthpiece for a dangerous form of denial that says, in effect, "Once we have been attacked, we are conveniently absolved from looking in the mirror; from critiquing our own choices; and from facing our own flaws."

The truth is that America as a nation is widely hated in the Middle East. (Significantly, this is often *not* the case for Americans as individuals.) There are only two possible explanations for such anti-Americanism. One is that there are unusually high numbers of evil, hateful people who happen to live in that part of the world. The other is that large-scale historical factors—including the actions taken by our own nation—have made a significant contribution to triggering that anger.

The truth lies largely in the latter. Crippling terrorist organizations like al-Qaeda and stopping international criminals like Osama bin Laden must legitimately be pursued to prevent more killing and destruction. But that is not the only important issue.

Learning to perceive our own flawed past actions, and seeking out better, wiser ones for the present and future, is itself a crucial priority for framing an effective long-term strategy in response to terrorism.

VIETNAM REDUX?

⁀

NOVEMBER 2001

I JUST HEARD AN INTERVIEW on public radio with Pakistani
president, Pervez Musharraf. He urged the United States
to suspend its bombings in Afghanistan during the Islamic
holy month of Ramadan in order to avoid further anti-American
backlash.

Musharraf's call for restraint is supported by only a small
minority of Americans and has already been publicly rejected
by President Bush. But overseas, including in Europe, the initial wave of unquestioning support for American military action
in Afghanistan is waning. A recent poll in Britain showed that
nearly half of Britons support such a pause for Ramadan (and for
the safety of relief convoys).

In effect, they are all saying, "Stop the bombing!" Those words
bear haunting echoes for people of my generation. It's a phrase I
heard (and shouted) many times in protests during the Johnson-
Nixon years, as the folly of our Vietnam bombings became more
and more apparent. After what we went through in Vietnam,
is this so-called war on terrorism becoming—heaven forbid—
another Vietnam?

Before discussing possible parallels to the Vietnam War, let me
first cite some differences. The threat to America resulting from

a possible "fall" of Vietnam to communism was a full-scale delusion, a figment of Cold War paranoia. It was part of what President Carter called our "inordinate fear of communism" (in his Notre Dame graduation speech of 1977). The mass anxiety of the Cold War produced the unholy trinity of McCarthyism, Korea, and Vietnam. It has now been more than a quarter century since we lost in Vietnam. As many of us foresaw, the only real threat to our country in that war turned out to be the fact that we waged it in the first place—not global communism.

By contrast, today's terrorism does contain some real level of threat to us, as 9/11 shows. This time, an attack on our own soil was not a fantasy but an actuality. And our fears for future violence are not paranoid but all too possible. As if September 11, anthrax, and the resulting body-blow to our economy were not enough, a scenario in which bin Laden and al-Qaeda might seek to gain and use nuclear (or biological) materials against population centers cannot be dismissed as mere paranoia. The "fire next time," to use James Baldwin's phrase, could be harsher—by many degrees—than what we saw on September 11.

There are many people today who want to build a new peace movement, and I am among them. But we who work for peace must do so with open eyes. Unlike the proverbial generals who prepare for the previous war, peace activists must now avoid formulaically recycling an analysis that once applied to Vietnam.

As an example, in the Vietnam days it was appropriate to advocate ending the war entirely. But "peace-work" today calls for something more nuanced. Our task now, in my view, is not to oppose *all* use of force against terrorist groups. Instead, we need to be advocating ways of working for peace that are, yes, minimally violent, but that are also effective in preventing the violence of terrorist acts themselves.

Those of us on the peace-work side of our national conversation mustn't overlook the fact that if a future terrorist attack is nuclear, or unleashes a pandemic, it could undermine the very functioning of our society itself. For any future peace movement, then, the prevention of such a catastrophe must itself be included as a legitimate and necessary goal.

One important help in sorting all this out lies in understanding the distinction between *policing* and *waging war*. Put simply, any use of force in response to terrorism must be of a policing nature (i.e., actions against specific people and groups who are responsible for past criminal attacks, or are planning future ones), but must fall short of starting and waging a new war (i.e., large-scale use of the military against whole nations or populations).

I well understand that this distinction is devilishly difficult to implement in real life. But the distinction is crucially necessary as a tool for framing and evaluating our future options. Yes, we need to identify and act on ways to weaken and move against terrorist groups. And, yes, that process may involve some targeted, armed action. But this must be done as a disciplined and measured police action, using only the least necessary violence, and doing so as a genuine last resort. And the actions we take must target only those who are directly culpable or actively threatening, and must avoid (to the degree humanly possible) innocent casualties.

Although I have written here about how dealing with today's terrorism is dissimilar from the political dynamics at work in the Vietnam debate, I also see some ominous parallels between how America acted in Vietnam and what we are currently doing in Afghanistan and the Middle East.

Next week I'll focus on what our mistakes and experiences in Vietnam can, in fact, teach us about wisely and effectively confronting terrorism today.

THE EMPIRE GAME

↴

NOVEMBER 2001

MY ARTICLE LAST WEEK discussed some differences between our approach to terrorists today and the way America waged war in Vietnam. The Cold War–era belief that our national security was threatened by the Viet Cong was fully an illusion. And because of that, American intervention in Vietnam was not only unjustified, but foolhardy. Today's threat of further terrorist attacks, however, is real. And that calls for a thorough rethinking of how to protect our population.

Having cited that difference, I'll turn now to the parallels between the Vietnam War era and our own time. For even though the threat level from today's jihadists is different in kind from that posed by the Viet Cong several decades ago, our current American attitudes about global action are remarkably similar to what they were in the Cold War. And they are often equally flawed.

One ominous parallel is America's unwillingness to educate itself about the historical background of these conflicts. Our Vietnam policy featured a willful refusal to learn about the fractures in Vietnamese society that originally triggered the war there. The fighting had been going on for years before the United States sent troops. Virtually all scholars agree that the original conflict within Vietnam itself was essentially a rebellion against

French colonial rule; that the Vietnamese people largely backed the revolt; and that their desire to end Western rule was fair and just.

As the United States became enmeshed there, however, it refused to acknowledge this anti-colonial dynamic as the root cause of the war. It decided instead to declare "global communism" as the cause. But communism was nowhere close to being the main engine of that attempt to oust the French (and, later, to push *us* out, after we took over for France). And since our assessment of the war's cause was wrong, our hopes for success were doomed.

But why was our analysis so wrong? In large part, it had to do with our own unacknowledged power agenda. Specifically, we refused to see the anti-French, anti-colonial dynamic in Vietnam precisely because we wanted to *be* the colonial power in Indochina ourselves. We wanted to *assume* colonial rule there. And we did so for the same reason the French first established it: to reinforce our wealth and power. The real, underlying American motivation for waging that war was not to oppose communist expansion, but to promote American expansion. Put frankly, we went there to establish one more foothold (among several) in the spread of what must be seen for what it was and is: an American Empire.

After World War II, with Britain and France depleted, America was the only unweakened world power. Given that position, we succumbed to the temptation to join history's stream of rulers who had tried their hand at empire. Like the Sumerians and the Persians, the Greeks and the Romans, the Ottomans and the British, we pledged allegiance to the game of global power and international preeminence.

This is a seductive game indeed. Few rulers who have a chance to play it can resist. And the head of state in each attempt at empire almost always calls it a noble enterprise, framing it as a chance to spread a higher good. It is an opportunity (so those rulers say) to bestow the blessings of Greek culture, or the Pax Romana, or the salvation of the Holy Roman Empire. It is labeled, variously, as a mandate to bear the white man's burden, to rid the world of godless communism, or to promote the blessings of free markets. That's the kind of thing the maximum leader virtually always asserts.

But those justifications are all for show. Whether for Alexander or Julius Caesar, Napoleon or Lyndon Johnson, this English queen or that Soviet premier, the real goal was, and is, always: power and domination. This is, in the end, a form of lust—an attempt to satisfy a longing in the loins, as it were, to become, if possible, "the world's sole remaining superpower."

But then, but then, but then. When one group of people seeks to impose the power of empire over another group of people, there is inevitable pushback from beneath. It comes from the actual human beings the empires are trying to control (whose natural resources these empires are eager to steal and get rich from). When this happens, each empire's head of state then labels the rebels as "wicked" and "evil." Always. Thus sayeth the Rules of Empire.

The playing of this Empire Game is the real root-system behind what's going on in the Middle East today. Just as colonial America tried to replace colonial France in Vietnam, so now colonial America is trying to replace colonial Britain in the Middle East. We were hated in Vietnam for the same reasons the French were hated there. And we are hated now in the Middle East for the same reasons the British were hated there (and in India). The locals see our presence for what it in fact is: power projection. (And, in this case, that very importantly includes oil protection—for the West, not for the local populations.)

I said earlier that empires virtually always put the label of "evil" on those who rebel against them. But even though those mounting a rebellion may be resisting a domination that is evil, that doesn't mean that the rebels don't sometimes undertake evil actions themselves. That is what makes this situation with terrorism today so mind-numbingly complex. There are precious few clearly white or black hats. Flawed as the American play at empire may be, peace activists must not be blind to the fact that today's terrorist threat is also a real and present danger. And dealing with that threat includes taking some necessary police actions to protect public safety. That is part of the complex ambiguity of our situation for the short-term.

For the long term, though, America and the West will never be free of terrorism until we are willing to let go of our own addiction to playing this generation's version of the Empire Game. As alcoholics and other addicts well know, you have to first move beyond denial, and admit you're hooked, before you can let go of the addiction.

More than anything else, our acknowledgment of and recovery from our national addiction to global domination is our real most urgent long-term need.

"HOW COULD GOD ALLOW...?"
(PART 1)

⟳

DECEMBER 2001

LAST MONTH, I co-led a workshop in Hilton Head, South Carolina, on the topic "How could God allow . . ." (the evil and senseless suffering we saw on 9/11)? Is there anything helpful at all that can be offered in response to that age-old question?

One thing that helps, I think, is to start by recognizing that this question speaks to—and expresses—two distinct aspects of our beings: the one cognitive, and the other emotional. Though usually *framed* cognitively, the very asking of this question often wells up as an eruption of emotional anguish and anger more than as a real request for cognitive explanation. Recognizing that can help us avoid the mistake of responding either from or to the wrong level when offering support to those who are grieving. For someone who is in emotional pain, a cognitive/theological answer becomes irrelevant, if not insensitive or offensive.

As an example of this, when I was a young minister a family in my church lost their son in a car accident. I can remember how hard it was to simply be in the presence of his mother's anguish, even as a bystander. She too, through her tears, asked this dagger of a question: "How could God have let my boy die?" I didn't know much back then, but I did know enough not to quote the

Bible about how "all things work together for good" (Romans 8:28). It pains me how often some of my clergy colleagues say just such things at times like that.

When someone is in that much pain, whatever help we may want to offer must come through personal presence, not doctrinal proclamation. If we use words at all, support can come through letting that person know: I'm with you; I'm ready to stay with you; I'm grieving with you; there's a lot of love around you here that can help get you through this.

Those kinds of sentiments can convey spiritual truths in their own right, and they can show at least a hint of the divine Love that is always at hand. But when someone is midstream in grieving, the only way any real comfort can be offered is through a relational-energetic modality, not a theological-cognitive one. There are major limits to what intellect has to offer when the question "How could God allow . . . ?" is asked from the level of emotional pain.

But having said that, we should also avoid assuming that no meaningful insights at all can be gleaned from the cognitive-theological level. When it comes to hard questions about the role of the Divine in human anguish, there are at least *some* clues and insights to be found. As our sense of the ultimate dimension grows, we can learn more of how and why life unfolds as it does, including the all-too-real predicaments of dealing with pain, loss, and victimization.

That cognitive level can and does serve a useful function in helping us frame working worldviews. And that is important because we humans have an inherent need for functional paradigms by which to organize our experience and our sense of the world. Our dilemmas of how best to respond to the questions we all ask about suffering, impermanence, loss, and human wrongdoing are intrinsically the most difficult parts of life. And in light of this, having some kind of working explanation for life's biggest challenges is an ongoing need of the human psyche.

Next week I'll continue with some thoughts that I think can, in fact, help us grapple—when the time is right—with this vexing question: "How could God allow . . . ?"

"HOW COULD GOD ALLOW...?"
(PART 2)

LAST WEEK I addressed the question "How could God allow evil?" and pointed to the importance of discerning whether the source of the question is to be found mainly in cognitive or emotional factors. When people are asking about this from emotional pain, that is not the time for an intellectual answer.

There are, however, appropriate times for using the intellect and doing the work of theology. As we turn to that today, it is important to acknowledge an initial conundrum: although theology inherently uses words and thoughts, the nature of the Divine is—also inherently—largely *inaccessible* to words and thoughts. But this fact of ineffability poses a problem. How can we even attempt to put into words what is fundamentally beyond words?

In response, I would say, first, that although ultimate things don't much lend themselves to verbal expression, we humans have a psychological need to *talk* with each other *about* ultimate things. And our main communication vehicle, our main language if you will, is, precisely: words and language.

Acknowledging this conundrum about ineffability can help point us toward an understanding that religious questions and ideas are, in a certain sense, more to be seen as conversation starters than as answer givers. The role of theology (and religion generally) is not to make fixed, final, or definitive statements about the Ultimate, but to offer us a framework in which to talk with each other *about* ultimate questions. It is, in fact, the process of *engaging* in that conversation that brings more insights into the larger divine Power than does merely embracing prepackaged verbalizations of religious belief or doctrine.

The function of theology, then, is not so much to state and proclaim The Truth as it is to spur us to *seek and find* more truths about things, where and as those insights are available to be glimpsed. And that happens, in part, through engaging in pro-active dialogue within our human communities about what is most real and important, and about what is creatively and newly possible in the living of our lives.

This leads to a second thought about how to handle the ineffability of the Divine. Although ultimate things may not be describable directly, they can be hinted at indirectly. This brings us into the realm of metaphor, and of poetic language generally.

It is crucial to see that the use of metaphoric expression is one of our best tools for offering the indirect hints and intimations about the spiritual realm. Although we can't make statements about the Godhead that are definitive, metaphor draws our attention to similarities between that which we already know in ordinary, tangible experience and that which we don't yet know (in this case, about the spiritual realm), but can, in time, *come* to glimpse increasingly more about.

As an example of how metaphor works, consider Shakespeare's words (in *Twelfth Night*): "If music be the food of love, play on . . ." The poetry here makes no attempt to describe music definitively. But it does tell us, metaphorically, something of value *about* music (and love). It does so by pointing to a similarity between what we already know (how we nourish and enjoy the body with the help of food) and what we can benefit from knowing more about (how we can nourish and enjoy love—in this case, with the help of music).

When we read poetry, it is usually clear which images are metaphoric and which are more literally descriptive. But it is an unfortunate reality that in the realm of religion many people, with distressing frequency, fail to acknowledge the metaphoric nature of the language they are using, especially about God.

These thoughts about theological language offer a helpful perspective, I think, regarding our question, "How could God allow evil?" Although this question is most often asked as an attempt to deal with a perceived problem in regard to God, I would suggest that the real problem is more to be found in regard to our own modes of thought and articulation. Specifically, one reason we often make so little progress on this question we are discussing (the relationship between God and evil), is our failure to notice a key metaphor within this question we are asking, one that is rarely noticed or discussed.

That key word here is *allow* (as in, God *allowing* evil). When we refer to "allowing" (or, similarly, preventing, deciding, choosing, acting, approving, disapproving, etc.), we are citing a function of *personhood*. It is a human person who has the functional capacity (and responsibility) to allow or disallow things. It is a human person who makes decisions and choices, who undertakes actions or fails to. And it is only a person whose actions can be evaluated through the category of personal responsibility. In short, it is only a *person* who is endowed with agency.

Thus it is that if or when we ask how God could allow something, we are projecting (in that unstated metaphor of "allowing") an attribute of human personhood and agency onto the Godhead. And this leads to a key theological question: When we do, in fact, use personalistic metaphors for the Divine, are we consciously aware of using them *as* metaphors? Or are we (as is more often the case, unconsciously) using them as a literal description?

There can, no doubt, be legitimate times for using personalistic metaphors for God. I think of the first line of the Twenty-third Psalm, "The Lord is my shepherd, I shall not want." That great spiritual poem has for centuries graced millions of people, including myself. Most of us, though, don't take that phrase to imply that God is literally a rural shepherd. And many, again including myself, find great comfort in those words without imagining that the divine "shepherd" is actually endowed with personhood.

Many people, though, do in fact let such phrases reinforce the idea that the Divine is an actual person. And that, in my view, is precisely why I think it is unwise and misleading to think about the question of evil by asking ourselves whether God does or doesn't "allow" it. The truth is that God does not, in fact, allow evil, because God does not *allow* anything at all. Allowing or disallowing are done by persons, and only by persons. But God is not a person and God is not person-like. Yes, God is real. But the nature of God is something wholly *other* than personal. We would do much better to think of God, to use Jung's term, as a reality that is *trans*-personal.

Next week I'll offer one final column on this complex subject.

"HOW COULD GOD ALLOW...?"
(PART 3)

↶

DECEMBER 2001

IN MY PREVIOUS TWO COLUMNS, I addressed the question of where God is to be found, if at all, in evil and suffering. I started by noting the importance of discerning whether the question itself is arising from current emotional distress, or from a more dispassionate intellectual inquiry. I suggested guidelines for how to frame our concepts, and how best to use language, when we discuss this question theologically. And I went on to emphasize that asking "How could God allow evil?" contains within it an often-undiscussed assumption: that some form of *personhood* exists within the Divinity—as indicated by use of the idea of "allowing," which is a function of a personal agent.

Framing our God-concept in terms of "allowing," in other words, is a form of anthropomorphic thinking. To think of God as a person (by imagining that God engages in the activities of "allowing" or "preventing"), and to do so in anything like a literal way is inherently misleading. Not only does it mislead people to think of the Ultimate in a personalistic way, but it also implies, more specifically, that the ways we might *evaluate* how the divine energies manifest in the world can be determined by the same standards, and through the same thinking processes, by which we might evaluate the behavior of human persons.

Here is an example. If human parents let their four-year-old child run unattended near traffic, and the child is then hit by a car, we might well ask, "How could those parents have allowed that to happen?" Asking that question would be fully *appropriate*, because a human parent is a decision-making person, who fulfills his or her function precisely by making choices and enforcing them. And given that a major function of a parent is to make the choices necessary to protect his or her child (given the fact that a parent is a decision-making person), it would be proper indeed to challenge someone's parenting if they allowed their child to run free near traffic.

But if we asked in a challenging way why an entity that is *not* a person—a dog, say, or a statue of a soldier—failed to protect the child, it would seem absurd. The invalidity of the question would be immediately obvious. Why? Because it would be a "category error." We would be utilizing a standard of evaluation that is applicable only to a person; but we would be mis-applying that standard to a nonpersonal entity, one that is not a decision-making agent endowed with responsibility. It is a category error to ascribe personal responsibility to a nonpersonal entity.

Here is another, analogous example. If someone were to ask "Why is justice blue?" or "Why does the sky allow income inequality?" we would "get it" immediately that these also are not validly posed questions, because, again, they contain category errors. The category of conduct (justice) does not correspond to the category of color (blue). The category of economics (income inequality) doesn't fit with a category of science (how the atmospheric makeup of the sky is perceived by the human eye).

The same principle applies to questions of explaining evil. The very question "How could God *allow* evil?" contains an inherent category error. Since God is not a person, God is not in the category of the kinds of beings endowed with the quality of allowing (or preventing or choosing) specific events that cause or relieve human suffering.

Consequently, I would suggest that one helpful way to approach this question is to acknowledge the importance of posing the question itself differently—and better. Instead of asking "How could God allow evil and suffering?" we would do much better to ask: "Where can God be *found*—or felt or known—when evil or suffering take place?" That *is* a valid theological question. It is category-consistent, because the Divine is *present*, and can be *felt*, in all places at all times. But to ask "How could God allow . . . ?" is to pose an *invalid* theological question, based on a category error, given that "allowing" belongs to the category of personal agency. But the Divine is not a person or a personalistic entity endowed with the same kind of agency found in a human person.

Learning to pose our theological questions more carefully and skillfully is an important key in parsing difficult questions like this. It continues to be deeply necessary that we *do* ask questions about the nature of evil and suffering—and also about the nature of our ultimate divine Source. But it is essential to be clear that when evil happens, it is a *human-only* event. Evil does not exist in the universe prior to or independent of human beings.

In light of this, the most important and truly legitimate question we need to ask is not "How could *God* allow evil?" but "How could we *humans* allow evil?" Only human persons allow or prevent. And from this it follows that it is we humans alone who allow—and can prevent—the doing of evil acts.

The more I reflect on all this, the more I am convinced that this phenomenon of asking about God's possible "allowing" of evil expresses a subtle form of denial. Instead of taking full responsibility for our own human behaviors, we try to convince ourselves that there might be an identifiable, external agent that is both the explanation for and the solution to our deepest perplexities about these hard questions. But, to paraphrase the cartoon character Pogo, when we have met evil, we have met a form of us—and *only* of us. The evil we meet is yet one more aspect—a vexing one, to be sure—of human patterns of thinking, attitude, and behavior that have become deeply habituated, but no longer serve us well at all.

So, having made this case—that God is not a person—what then might we say about what God *is*, stated positively? It is beyond the scope of these articles to present any lengthy or definitive answer for that. But here is at least one important starting place: to develop a theology that depicts the Divine not as an external entity to be beseeched, but, much more so, as an internal energy to be released.

In line with this way of thinking, one way to approach the Ultimate Reality is to conceive of it as the Life-Force itself, a power that presents itself to us internally as our own aliveness. As such, the grace of God is radically available to help us master, and transcend, our all-too-human tendency to inflict hurt and harm. That tendency is a strong and persistent engine by which our species does such horrific damage to our own kind, and to our physical surroundings.

How, then, could *we humans* allow so much evil? Any working answer must start with acknowledging the existence of this tragic tendency toward harm-infliction that so often erupts from within us. And it must continue with studying and learning why and how that tendency toward wrong action operates and manifests.

A second element of approaching the Ultimate lies in trusting and surrendering to the divine Life-Energy that we *also* find at work within our own beings—side by side with our willingness to inflict hurt and harm and keep on doing so. That inner Life-Source is the one resource we most need to access and take advantage of, in order to help turn the human race back toward the things that make for life and love, for trust and growth—and for a more hopeful collective future.

TWO PAPER BAGS

⟨⟩

DECEMBER 2001

As THIS WATERSHED YEAR OF 2001 nears its end, what next? Despite these harsh times, the turning of one year to the next can remind us of new beginnings, and of the opportunities they bring for shaping a better future. As our spiritual traditions remind us in their varying ways, there is a "starting now" side of life that is ever at hand, if and as we proactively seek and find it. One way to start again now is to retrain our minds to look at long-known things in fresh new ways.

The Unitarian minister Robert Fulghum tells a story about his then seven-year-old daughter, Molly. As he left for work one day, she handed him two brown paper bags. One held his lunch. When he asked Molly what the second held, she said, "Just some stuff. You can take it with you."

At noon, Fulghum opened the first bag and started eating. He then curiously opened the second, mystery bag. When he emptied it out, here's what he saw: three small stones, one pencil stub, two hair ribbons, a plastic dinosaur, one tiny seashell, two partially nibbled animal crackers, a marble, some used lipstick, a small tattered doll, two chocolate kisses, and thirteen pennies. A few hours later, after a busy afternoon, Fulghum was running late.

As he tried to restore some order to his desk before leaving, he absentmindedly dumped both bags into the trash.

When he got home, up came Molly, saying excitedly, "Daddy, Daddy, did you like my bag?"

"Why, yes, Molly, I loved it," he answered.

Right away she said, "Where *is* my bag?"

He mumbled something about having left it at the office, and then said, "Why do you ask?"

The little girl said, "Those are my things in the sack, Daddy, the ones I really like. I wanted you to have fun with them during the day while I was at school, but I'd like to play with them now. You didn't lose that bag did you, Daddy?"

It's all in how we see things, isn't it? To a still-young Robert Fulghum, busy building a career, the ribbons and stones and the rest didn't seem like much. To his auto-pilot adult mind, those items were old and worn-down. They came in a crumpled bag of a kind we often use once and throw out. Because he saw only the used and childish element in them, he saw them as throwaways.

But to Molly they were priceless because she *saw* them differently. Her child's heart and wide-flung imagination could still see their specialness, despite their ordinariness. And letting her dad play with them at work, even for a day, was a child-gift of love. But Robert Fulghum couldn't see it—or at least, not at first. The Hebrew prophet Isaiah once wrote about how "a little child shall lead them" (Isaiah 11:6). This was a moment for the Reverend Fulghum to learn a slice of that wisdom at work in real life.

As we step toward an uncertain future, filled with the decidedly "mixed bag" that 2001 has left us, one way we can face into these coming days is to look forward with a child's eye of possibility. We can look with the same beginner's mind that can turn some simple pebbles into priceless gems; a broken-off pencil into a Shakespearean quill; a plastic dinosaur into a time-travel machine; an old, worn-out doll into a gracious queen; a small cracked shell into a trip to the shore; two chocolate kisses into kisses sweeter than wine; thirteen pennies into the gold of Fort

Knox; and two partially nibbled animal crackers into the Bread of Life itself.

The creative innocence in children that can see such things is still available to empower each of us, of whatever age, to share in the work of imagining and building a humane future for those same children—and, yes, for us grown-ups too—one that is structured around real love, around kindness and caring, and around creative possibilities and the willingness and daring to bring them into form and aliveness.

We need that kind of creative imagining greatly. It's the one thing, if not the main thing, of lasting hope and value.

ABOUT THE AUTHOR

‹➔

ANTHONY ACHESON grew up near New York City. After graduating from St. Mark's School (cum laude, 1965) in Southborough, Massachusetts, he earned a BA in Social Relations from Harvard College (cum laude, 1970) in Cambridge, Massachusetts, and a Master of Divinity from the Episcopal Divinity School (1976), also in Cambridge. He was ordained a minister in 1977 in the United Church of Christ, a nondogmatic and inclusive Protestant denomination.

Since ordination, he has led several UCC congregations, as well as one Unitarian-Universalist church, in the Midwest and New England, including his final pastorate, of nearly seventeen years, in Greensboro, Vermont. He is also a lifelong musician who has recorded a CD of original compositions.

Since retiring from pastoral ministry in 2015, Rev. Acheson continues to be active as a guest speaker, workshop leader, and writer. He and his partner, Nancy, have a daughter born in 1984, and three granddaughters. Tony and Nancy consider themselves fortunate to live amid the great beauties of the state of Vermont.